Regional Developmentalism through International Law

Offering a study of regionalism in Africa and investigating the ways in which law can be used to address the issues raised by regional processes on the continent, this book examines the African Economic Community, considering that it has been entrusted to coordinate and to harmonise policies between various Regional Economic Communities (RECs) across the continent, thereby influencing the continent's approach towards regional integration.

It seeks to identify how law can be used to strengthen the African RECs while ensuring that they achieve their goal of promoting regional development across the continent. Drawing upon economic and political theories, and using a critical doctrinal analysis of legal texts and norms, the book uncovers the legal and economic underpinnings of the model of regional integration followed by the regional schemes operating under the banner of the AEC, aiming to contribute to the search for effective methods to ensure the success of these various initiatives.

Proposing the concept of "Regional Developmentalism Through Law" as the most suitable conceptual framework to support the effective establishment of an African Economic Community, this book will be of interest to researchers, academics and policy makers interested in the correlation between law, regional integration and development in Africa.

Jonathan Bashi Rudahindwa is a Post-Doctoral Research Associate at the School of Law at SOAS, University of London and a Law Lecturer at Université Protestante au Congo, Democratic Republic of Congo.

Routledge Research in International Law

Available:

The Rule of Unwritten International Law
Customary Law, General Principles, and World Order
Peter G. Staubach

State Interest and the Sources of International Law
Doctrine, Morality, and Non-Treaty Law
Markus P. Beham

Demilitarisation and International Law in Context
The Åland Islands
Sia Spiliopoulou Åkermark and Saila Heinikoski

International Criminal Law and Sexual Violence against Women
The Interpretation of Gender in the Contemporary International Criminal Trial
Daniela Nadj

Unilateral Acts
A History of a Legal Doctrine
Betina Appel Kuzmarov

Regional Developmentalism Through International Law
Establishing an African Economic Community
Jonathan Bashi Rudahindwa

China's One Belt One Road Initiative and Private International Law
Poomintr Sooksripaisarnkit and Sai Ramani Garimella

For a full list of titles in this series, visit www.routledge.com/Routledge-Research-in-International-Law/book-series/INTNLLAW

Regional Developmentalism through International Law

Establishing an African Economic Community

Jonathan Bashi Rudahindwa

Routledge
Taylor & Francis Group
LONDON AND NEW YORK

First published 2018
by Routledge

2 Park Square, Milton Park, Abingdon, Oxfordshire OX14 4RN
52 Vanderbilt Avenue, New York, NY 10017

Routledge is an imprint of the Taylor & Francis Group, an informa business

First issued in paperback 2020

British Library Cataloguing-in-Publication Data
A catalogue record for this book is available from the British Library

Library of Congress Cataloging-in-Publication Data
Names: Rudahindwa, Jonathan Bashi, author.
Title: Regional developmentalism through international law : establishing an African Economic Community/Jonathan Bashi Rudahindwa.
Description: New York, NY : Routledge, 2018. | Series: Routledge research in international law | Includes bibliographical references and index.
Identifiers: LCCN 2018006647 | ISBN 9781138060197 (hardback)
Subjects: LCSH: Law and economic development—Africa. | Law—Africa. | Africa—Economic policy.
Classification: LCC KQC738. R83 2018 | DDC 341.24/9—dc23
LC record available at https://lccn.loc.gov/2018006647

ISBN: 978-1-138-06019-7 (hbk)
ISBN: 978-0-367-59042-0 (pbk)

Typeset in Galliard
by Apex CoVantage, LLC

For my father, Joseph Bashi Rudahindwa Cishibanji, in memoriam.

Overview of the Chapters

Contents

Foreword

Trade has been a defining feature of human life from the days of the earliest and most primitive human societies. Climatic conditions, the flora and fauna in our living environments and the gradual specialisation of human know-how and work have always produced different economic outcomes for different people. The herders had animals and animal products, while the settlers had crops. By getting together in the marketplace, they were able to trade some of their surplus for those goods (and services) they could not produce themselves. If an individual or a group of people has an abundance of one thing while another individual or group does not have and cannot make the thing at all, we may speak of an absolute advantage or disadvantage. If it is just much harder for an individual or group to make the thing than for another, we may speak of relative advantage and disadvantage. Trade will benefit both sides as long as each side has something to give in exchange of the things they would like to get.

David Ricardo was the first to explain that societies can trade for mutual benefit even if one side is better than the other at making all the goods and services they may wish to exchange.

Constraints of time and resources suggest that nobody should make all the goods and services she needs by herself. Since we will be better at making some good or services than at others, we should focus on those where we have the greatest advantage and can add the greatest value and trade for the others. Ricardo called this comparative advantage and disadvantage.

In combination, the three types of advantages and disadvantages have been the driving forces of trade for millennia. In combination, they have also allowed virtually all groups and societies around the globe to participate because virtually everyone has something to give in exchange for what they would like to get.

Furthermore, these motors of trade have generally been forces for good. Access to trading opportunities has enriched individuals and societies in many ways. Diets became more diversified and nutritious, in particular during long winters or when staple crops failed during adverse weather. Living conditions improved in many other ways and choice rather than need has become the defining condition in the life of a majority of human beings on the planet.

"I am, therefore I trade" rather than "I trade, therefore I am" is the closer description of the human condition.

However, trade relations are also subject to an uneven distribution of power. Physical strength or military might has always allowed some groups to take more than they were willing to give in their interaction with others. Unequal information or knowledge has been another factor causing imbalances in exchanges, for example, when the usefulness or value of a good or service is deliberately misrepresented. Even in trade between equals, some products or services are valued or at least priced higher than others because the seller has a monopoly or the buyer has a real or perceived dependence. Decisions to undersupply a market to drive up the price or to oversupply it to ruin a competitor usually have little or nothing to do with absolute, relative, or comparative advantages and disadvantages. They are just human manipulations, abuses of power.

Since economists can show that the overall prosperity of humankind is always greater if trade exchanges are conducted in a fair and transparent manner, with an objective or at least neutral valuation of the goods and services to be exchanged, trade law has the important function of constraining the powerful or ruthless and protecting those who are weaker or in need, or simply more honest and less willing to maximize their gains at any cost.

In the village market, this trade law is usually referred to as contract law with a growing dose of consumer protection. Anti-trust and anti-fraud statutes, environmental laws, labour laws and other modern rules and regulations apply between corporate entities at the local and national levels. Regional integration treaties and the World Trade Organization are charged with the provision of equitable trading rules at the regional and global level.

A comparison of different regional integration schemes will quickly show that some of them have done better than others when it comes to the allocation of goods and services, opportunities for growth and development, the promotion of fairness and equality and the prevention of abuses of power. Bela Balassa, in his book *The Theory of Economic Integration*, defined as early as 1961 the different stages or models that can be pursued when countries want to subject their bilateral or multilateral (trade) relations to more advanced rules than those applicable for everyone around the globe. Free Trade Agreements like the one that created the North American Free Trade Area (NAFTA) require only modest levels of concessions and collaboration. By contrast, an advanced Monetary and Economic Union like the European Union (EU) implies a significant transfer of sovereignty and high-frequency interaction for joint decision-making. Regional partners like the members of the Association of East Asian Nations (ASEAN) or the member of the African Union (AU) have to consider many factors to pick the level of integration that is most suitable for them and then make it a reality.

The present study by Jonathan Bashi is not only a comparison between different levels of integration. Bashi digs deeper and looks at the actual rules in a number of regional and international contexts to show what does and does not work. After a discussion of the proper role of law in the context of regional development, Bashi examines in some detail the rules provided in the Treaty of Abuja for African economic integration and their suitability in principle and relevance in practice. In this part, he is appropriately critical of the emphasis on trade liberalisation and market-led economic integration and calls for more sophisticated regulatory frameworks. To build his case, he frequently cross-references the rules and results observed in the context of NAFTA, ASEAN and the EU. Importantly, Bashi understands and showcases the pivotal role played by the European Court of Justice in the development of the legal framework and ultimately the success of the EU. Last but not least, Bashi applies the lessons learned in the comparative study to the African context and develops a set of recommendations for Africa in general and for the East African Community in particular, since the latter is currently the only regional integration scheme in Africa that combines state-led regulatory and judicial integration procedures with market-led liberalisation. The Organization for Harmonization of Business Law in Africa (OHADA) is seen as an impressive start by Bashi, but also hobbled by its limitations and shortcomings.

Overall, the present volume makes a powerful argument in favour of the rapid and purposeful development of a stronger and more comprehensive regulatory framework for economic integration in Africa. Bashi demonstrates that the current focus on liberalisation and removal of barriers to trade needs to be supplemented by smart regulation at the supranational level, combined with effective supranational judicial supervision and enforcement, if Africa wants to maximize capacity-building and development for the benefit of the greatest possible number of its people. In so doing, the book advocates for specific African solutions that address the need for infrastructure and human development, industrialisation and economic transformation. It should be required reading for everyone professionally charged with or privately interested in leading and developing economies and societies in Africa.

Prof. Dr. Frank Emmert, LL.M., MCIArb
John S. Grimes Professor of Law and
Director of the Center for International & Comparative Law
Indiana University, Robert H. McKinney School of Law

Cases

East African Community (EAC)

Anyang' Nyongo and others v Attorney General of the Republic of Kenya and others, East African Court of Justice, Reference No.1 of 2006

East African Law Society and others v Attorney General of Kenya and others, East African Court of Justice, Reference No.03 of 2007

James Katabazi v Secretary General of the EAC, East African Court of Justice, Reference No.1 2007

Ololosokwan Village and 3 others v Attorney General of the United Republic of Tanzania, Application No.15 of 2017, arising from Reference No. 10 of 2017

Economic Community of West African States (ECOWAS)

Afolabi Oladjide v Nigeria, Case ECW/CCJ/JUD/01/04

Konso Kokou Parounam v République du Togo, Case ECW/CCJ/JUD/02/16

Société Anonyme Maseda v République du Mali, Case ECW/CCJ/JUD/02/17

Wing Commander Danladi Angulu Kwasu v Republic of Nigeria, Case ECW/CCJ/JUD/04/17

European Economic Community (EEC)

Case 26/62 *Van Gend en Loos v Nederlandse Administratie der Belastingen* (1963) ECR 1

Case 6/64 *Flaminio Costa v ENEL* (1964) ECR 585

Case 41/74 *Van Duyn* [1974] ECR 1337

Case 148/78 *Ratti* [1979] ECR 1629

Case 120/78 *Rewe-Zentral AG v Bundesmonopolverwaltung für Branntwein [1979] ECR 649*

Southern African Development Community (SADC)

Mike Campbell (Pvt) Ltd and Others v. Republic of Zimbabwe (2/2007) [2008] SADCT 2 (28 Nov.2008)

Acknowledgements

I would like to express my sincere gratitude to the many people who saw me through this book; to all those who provided support, debated things over, read, offered comments, inspired some of its content and assisted in editing and proofreading.

Firstly, I would like to thank my doctoral supervisor, Professor Diamond Ashiagbor, for the continuous support of my doctoral research, of which this book is the product. I would like to thank her more particularly for her patience, motivation, immense knowledge and challenging questions, as her exceptional guidance helped me at all times of the research. I could not have imagined having a better advisor and mentor at SOAS, University of London.

I would like to also thank Dr Scott Newton for his insightful comments and encouragements, but also for offering me the opportunity to teach in his SOAS law and development course. Teaching under his guidance helped me widen my research and engage with more theories and approaches to law and development in general and international inequality in particular.

My sincere thanks also go to all my SOAS colleagues from various departments for their stimulating discussions and moral support during my doctoral studies. In particular, I am grateful to Demetra Loizou, Prince Olokotor, Sahil Warsi, Xinchao Wang, Virginie Rouas and Jean-Baptiste Damestoy for enlightening my time at SOAS with their enjoyable company. Here, I would also like to include other SOAS members of staff, especially Thiago Tonussi, Matthew Richards, Isaac Apau, Ishola Ajisegiri, Aaron Barnett and Bassam Zafar, for all the laughs, the advice and the encouragements when I needed them the most.

Special thanks both to my aunt Alphonsine Kabangu and to the Ocholla family for opening their door to me during my stay in London and for adopting me as their son and brother. I will always be grateful for the unconditional love and support that they provided me during my doctoral studies.

Last but not least, I would like to thank Routledge Editorial Assistants, Nicola Sharpe and Siobhán Poole, for their help during the preparation and the submission of my manuscript.

1 Introduction

I. Introduction

This monograph provides a study of regionalism in the context of Africa and investigates the various ways in which law can be used to address the particular issues raised by regional schemes across the continent. Given the relatively slow pace and the apparent failure which seem to have characterised regional initiatives in Africa to date, this study is intended to contribute to the search of effective methods to ensure the success of those initiatives. This is conducted through the contemplation of the role that law can play to help achieve the various objectives assigned to regional schemes in the context of the Treaty of Abuja.

Throughout the monograph, a particular emphasis is placed on the African Economic Community (AEC), considering that it has been entrusted with the coordination and the harmonisation of policies between various Regional Economic Communities (RECs) across the continent[1] and thereby to influence the continent's approach towards regional integration.[2] The Treaty of Abuja, which was signed in 1991 by the Member States of the former Organisation of African Unity (current African Union) and provides for the establishment of the AEC, therefore constitutes the major focus of the analysis conducted throughout this monograph.

Development occupies a prominent place in regional initiatives across the continent and appears to be the ultimate objective which motivates African states to engage in regional integration processes. This is evidenced in particular in the wording of the Treaty of Abuja, which has provided for the establishment of a continental Common Market under the auspices of an AEC in order to promote development across the continent. For this purpose, the establishment of the AEC is aimed, inter alia, at "promot[ing] economic, social and cultural development and the integration of African economies", "establish[ing] . . . a framework for the development, mobilisation and utilisation of the human and material resources of Africa" as well as "promot[ing] co-operation in all fields of human endeavour in order to raise the standard of living of African peoples".[3]

Regional economic integration seems to be the main approach adopted by the Treaty of Abuja to promote development across various regions, particularly when it provides for the "the liberalisation of trade through the abolition, among the Member States, of customs duties levied on imports and exports . . . [as well as] non-tariff barriers . . . to establish a free trade area at the level of each [REC]" and "the harmonisation of national policies in order to promote Community activities, particularly in fields [such as] agriculture, industry or natural resources".[4] This approach towards regional integration, which is presented as being the most appropriate to promote development in the AEC Member States,[5] raises several issues which need to be addressed in order to ensure the successful achievement of the objectives assigned to the AEC.

Given the set of goals provided by the Treaty of Abuja, which place a strong emphasis on the development of the AEC Member States, this study is particularly aimed at identifying the particular type of regional arrangement most likely to support the successful establishment of the AEC and the achievement of its objectives. A particular focus is placed on the various characteristics that law is likely to take under the model of regionalism adopted by the Treaty of Abuja, with a view to assessing their relevance and limitations in light of both the circumstances and the particular context of the African continent. This analysis is conducted with a view to evaluating the suitability of the regional legal processes conducted under the banner of the AEC for the promotion of regional development in Africa.

For this purpose, the different chapters include discussions on several legal principles and mechanisms which are offered in the Treaty of Abuja, providing for a critical analysis which focuses more particularly on the economic and political aspects of regional legal frameworks.

On the one hand, the analysis focuses on trade liberalisation and the promotion of the AEC's economic activities in specific sectors and considers the various issues likely to be raised by these concepts given the particular circumstances of the Africa continent. This analysis engages more particularly with the debate between the proponents of a market-led (liberalisation) and state-led (interventionism) development and highlights the rationale for and the various limitations of the approach to regional integration promoted by the Treaty of Abuja.

On the other hand, discussions on the coordination and harmonisation of the RECs' policies and, subsequently, the strengthening of the various RECs across the continent, engage with specific political discourses which highlight the need to identify various legal mechanisms, techniques and methods, as well as institutional arrangements which are necessary in order to achieve these objectives. A particular emphasis is placed on the extent of the actions that states and other actors are expected to take, highlighting the dichotomy between supranationalism and intergovernmentalism and considering regional governance mechanisms that seem the most suitable in the African context.

Moreover, a particular emphasis is placed on the apparent paradox between the multiple constraints and challenges still faced by the continent today and the law-making process that has shaped regionalism in Africa to date. Drawing upon economic and political theories and using a comparative study, this study argues for the adoption of an overall regulatory framework which places a stronger emphasis on capacity-building in addition to economic integration and focuses more particularly on the need for a comprehensive approach to regional legal processes which would be adapted to each region's particular circumstances as well as to the specific objectives pursued by each REC.

It is against such a backdrop that the study seeks to identify the specific manner in which law can be used to address the particular issues raised by regionalism in Africa while ensuring that it achieves its goal of promoting economic development on the continent. By using economic and political theories, the analysis conducted in the monograph allows us to distinguish the various factors and processes that need to be taken into consideration in the formulation and further development of both regulatory and institutional frameworks which are needed to support regional integration processes in Africa.

II. Methodological Approach

The methodology adopted in the monograph combines both a doctrinal analysis of legal texts and legal norms and a critical approach to regionalism. Rather than focusing solely on the various legal processes that arise from regional integration initiatives, the methodology used throughout the monograph highlights both the particular circumstances in which these processes were developed and the specific context within which they are expected to operate. This particular approach is adopted in order to uncover the underpinnings of specific legal principles and legal concepts used in the context of regionalism. Regional legal processes are therefore analysed in light of the specific historical, economic and political contexts within which they are conducted, with a view to grasping their particular essence and appraising their suitability for regionalism in the context of Africa.

This study distinguishes itself from other similar studies in the fact that, beyond an analysis of the various regional legal processes conducted across the African continent,[6] and the acknowledgement that the African regional schemes should be studied as regional legal regimes on terms,[7] it engages with law and development theory and sets out both to question the relevance of the different African legal processes and to explore the various ways in which they can be used to achieve the objective of the Treaty of Abuja, i.e. promoting regional development across the continent.

This approach also focuses to some extent on the impact of law in action and the role played by public policy in shaping regionalism in Africa. This particular approach has been adopted to allow us to understand the different aspects of the policy-making process in the context of regionalism and to consider the crucial role that a suitable legal framework is expected to play in determining the success of regional initiatives in Africa.

The main research method used in this study builds primarily on a doctrinal analysis which focuses in particular on official documentation and policy documents produced under the auspices of the Organisation of African Unity (OAU) and the African Union (AU). This documentation includes, in particular, the Treaty of Abuja, the Charter of the OAU, the Lagos Plan of Action (LPA), the New Partnership for Africa's Development (NEPAD), the Constitutive Act of the African Union and the regional trade agreements which established the various RECs which constitute the AEC.

This study also includes a particular focus on comparative regional integration, drawing insights and conclusions from regional processes in other parts of the world, including the North American Free Trade Area (NAFTA), the Common Market of the Southern Cone (MERCOSUR), the Association of East Asian Nations (ASEAN) and the European Union (EU), with a view to better understanding the multiple facets that law can take in the context of regionalism and using these to build the main conceptual framework of the monograph. This comparison is also aimed at highlighting the need for regional regulatory frameworks to correspond to the particular needs of the regional processes to which they apply.

Several reports produced by organisations such as the United Nations Economic Commission for Africa (UNECA) and the United Nations Conference on Trade and Development (UNCTAD) are also consulted and provide critical insights on both economic and social aspects of the African regional processes.

III. Research Axes and Outline

As mentioned above, a discussion on regionalism in the particular context of Africa raises various issues which need to be both explored and addressed in order to identify the most effective way in which law could be used to support regional integration in Africa. These issues are linked to several axes/questions which are used to explore the different aspects of the analysis conducted in the monograph.

The main study question of the monograph, therefore, explores the key role that law could play to address the issues arising in the context of regionalism in Africa and thereby support the establishment of an AEC which corresponds to the particular circumstances of the African economies.

In particular, Chapter 2 provides the main conceptual framework developed throughout the monograph and sets out to identify the key aspects of regional legal processes in general. The chapter focuses particularly on the underpinnings of and the correlation between the key concepts analysed in this study, namely law, regionalism and development, focusing especially on the economic, political and historical aspects of regional integration in general and regional integration in Africa in particular. A strong emphasis is also placed on the particular *nature* of law in the context of regional integration and the specific ways in which it is expected to support the achievement of development through regional integration.

While Chapter 2 provides a political economy of regionalism efforts in Africa, highlighting different factors and trends which are specific to the African context, Chapter 3 offers an initial insight on the practical ways in which law can be used in the context of regional integration and is used to identify the key legal instruments used by countries to achieve their regional objectives. The chapter also assesses the particular legal rules, policies and legal institutions that are needed to promote economic growth and development in this specific context and explores the particular way in which regional integration is expected to achieve specific goals.

To ensure that the objectives assigned to the model of regional integration that has been adopted by the Treaty of Abuja are achieved, Chapter 4 investigates the legal mechanisms, techniques and methods that were used to ensure the successful establishment of a Common Market within the European Economic Community (EEC), placing a stronger emphasis on the various institutions and regulatory frameworks that were needed to coordinate the efforts towards deeper regional integration.

Chapters 6 and 7 are used to consider the application of the legal concepts identified in the previous chapters in the African context, with a view to assessing their suitability to support the establishment of an AEC and to achieve the goal of promoting economic growth and self-sustained development assigned to regional integration in Africa.

The concluding chapter sums up the finding of the previous chapters and argues for the adoption of a regional legal framework suitable to promote economic development on the continent in light of the particular needs of the African economies.

In details, the structure of the monograph is as follows:

Chapter 2 offers the conceptual framework within which the study is developed. The chapter, therefore, provides for both theoretical and historical backgrounds which will inform the analysis developed in the rest of the monograph.

The chapter focuses on the concept of *regional developmentalism through law*, which is presented as a suitable conceptual framework to consider the role of law in regionalism in light of its goal of promoting regional development. In an attempt to better understand the different aspects that law can take in the context of regional integration and identify the different roles that it can play to support the smooth progression of regional processes, the second section focuses on the various theoretical approaches to the concept of regional integration and highlights both the economic and political components of the concept. These different approaches are analysed with a view to identifying the key issues that law is expected to address in the context of regional integration and their correlation with development.

It is against such backdrop that the next section of this chapter provides an initial insight into the different stages in the African efforts towards regionalism—from the OAU to the AU—with an emphasis on the different organisations created in parallel to promote regional development at a sub-regional level. Through an overview of the progress achieved by the African RECs, the chapter also highlights various issues raised by this process, including the fact that the different RECs appear to be progressing at such different paces that it seems rather unlikely to have them merge by the deadline provided in the Treaty of Abuja. In light of these observations, the last section of the chapter provides the rationale for the use of the concept of regional developmentalism through law, which provides the main conceptual framework upon which the analysis conducted in this monograph is built.

Chapter 3 focuses on the substantive rules provided in the Treaty of Abuja and the various RECs and considers their relevance and their suitability to address the key issues faced by most African countries. The chapter focuses more particularly on the various factors that have influenced the different stages of regional initiatives on the continent and places a particular emphasis on three key periods which have been affected by different approaches to/theories of development and have subsequently produced various sets of different legal rules and processes: the period of self-reliance and state interventionism (1960s to early 1980s), which influenced the adoption of the Charter of the OAU and the LPA; the period of structural adjustment and trade liberalisation (1980s to 1990s), which witnessed the significant reduction of the role of the state and the adoption of the Treaty of Abuja; and the period of post-Washington Consensus (2000s) with the adoption of NEPAD.

In light of the different constraints and challenges still faced by the continent until today, the chapter critically analyses the benefits and limitations of the approach to regionalism adopted by the Treaty of Abuja, which is mostly based on trade liberalisation and market-led economic integration, and questions the law-making process which has shaped regionalism in Africa so far. The chapter argues for the need for the adoption of comprehensive regulatory frameworks in the African context which, in addition to trade liberalisation and economic integration, would also focus on trade facilitation, market regulation and industrialisation, in light of some of the various topics discussed in Chapter 3. Taking these various observations into consideration, the remaining chapters of the monograph consider the use of law to support the establishment of an AEC which would be particularly designed to address the key issues faced by a majority of African economies.

Aimed at highlighting the critical role that law can play in the context of regional integration, Chapter 4 provides an overview of three different types of regional integration projects, namely NAFTA, the Common Market of the Southern Cone and ASEAN. In particular, the chapter is used to identify the various legal instruments provided under these processes and presents the different sets of coordination and implementation mechanisms used by these organisations while also highlighting the particularities of each mechanism based on its objectives and its particular circumstances. While identifying the key components of the concept of regional developmentalism through law, the chapter also emphasises the need for both regulatory and institutional frameworks provided at the regional level to correspond to the objectives and the particular needs of the region that they have been created for.

With a view to identifying the particular rules, mechanisms and techniques needed to support regional processes leading to the establishment of a Common Market, Chapter 5 focuses on legal integration in the EEC, later the European Community, and emphasises the critical role played by law in the establishment of a Common Market within the EEC. The first section provides a brief overview on the history of the establishment of the EEC Common Market—from the European Coal and Steel Community to the EU—and highlights the different factors which have contributed to the establishment of the Common Market and the particular way in which it is expected to promote economic growth. The section focuses in particular on the manner in which the successive treaties have been used concurrently either to create the impetus for more integration or to reflect a development which had already been induced by the supranational institutional framework established to this effect.

The second section focuses on the European Court of Justice (ECJ) which, through the strong legal framework that it established as the backdrop of the European Community and the authority that it gave to the foundational treaties, played a critical role in the development of the EEC. The section focuses in particular on the preliminary reference procedure, which was used by the Court to establish its authority within its jurisdiction and to produce the different principles upon which the legal framework of the EEC Common Market was developed. The third section of this chapter focuses on the principles of direct effect, supremacy and mutual recognition that were created by the Court to ensure the implementation of the Foundational Treaties and of the law emanating from them. Through the study of various ECJ cases, the section highlights the role that each principle played in the establishment of the European Community legal order.

Chapter 6 is used to analyse the use of law to promote regional development in the context of the AEC. The chapter focuses on selected RECs, namely the Southern African Development Community (SADC), the Economic Community of West African States (ECOWAS) and the East African Community (EAC), as these three RECs are believed to provide various aspects of the key issues faced by RECs across the continent which are relevant to the overall argument of the monograph. With a particular focus on regional legal processes, the chapter focuses on both the regulatory and institutional frameworks established to manage and monitor the development of these RECs. A particular emphasis is also placed on the RECs judicial institutions and the key role that they have played or could potentially play in the advancement of the integration efforts in the region. Different concepts such as the preliminary reference procedure and the contribution of national courts and private litigants in the implementation of Community law are used to highlight the key role that judicial integration could potentially play in these RECs. The last section of this chapter focuses more particularly on the EAC, which is presented as the only African regional scheme which has adopted a comprehensive model of regionalism in which both state-led and market-led processes are used to achieve the goal of promoting regional development.

In light of the analysis in the previous chapters, Chapter 7 focuses on the issue of legislative harmonisation within the AEC and considers both the relevance and the use of various harmonisation processes and methods to achieve regional development in the African context.

The chapter also places particular emphasis on the Organisation for Harmonisation of Business Law in Africa (OHADA), which constitutes the largest continental initiative which focuses exclusively on legal integration. The chapter is used to highlight the particular features of OHADA which, through trade facilitation and harmonisation of national policies, are intended to promote regional development on the continent.

After a short overview of the circumstances in which OHADA was created, the chapter focuses on the different methods chosen by OHADA to achieve its goal of facilitating trade and promoting regional integration within its jurisdiction. The second section of the chapter provides a general introduction to OHADA and provides a critical analysis of the organisation, highlighting the two methods used in the process carried out by OHADA: unification and judicial integration. The following section of the chapter focuses on the OHADA judicial system headed by the OHADA Common Court of Justice and Arbitration (CCJA), with a particular emphasis on the interaction between the CCJA and the OHADA Member States' national courts and its role as a regional arbitration centre. This section also focuses on the application of the direct effect and supremacy principles in the OHADA context and distinguishes it from the ECJ approach. The last section of this chapter is used to highlight the limitations and shortcomings of the OHADA process and the need for a legal framework which would promote selective state intervention and the industrialisation of African countries.

By way of conclusion, Chapter 8 draws together the different arguments developed throughout the monograph and refocuses on the need for a regional regulatory framework adapted to the particular circumstances of the African economies as well as an institutional framework with techniques and methods to ensure the effective implementation of regional rules. The discussion in this chapter is used to corroborate the concept of regional developmentalism through law and argues that, instead of concentrating all the efforts exclusively on trade liberalisation and the removal of barriers to cross-border trade, regional legal processes should be considered as means to promote regional development as much as state interventions aimed at promoting capacity-building. These various observations and considerations are presented as prerequisites to ensure the effective establishment of an AEC which would be adapted to the particular circumstances of the African economies.

Notes

1. While the coordination and harmonisation of policies between existing and future RECs is listed as one of the objectives of the AU (article 3(l) of the Constitutive Act), this role has been assigned to the AEC in article 4(1)(d) of the Treaty of Abuja. Throughout the monograph, the term *African Economic Community* will be used to refer both to the Economic Community which is expected to be established through the merger of the various African RECs and to the group of the same African RECs which are supposed to be coordinated through the Treaty of Abuja.
2. The term *regional integration* is used when referring to the particular approach towards regionalism adopted by the Treaty of Abuja and other similar initiatives, while the broader concept *regionalism* is used to encapsulate the various considerations covered in the monograph.
3. These objectives are listed in article 4 1(a), (b) and (c) of the Treaty of Abuja.
4. These strategies are provided in article 4 2(a), (d) and (e).
5. See Kararach, G. (2014) *Development Policy in Africa, Mastering the Future?* Basingstoke: Palgrave Macmillan, p. 18. See also Ilorah, R. (2012) 'The Realities of Regional Integration: The NEPAD Perspective' in Bobo, B.H. and Sintim-Aboagye, H. (eds) *Neo-Liberalism, Interventionism and the Developmental State: Implementing the New Partnership for Africa's Development*, Trenton, NJ: Africa World Press.
6. See Oppong, R.F. (2011) *Legal Aspects of Economic Integration in Africa*, Cambridge: Cambridge University Press. This book constitutes one of the first in-depth studies of the various legal processes conducted across the African continent.
7. Gathii, J.T. (2011) *African Regional Trade Agreements as Legal Regimes*, Cambridge: Cambridge University Press. This book offers a critical analysis of the African Regional Trade Arguments both in their own terms as flexible legal regimes and in light of their consistency with the multilateral trade regime.

2 Regionalism, Law and Development

I. Introduction: Integration Through Law

This chapter is used to construct the analytical framework for considering regional integration throughout the monograph and for identifying and exploring the various ways in which law can be used to successfully achieve the objectives of the Treaty of Abuja and thereby support the establishment of an African Economic Community (AEC). The chapter focuses more particularly on the three key concepts which form the core theoretical framework of the study, namely law, regionalism and development, placing a particular emphasis on the various theories underlying these concepts and highlighting the correlation between them. This chapter is used to develop the concept of *regional developmentalism through law* which, deriving from the concept of *integration through law*, is presented throughout the monograph as a suitable analytical tool through which law is considered both as a foundation upon which regional schemes can be built and as an instrument that can provide the impetus necessary to achieve the objectives assigned to the African regional schemes, of which regional development occupies a prominent place.

The concept of integration through law—which originates from the theory and experience of regional integration—can be defined as a theory concerned with the various ways in which law can be used to support economic integration.[1] In particular, the law is considered as an instrument harnessed in the context of regional integration with a view to achieving the objectives of different regional schemes by providing for the regulatory and institutional frameworks necessary to coordinate the participating countries' collective action.[2] Integration through law is therefore used in the monograph both as a descriptive tool to clarify the underlying norms, mechanisms and policies adopted in the context of regional integration and as a normative tool aimed at identifying the legal rules, legal principles and institutions likely to be prescribed in the context of regional integration and which are necessary to promote development in the African context.

For this purpose, and to ensure that the analysis provided in this chapter is both thorough and comprehensive, the concept of *law* will be deemed to include the rules and policies contained in Regional Trade Agreements

(RTAs)—rules which provide for the objectives to be achieved—as well as the various coordination mechanisms provided to ensure that these objectives can be achieved successfully.[3] These mechanisms may include the elaboration of techniques and methods specifically designed to ensure the implementation of the RTAs and the establishment of special institutions responsible for monitoring and coordinating the effective and successful enforcement of the RTAs. These techniques may also include a dispute settlement mechanism to handle the conflicts likely to arise between participating countries or other stakeholders regarding the provisions of the RTAs.[4] An appropriate dispute settlement mechanism proves crucial in the context of regional integration, given the significant damage that unresolved disputes are likely to cause to the participating countries' relations.[5]

The rationale for the prominence given to law throughout the monograph therefore resides in the fact that, in the particular context of regional integration, whether in the form of rules, methods and techniques or institutions, law plays a key role, as it is used to assist in the coordination of the RTAs by dictating certain behaviour to be adopted by the participating countries and other stakeholders.[6] As will be discussed in this chapter, when entering into an international agreement, and more particularly in the context of regional integration, countries are usually in search of a solution to a common problem that they seek to address by using a wider range of resources for their common good.[7] RTAs, which are the particular focus of this study, therefore provide for various rules and provisions representing the participating countries' commitment to regional integration efforts.

This analysis is especially concerned with international economic law, which is described as the area of law providing the rules of regulation of economic activities by states and international organisations, as well as the legal principles and procedures governing the allocation of jurisdiction between states.[8] For this purpose, this study focuses on rules regulating various economic activities and commercial transactions, including the production and distribution of goods, international and cross-border business transactions and the status and particular role of the various actors involved in such processes.[9]

Equally important, the study examines the particular nature of international law and highlights its potentiality to be used both as a factor for, and a restraint to, development.[10] Moreover, the use of law in this analysis allows us to grasp the contrast between endogenous and externally led development and to emphasise the particular effect of these two approaches on both political and economic aspects of regional integration in Africa. For this purpose, economic and political theories of regionalism are used to emphasise the various ways in which law has been used to reflect either approach, with the view to assessing their effectiveness in the African context. This analysis also engages with both modernisation and neoliberal theories of development and focuses especially on the rules stemming from past and current international legal orders, highlighting the particular way in which they have been used to shape the African regional schemes.

The chapter is organised into different sections which are used to develop the conceptual framework of the monograph.

Firstly, given the particular emphasis that is placed on both concepts of poverty and development in the context of Africa, the chapter is concerned with the evolution of the development discourse on the continent and the particular role that law is expected to play in this context. Here the chapter emphasises the significance of the historical past of the African continent—of colonisation in particular—which is considered as an essential element allowing us to highlight the particular context and historical background in which this study is developed. The chapter also builds on the insights of post-colonial theory and critically engages with concepts such as developmentalism, modernisation and dependency, highlighting the particular ways in which these notions have influenced the approach that African countries have adopted towards law, regionalism and development.

Secondly, the chapter focuses on the main narratives on regional integration and includes the various principles underlying the concept and the different forms that it can take, as well as the specific ways in which it is generally expected to promote development. A particular focus is placed on trade theory and the various ways in which countries are expected to benefit from international trade through comparative advantage. This section also focuses on both economic and political aspects of regional integration and reviews the different theories that have been developed to analyse the various stages and sequences of regional integration processes. A particular emphasis is placed on the need for the adoption of legal rules and mechanisms specifically designed to regulate cross-border trade and the different stages of integration to ensure that the participating countries can benefit from the overall process.

Thirdly, the chapter provides a first overview of both sub-regional and continental efforts towards regional integration in Africa and conducts an initial assessment of the progress made by the different African Regional Economic Communities (RECs). In particular, this section is used to highlight the key challenges faced by most regional schemes conducted under the banner of the AEC, including coordination and implementation issues, as well as the limitations of the model of regional integration adopted by these RECs. It is against such backdrop that the last section introduces the concept of *regional developmentalism through law*. This concept, which is inspired from the new developmental state paradigm, argues for the adoption of an approach to legal regionalism that places a stronger emphasis on regional development and the various mechanisms needed to achieve it.

This conceptual framework—which is built upon the two key concepts of *integration through law* and *regional developmentalism*—is used throughout the monograph both to inform the analysis conducted in each chapter and to identify the regional rules and legal mechanisms that are deemed suitable to the specific needs and particular circumstances of the African countries.

II. Colonisation and Early Attempts Towards Regional Groupings

Regional integration in Africa, in its contemporary form, has a long history, dating back to the end of the nineteenth century during the colonial period, when early attempts towards the grouping of countries could be observed in several parts of the continent. The Federation of French West Africa, which was established in 1895 to provide for a central administration aimed at controlling various French colonial territories in the region, constitutes one of the earliest forms of such initiatives.[11] Other early groupings also include the creation of the Southern African Customs Union (SACU) in 1910[12] and the establishment of the East African Community (EAC) in 1917.[13] This account of early efforts towards regional groupings raises various questions on the political economy of these initiatives, including the creation nation-states as well as the political and the economic underpinnings for such initiatives. These various considerations prove important insofar as they provide the historical context which has determined the patterns of the continent's economic development as well as the various issues and challenges to be addressed by current efforts towards regional integration.

The reasoning behind the initial efforts towards regional integration in Africa is believed to reflect the very objectives of the proponents of colonisation. On the one hand, colonisation is understood to have been motivated by European states' capitalist interests in the search for new territories to control and both labour and primary resources to exploit in order to increase their profits.[14] On the other hand, and as a corollary to the economic consideration, colonisation was presented as a civilising mission through which colonised territories and populations, considered as less advanced and traditional, ought to be transformed through the establishment of new sets of economic, political and social institutions considered as *modern*.[15] Under both views, colonisation was therefore seen as the expansion and the internationalisation of the capitalist system as well as the integration of African colonial territories into the world economy.[16]

Several institutions were established to achieve this purpose. Modern African states were created as colonial administrations with a view to regulating the exploitation of the various territories under control and transforming pre-existing traditional societies into labour forces supposed to work in plantations and mines.[17] Through the implementation of new legal rules and institutions, these modern states were used to establish the adequate frameworks in the form of nascent markets, considered as necessary to regulate the export of commodities produced in the colonies.[18] Alongside these colonial states and central administrations, transnational trading companies were also established with the specific goal of transferring the commodities produced by colonial labour from the colonies to European metropoles. These trading companies focused mostly on the production and the subsequent export of raw materials and primary commodities from different colonies across the continent and the importation from the metropoles of European goods for local consumption.[19]

This is the context in which efforts towards regional groupings in Africa were initiated, with the aim of serving imperial purposes by organising regional labour and coordinating the production of primary commodities, as well as regulating the international flow of goods between the colonies and their European metropoles. Initial groupings were established for this purpose and provided for central administrative entities and legal rules aimed at encouraging the free movement of labour between colonies and at regulating economic activities across regions, including the transportation of goods to and from European metropoles.[20] The original Federation of French West Africa and the first EAC were established in this context and significantly influenced both international and regional trade patterns, including through the adoption of rules which promoted the concentration of the African countries' production on raw materials and primary commodities.[21]

It is this legal and economic apparatus, established during the colonial period with the aim to serve colonial mercantilist interests and provide the metropoles with resources for both their industries and their consumer markets, which most African countries inherited upon independence. The majority of these countries received limited state infrastructures and inappropriate institutional frameworks, as well as asymmetrical and truncated economic structures heavily dependent on their former colonial metropoles. This situation seriously limited their ability to promote an autonomous and self-sustaining economic growth once they became politically independent.[22] These various factors were found to be crucial in determining both the pattern and the content of the different regional integration initiatives which were established by the African countries upon independence.

III. Independence, Old Regionalism and the Role of Law in Regional Development

Upon independence, which for the majority of African states occurred in the 1950s and the 1960s, the newly established African states joined a pre-established international legal order with a set of rules and principles designed mainly to serve European interests which were aimed at dictating selected activities that the new states could participate in as well as particular ways to conduct their international relations.[23] However, despite the proclaimed political equality among all independent states based on fundamental international legal principles, a putative hierarchy was maintained between the new African states, considered economically backward, and the former European colonial powers now referred to as "developed countries".[24]

Accepting the idea of their economic backwardness, which they considered as a detrimental consequence of colonisation, the new states asserted their need to develop and modernise in an attempt to *catch up* with the developed world.[25] The economy was therefore recognised as the means through which the new states could reach their goal of achieving progress and reaching the status of "developed" nations.[26] These various considerations determined the different connotations of the concept of development in the African context as well as the various mechanisms prescribed to achieve it, including regional integration. Understanding these various connotations proves important, as it allows us to grasp the various ways in which African countries are expected to use both law and regional integration to achieve development.

II.1. Defining Development

Development can be defined as the understanding of the different factors and conditions required to achieve human well-being and increased living standards.[27] While this definition could be the subject of different interpretations depending on the context and circumstances of particular regions, over the years, development has come to be understood to include both a goal to achieve—i.e. human well-being and increased living standards—and the process that is necessary to achieve it. Economic development, in particular, has historically been associated with the measurement of the wealth of countries and used to distinguish between rich and developed countries on the one hand, and poor or develop*ing* countries on the other hand.[28]

Over the years, a particular model of development—the Western model—has come to be presented as *a universal* or *ideal* model, thereby providing for specific processes, structures and particular policies needed for poor countries to achieve development.[29] As discussed earlier, this fact is used later in the monograph to explain the adoption of particular models and paradigms of regional integration which, despite the fact that they are not particularly suitable to the particular circumstances of the African countries, are nevertheless expected to help them achieve the same level of development as industrialised countries in the Western world. Economic growth plays an important role in this conception of development, as it is seen as an effective instrument to eliminate poverty and thereby increase living standards.[30] This is the particular conception of development that was adopted by most African countries at independence, which accepted the idea of their backwardness and acknowledged the need for them to achieve development (goal) through modernisation (process).

Law was expected to play a key role in the transformation process, which explains the particular use of legal transplants or the adoption of particular legal institutions from the developed world believed to be *modern* and thereby more suitable to promote economic growth and development.[31] These modern legal institutions included, *inter alia*, rules regarding the possession and exploitation of natural resources; the production and trade of various goods; and the status of persons participating in such activities.[32] Law was therefore expected to support the gradual adoption of specific structures and institutions found in developed countries, including an economic structure based on a market system.

Given the central role that the state was expected to play in this process, the next section is dedicated to the developmental state paradigm and analyses the particular ways in which states were expected to address the various issues and economic challenges that they inherited from the colonial period.

II.2. Old Regionalism and the Developmental State Paradigm

The concept of developmental state occupies a prominent place in this analysis, given its particular focus on the use of the state as an instrument to achieve development through different processes and mechanisms, including through interventionism and protectionism. This analysis proves particularly important, as it allows us to consider the various characteristics of a developmental state, the various actions that the state is expected to take in this context, and the particular way in which these various factors are expected to promote development in the African states. These considerations are used to inform the analysis conducted throughout the monograph, in particular when developing the concept of regional developmentalism as well as when considering the various actions that could potentially be undertaken by both the states and the institutional framework established to this effect to promote development in the context of regionalism.

The developmental state can be defined as a state which essence is determined by "developmentalist" ideological underpinnings or a state that conceives its primary mission as that of promoting economic development.[33] In addition, the developmental state can also be defined as one that has the capacity to regulate its economy in an effective and functional manner.[34] The developmental state literature has identified several features which characterise this specific type of state and has placed a particular emphasis on the special attributes that are necessary for the developmental state to successfully achieve its goal. These features and attributes have been analysed and developed under two different schools, namely the economic and the political schools.[35]

On the one hand, the economic school focuses on the ideological aspect of the developmental state, more particularly on state intervention as well as the various sets of policies that are required for a state to achieve economic development.[36] These policies include, *inter alia*, appropriate trade and industrial policies, the coordination of investments within and across various sectors and the promotion of sustainable economic growth, taking into consideration both domestic and international factors and opportunities.[37] On the other hand, the political school is concerned with the nature of the state and its capacity to both devise and successfully implement its economic policies.[38] A particular emphasis is placed here on the autonomy of the state and its ability to curb particular interests and ensure the independence of its policy-making process.[39] The developmental state paradigm, therefore, provides for a particular state model which has the ability both to devise appropriate economic policies and to effectively implement them.[40]

At the regional level, this paradigm was translated into the concept of *developmental regionalism* or *old regionalism*, which was associated with the promotion of regional self-reliance through industrialisation and protectionism.[41] This approach highlighted the need for countries to adopt appropriate industrial policies in order to promote a few industries considered as crucial to promote economic growth.[42] Given the particular challenges faced by the African states, which inherited truncated economies and weak legal and institutional frameworks upon independence, this strategy was deemed appropriate for their economic transformation and the diversification of their exports and therefore for the promotion of sustainable economic growth and development.[43]

Moreover, under old regionalism, protectionism was particularly designed to counter the effects of an international trade regime established during the colonial period which was believed to be unsuitable to the needs of the continent, especially given the international division of labour in which African states were expected to specialise in the production of raw materials and primary commodities.[44] This particular issue was analysed by the proponents of the dependency theory, who argued that the international (capitalist) trading regime was set in a specific way to maintain unfair economic relations between core countries—former colonial powers—and peripheral countries—former colonies—which were expected to specialise in the production of goods to sustain the core countries' economic growth.[45]

In this context, the (core) industrial countries are expected to provide foreign investment (often with a set of limited resources in technology and capital) to peripheral (developing) countries, while the latter provides cheap raw materials and agricultural products. Given the relatively low price of primary products produced by developing countries compared to the manufactured products that they imported from industrial countries, this situation was believed to contribute to the maintenance of the developing countries' subordination to the former colonial powers. What became known as Import Substitution Industrialisation (ISI) was therefore specifically designed to eliminate any dependency through the imposition of higher tariffs to limit the flow of imports and instead develop local nascent industries.[46]

The need for states to adopt appropriate industrial policies in order to diversify their production and to opt for a protectionist regulatory framework to promote the development of local industries is a key distinctive feature of the early forms of regionalism, which highlighted the central role that international trade can play in the development process of a country. This also explains the tendency of the law, in the context of regionalism, to focus mainly on the regulation of both the production and the external trade of the countries involved. The correlation between these two components of regionalism was further developed through the trade theory and the notion of comparative advantage.

II.3. Trade Theory and Comparative Advantage

International trade is believed to play a crucial role in the development process of a country, as it allows countries to increase their wealth and income through exports and to buy goods that are needed in their domestic markets through imports.[47] In addition, international trade encourages the specialisation of countries in the production of goods in which they have comparative advantage, thereby increasing efficiency in the use of their various resources.[48] According to comparative advantage theory, countries will predictably specialise in goods that they can produce more efficiently and by using fewer resources—thereby using their local industries at their greatest advantage—while they import other goods from countries that can supply them at a cheaper price.[49] Under this conception, comparative advantage determines international specialisation, and most countries are therefore expected to benefit from international trade.[50]

This notion of comparative advantage—considered as classical or *static* comparative advantage—is complemented by the concept of *dynamic* comparative advantage, which seems more appropriate in the context of both dependency theory and the developmental state paradigm. A dynamic comparative advantage consists of the development by countries of new comparative advantages in activities and sectors which they consider more likely to increase their international competitiveness and, thereby, promote their long-term developmental goals.[51] The development of a dynamic comparative advantage involves the adoption of adequate regulatory frameworks and the appropriate allocation of resources to specific sectors, taking into account both the internal resources of the concerned countries and the opportunities and risks provided by international trade.[52] This is achieved through the adoption of particular regulatory and institutional mechanisms, which are expected to influence the interaction between opportunity costs and product and country characteristics.[53]

So far, this analysis has mainly focused on development as a state-led process, highlighting the various roles that the state, through the adoption of appropriate rules, is expected to play in the context of development, as well as the different mechanisms and rules that are supposed to promote sustainable economic growth, thereby development. The next section focuses on globalisation and the rise to prominence of neoliberalism, emphasising the shift from states to markets as the preferred instruments to achieve development. This paradigm shift and the subsequent focus on free trade provide the context in which the most recent model of regional integration has been developed as a process designed to promote economic growth and development.

IV. Globalisation and the Shift to New Regionalism

Globalisation constitutes a major process which has significantly altered the global economic discourse and thereby inspired a new approach towards the achievement of development. The concept has been used to define the process through which the world is becoming increasingly interconnected as a result of increased capital movement and the intensification of international trade, through and beyond nation-states.[54] The advent of globalisation has been accompanied by the emergence of various concepts, theories and institutions which are presumably shared by the global community, therefore deemed to be universal or global. Moreover, several of the economic issues and challenges analysed in previous sections are now supposedly approached with a global perspective, thereby providing for a set of remedies deemed universal and specifically designed to be applicable in developed and developing economies alike.[55]

It is in this context that neoliberalism has risen to prominence in the development discourse and is believed to provide a global and more effective approach towards development. Neoliberalism can be defined as an ideology deriving from classical liberalism, which places a particular emphasis on the belief that free or self-regulating markets, and not states, are the preferred instruments used to promote the appropriate allocation of resources.[56] In this context, neoliberalism is believed to provide the most appropriate definition for development and the best approach to achieve it.

IV.1. Regional Development Through Legal and Economic Integration

Under neoliberalist theory, development—which was initially understood as human well-being or increased living standards—is believed to best be achieved by the advancement of private enterprise through free trade and a self-regulating market, and the promotion of property rights and individual liberties.[57] These measures are intended to promote economic growth, which is considered as a prerequisite for development. Over the years, the internationalisation and subsequent rise to prominence of neoliberalism through globalisation[58] has managed to alter the meaning of development both as a concept and a process, with the advancement of countries now measured based on their ability or not to promote economic integration through open and competitive markets or on the conformity of their national economies with the liberal model, which is believed to be the ideal approach towards development.[59]

The central argument of this approach is that, in order to access the capital and resources which are necessary to promote economic growth and thereby achieve development, countries need to promote international economic integration by linking their national economies to the world economic system. Countries are therefore encouraged to open up their economies to the global market and the international economic order through freer trade and the implementation of liberal economic rules. Development is presented as a universal concept and as a goal which can be achieved through various reforms based on neoliberal policies, which are deemed to be suitable to both developed and developing countries, irrespectively of their particular circumstances.[60] These are the considerations that have influenced the adoption of a new approach towards regionalism which places a stronger emphasis on the promotion of freer regional and international trade and constitutes what is referred to as *new regionalism*.[61]

In the African context, this approach has been presented as the most suitable remedy to the various challenges that most states have been faced with in their attempt towards economic transformation and development since the independence era. Similar to the modernisation theory, neoliberal development is presented as an externally led process through which Western economic and social models are supposed to be implemented by countries in an effort to promote international economic integration and economic growth and thereby raise their living standards.[62] These models are expected to be implemented through various reforms which include trade liberalisation and the establishment of a market economy, which are deemed suitable for the efficient allocation of economic resources and economic growth. In contrast with the developmental state paradigm, neoliberalism focuses on the prominent role played by markets to achieve development and reduces the role of the state to that of the provider of a favourable environment in which markets can operate.[63]

As a consequence, in the context of regional integration, rather than regulating state activities which are supposed to promote development, regional regulatory frameworks are expected to focus on the establishment of a market economy and the creation of an environment that is favourable to the enhancement of cross-border business transactions. These regulatory frameworks include rules designed to eliminate any constraints that are likely to prevent the flow of capital and to restrict the growth of business activities in a particular region as well as their expansion across national borders.

IV.2. Economic and Politico-Legal Approaches to Regional Integration

Regional economic integration, as one of the various instruments promoted by new regionalism, can be defined as a process through which two or more countries undertake to combine their resources and unify their economic policies with a view to creating a larger and more open economy, which is believed to benefit them.[64] Moreover, as mentioned above, in order to promote economic development countries are encouraged to promote international economic integration by opening up their economies to the international economic order, using regional economic integration and regional rules as means to achieve this particular goal.

Through several attempts since the independence era, African countries have positioned themselves on the path to regional integration, with a view to using integration as a strategy for achieving sustainable economic growth and thereby promoting development. There is a general assumption that by merging their economies, African countries will be able to overcome the enormity of development challenges faced by the continent and to promote a better allocation of economic resources, thereby inciting economic growth and achieving development. The central argument is that, through regional integration, African countries will access the resources that are necessary for poverty alleviation and increased living standards.[65]

However, there is a broad consensus that these efforts towards regional integration have not been successful in general.[66] Given the proliferation of regional integration initiatives on the continent and the ambitious mandates assigned to the majority of them, it is necessary to analyse the concept of regional integration in more details by considering the various theories and models underlying the particular approach to regional integration that is followed by the majority of countries in Africa. Similar to the developmental state paradigm, the concept of regional integration has been analysed under both economic and political perspectives in order to identify the various goals that regional integration is expected to achieve and the different mechanisms and models that are needed to ensure the effective implementation of those objectives. This two-part analysis proves important as it enables us to identify with precision the different roles that law is likely to play as well as the different areas that it is supposed to regulate in the context of regional integration.

III.2.1. Economic Approach to Regional Integration

Different theories have been developed over the years to understand the various perspectives which have been used to approach the concept, in an attempt to grasp the different forms of regional integration that have emerged across the world. This section focuses more particularly on the classical model of regional integration, also referred to as the *Customs Union* or *Vinerian* model,[67] given that it is the model that has been adopted by most countries in Africa.[68] This approach, which is mainly based on the trade theory, focuses primarily on market dynamics between goods and factors of production within a region and considers the various implications and benefits of discriminating against members of such markets. In this context, the establishment of a Customs Union involves the elimination of intra-area trade barriers and the equalisation of tariffs on imports from non-member countries.[69]

Trade creation is expected to occur as countries gain access to larger markets, thereby benefiting them through comparative advantage, as cross-border trade provides both new markets for exports and cheaper imported goods, thereby increasing consumer's surpluses and allowing production gains.[70] Under this model, regional integration is achieved through various stages in linear succession, which include preferential and free trade areas—in which participating countries scale down or completely abolish tariffs and other quantitative restrictions on trade among them; a Customs Union—which includes both the abolition of tariffs among participating countries and the adoption of a common external trade policy by all participating countries; and a Common Market—which involves the abolition of all barriers to trade and the movement of factors of production (labour and capital).[71] More advanced forms can also include an Economic Union, with the adoption by participating countries of common economic policies or a Monetary Union, in which participating countries adopt a common currency.[72]

In this context, law is used primarily to conduct a discriminatory integration, to ensure that only participating countries can benefit from the preferential treatment offered by a specific regional scheme.[73] At the initial stage, which can include the establishment of a Preferential or a Free Trade Area, this is achieved through the adoption of appropriate rules of origin (ROOs), which constitute an import instrument that lists all the goods originating from the Member States which are exempt from customs duties within the region. A Common External Tariff (CET) constitutes another legal tool used to generate deeper integration and to allow countries participating in a regional scheme to control all trade flows coming into their region. A CET differs from the ROOs by the fact that it requires the adoption of a more sophisticated and more condensed regulatory mechanism aimed at managing the collective actions of the participating countries. In the same vein, the establishment of a Common Market and an Economic Union requires the adoption of a significant number of common rules to regulate the participating countries' trade and financial policies with a view to achieving their common goal of ensuring the free flow of goods and factors of production.

Under the Vinerian paradigm, there is a general assumption that the gradual establishment of a Common Market will be influenced by the spillover effect of increased trade and free movement of factors of production, thus making deeper integration a necessity.[74] This approach, however, has been heavily criticised for not taking into account the differences across regions regarding resources endowment, the participating countries' ability to successfully implement the various stages of deeper integration as well as the specific opportunities available to countries involved in such initiatives.[75] This model has been depicted as being inappropriate for the needs and circumstances of developing countries in general and African countries in particular.[76]

Moreover, this approach is believed to be particularly suited for the European integration process from which it originated, therefore providing for economic and political models that are more suitable for European circumstances that are different from the circumstances of most African countries.[77] In addition to trade creation and trade diversion and trade issues, in the African context, a greater emphasis is placed on economic transformation and the need for industrialisation and export diversification.[78] This particular issue, which could explain the limited progress experienced by regional integration initiatives in Africa, calls for an alternative approach to regionalism, a subject which is covered in the section discussing the concept of regional developmentalism through law.

III.2.2. Political and Legal Approaches to Regional Integration

The primary focus of the political approach to regional integration is the understanding of the institutional and regulatory dimensions of integration.

In particular, this approach provides various theories that help identify the political context in which integration takes place, the particular role played by the state in this context and the different factors that influence the successful development of regional integration processes. Moreover, similar to the political school under the developmental state paradigm, rather than focusing on the ideological paradigm followed by a particular regional process, this approach places a stronger emphasis on the various characteristics that both regulatory and institutional frameworks need to take in order to ensure the successful achievement of the participating countries' objectives.

Several theories have been developed for this purpose, including functionalism and institutionalism—which focus either on the objectives of a particular integration process or the political institutions established to achieve them—as well as intergovernmentalism and supranationalism—which highlight the particular role played by, as well as the different power dynamics between, the common institutions created to coordinate regional processes and the states involved in those processes. These dynamics often determine the type of regulatory framework adopted by the participating countries and regulate the demand for secondary rules aimed at the implementation of their common objectives.

Functionalism is concerned with identifying particular issues and needs that exist outside the realms of politics—including economic, social and technical issues—and concentrates on various measures required to solve them. Under this perspective, regional integration can be achieved by indirectly seeking out areas of mutual interest and allocating resources with a view to solving them.[79] Regional organisations are therefore created to address the participating countries' needs in a particular sector. The assumption here is that successful integration in particular sectors will create a "spillover effect" which will, as a result, foster a deeper integration by spreading to other sectors. The functionalist approach is based on the principle of a gradual transfer of sovereignty in particular policy areas that are considered as a priority by the participating countries.[80] In this context, rather than focusing on the participating countries' economies in general, regional rules are used to target specific sectors that seem particularly promising in terms of profit and economic growth, as well as to implement measures that aimed at increasing the production in those sectors.

As a corollary of the functionalist theory, neo-functionalism focuses on the various factors that influence decision-makers in favour of further integration in the countries participating in regional integration initiatives.[81] Neo-functionalism emphasises the various sets of interests and different groups involved in the advancement of integration processes, which could include common institutions such as the European Court of Justice, regional interest groups such as the East African Law Society and corporations involved in cross-border trade.[82] This approach highlights the need for regulatory frameworks to include rules and mechanisms that reflect the views and contributions of a wide range of actors and which gives them the possibility to influence the progression of the integration process and the achievement of the regional objectives.

In contrast, institutionalism places a particular emphasis on the role of common institutions rather than particular issues and highlights the ability for these institutions to support the countries' efforts in solving a wide range of different issues, including economic, political and social issues. Under this theory, it is argued that institutions are likely to support countries in solving collective action issues and other challenges faced by countries participating in economic and political integration.[83] Furthermore, institutions are believed to be created and specifically designed to promote cooperation through the facilitation of reciprocity and in linking the various issues at hand. Instead of focusing on particular sectors as prescribed by the functionalist approach, this theory highlights the role of regional organisations which are deemed to provide an avenue for participating countries to address multiple issues arising over a longer period of time.[84]

Similar to institutionalism, the proponents of supranationalism argue that successful regional integration can only be achieved through the establishment of regional institutions with increased power and autonomy, which are independent of the participating countries. Here a particular emphasis is placed on the rules and mechanisms that are needed to ensure that the regional institutions are effectively operational and that they have the capacity to monitor and steer the regional process. Correspondingly, this approach also includes the adoption by these institutions of regional laws which are expected to prevail over the municipal laws of the participating countries.[85] This is explained by the fact that these supranational institutions are considered as representative of the interests of a nascent transnational society and are therefore expected to work with public and private actors at both regional and national levels to ensure the advancement of the regional process through the expansion of the domain of supranational governance.[86]

Intergovernmentalism builds upon the previous theories and acknowledges the key role played by economic interests in advancing integration efforts as well as the importance of regional institutions in facilitating the participating countries' collecting action and cooperation. However, it differs from both institutionalism and supranationalism in that it highlights the crucial role played by the states as the driving forces behind regional processes, and emphasises the fact that common institutions and supranational actors are largely dependent on state action.[87] According to this approach, which accords priority to the actions taken by the participating countries' governments, there is no particular need for either a significant number of common policies or strong regional institutions, as each participating country is supposed to adopt laws and policies that are relevant to their national needs and particular circumstances.

In this context, intergovernmental institutions are usually weak and are likely to include a secretariat with no special autonomy and which operates only to facilitate cooperation among the participating countries.[88] As a consequence, regulatory frameworks under the intergovernmental approach tend to be very limited, providing only for the general objectives to be achieved by a particular region but relying primarily upon both national institutions and legal systems for the implementation of those objectives. This approach is deemed particularly suitable for the accommodation of the participating countries' concerns over their sovereignty or any external interference with their international affairs.

These various approaches are used throughout the monograph to consider the different aspects of the law and the crucial role that it could play in advancing regional integration in the African context. This proves particularly important given the general assumption that states in Africa are weak and therefore likely to lack the capacity needed to effectively coordinate complex regional integration processes. State capacity is believed to be further limited by the fact that state apparatus in a majority of African countries represent the perception of a small group of actors, including national elites and key bilateral and multilateral donors with particular interests often are not in line with the countries' needs.[89] Moreover, this analysis also engages with the particular emphasis on formal and absolute state sovereignty[90] by national political leaders and the detrimental effect that this is likely to have on regional processes which are often considered as a means to increase the national elites' credibility in their international relations rather than formal commitments to regional objectives.[91]

It is against this theoretical background that the section provides an initial overview of major regional processes which have been initiated in Africa, highlighting the evolution towards the Vinerian model of regionalism through the establishment of Customs Unions and Common Markets across the continent.

V. Overview of Regional Integration Efforts in Africa

As mentioned in the introduction to this chapter, regional integration initiatives in Africa have a long history whose origins can be traced back to the colonial period. Since the independence era (the late 1950s, early 1960s), there has been a proliferation of regional organisations on the continent, each of them being given the ambitious mandate of supporting integration and tackling the development challenges of a specific region. Regional integration has been considered as an avenue for the promotion of measures for economic cooperation and a necessary tool to help address the multiple issues faced by the majority of African countries, including the balkanisation of the continent, state structural deficiencies and economic challenges.[92]

It is for this purpose that the Organisation of African Unity (OAU) was established in 1963 in Addis-Ababa, with a view to being the most inclusive regional initiative on the continent.[93] The establishment of the OAU was the first comprehensive effort to promote African-wide cooperation with the long-term vision of promoting unity and solidarity amongst African states; to protect and defend the sovereignty, territorial integrity and independence of its

Member States; and to overcome all forms of colonialism.[94] The organisation was aimed at promoting the common interests of its Member States through the coordination and the harmonisation of their general policies in economic and other critical areas.[95] Initial efforts were therefore based on a strong intergovernmentalist approach, the establishment of the OAU being aimed at promoting cooperation among the participating countries while highlighting their desire to retain their newly acquired autonomy and independence.[96]

However, the OAU's efforts to achieve African unity and promote a continent-wide cooperation proved unsuccessful, prompting the shift to a new strategy for the promotion of economic development in Africa which included, inter alia, the establishment of sub-regional organisations and the strengthening of existing ones in the view to establish an African Common Market. This new strategy was laid out in the Lagos Plan of Action for Economic Development in Africa (LPA), a document adopted by the OAU Heads of State and Government in Lagos, Nigeria, in April 1980, which paved the way for the shift to economic integration and the adoption of the Vinerian model of regionalism.[97]

This new vision was further expanded and developed in the Treaty of Abuja, which provided for the establishment of a continental Common Market in the form of an AEC. Through the Treaty of Abuja, a stronger emphasis was placed on economic issues and on various factors supposed to promote economic growth across the continent.[98] The establishment of an AEC was seen as an attempt to put in place a framework providing the pre-requisites for regional integration to be adequately pursued in Africa.[99] For this purpose, the Treaty of Abuja provides for a six-step process towards the achievement of continent-wide economic integration over 34 years, which include the "gradual removal of obstacles among Member States to the movement of persons, goods, services and capital".[100] The AEC constitutes a component of the African Union, which was established on 26 May 2001 and launched on 09 July 2002 to replace the OAU.[101]

The reliance on RECs as building blocks to achieve continent-wide economic integration constitutes one of the distinctive features of the Treaty of Abuja. In particular, the AEC is expected to be established through the coordination, the harmonisation and the gradual integration of the activities of the various RECs. This strategy, which is provided in article 4(1) (d) of the AEC Treaty, is intended to provide some degree of manageability that is expected to accommodate sub-regional particularities with a view to gradually develop a continental Common Market.[102] Through the coordination and the harmonisation of the RECs' policies, the AEC is therefore expected to play a crucial role in the implementation of regional integration as a means to promote development across the continent.[103]

Eight RECs have been selected as the pillars upon which the AEC is expected to be established. These include the Arab Maghreb Union (UMA), the Community of Sahel-Saharan States (CEN-SAD), the Economic Community of West African States (ECOWAS), the Intergovernmental Authority for

Development (IGAD), the East African Community (EAC), the Economic Community of Central African States (ECCAS), the Common Market of East and Southern Africa and the Southern African Development Community (SADC).

However, despite the establishment of the RECs and the fact that most of them include the establishment of Economic Unions and Common Markets, progress towards deeper regional integration has been rather unsatisfactory.[104] As of 2013, only COMESA, EAC, ECCAS, ECOWAS and SADC had managed to set up a Free Trade Area; COMESA had initiated the establishment of a Customs Union, while the EAC was the only REC that had managed to establish a fully functioning Customs Union.[105] This situation can be attributed to various issues, including the particular economic approach adopted by the RECs, the complex institutional framework which has been established by each REC and the numerous and overlapping memberships of countries in different organisations.[106] In addition, the different RECs designated as the pillars of the AEC have been evolving and developing on separate pace and path, a situation which, if it not addressed properly, could result in the impossibility to merge them into a single continental Community.[107]

As highlighted in the previous section, the particular model of regionalism adopted by the majority of RECs, which is based on neoliberal underpinnings and therefore promotes trade liberalisation and economic integration as instruments to promote development across the continent, has been criticised as being inadequate to the particular circumstances of most African countries.[108] A particular emphasis is placed on the fact that this model was developed in the context of industrialised countries with pre-existing cross-border trade activities, a context which is in contrast with that of the majority of countries in Africa, where both cross-border trade and industrial levels are low.[109]

It is against such backdrop that the concept of regional developmentalism through law is used as theoretical basis throughout the monograph, with a view to providing an approach to regionalism that is both comprehensive and adapted to the particular circumstances of the African countries.

VI. Regional Developmentalism Through Law

The broader concept of regionalism—which can be defined as a process providing common rules, regulations, and policies with the view to meeting the needs of a specific region[110]—is used to describe regional developmentalism through law and allows us to assess the African RECs in their own terms and contexts rather than focusing solely on their progress towards economic integration and trade liberalisation.[111] The analysis conducted throughout this study, therefore, focuses on regionalism as a particular scheme to achieve development, given the fact that in the context of Africa, regionalism is considered as a key instrument to promote the social-economic transformation of the continent rather than resulting from the development of the participating countries.[112] Socio-economic transformation is considered as a pre-requisite for development across the continent and constitutes the particular concern of the majority of countries involved in regional schemes.

Inspired from the new developmental state paradigm,[113] regional developmentalism through law is aimed at providing an approach to regionalism that investigates the various rules, methods and legal mechanisms most likely to promote regional development in the particular context of Africa. This approach departs from the focus on modernisation as the main development strategy and, rather than focusing on particular concepts and models which are considered as universal and deemed to be applicable to industrial and developing countries, argues for the adoption of a dynamic approach to development which is adapted to the particular circumstances of a specific region.

In particular, this vision departs from the focus on neoliberal or market-led regionalism, which prescribes trade liberalisation and both regional and international economic integrations as objectives to be achieved by all means in order to promote development. Instead, this approach places economic development at the centre of regional efforts and seeks to identify the various barriers preventing countries from achieving this particular goal. The capacity for law to foster regional development is analysed in light of those considerations. For this purpose, alongside economic integration, a particular attention is also placed on cooperation-led regional development, which involves the coordination of actions and projects determined by the participating countries' areas of common interest and intended at accommodating concerns over their autonomy and sovereignty.[114] The main focus of the study remains, nevertheless, the economic challenges faced by the African countries in general, and trade issues in particular.

The monograph provides a holistic approach to regional development in which trade liberalisation and both regional economic integration and regional cooperation are examined as means among others used to achieve human well-being and increased living standards through increased economic growth and capacity-building. Given the particular circumstances and historical background of most African countries and the specific needs of their economies, the analysis conducted in each chapter also investigates other means used in the context of regionalism to promote economic transformation and support national development policies, including infrastructure building, the adoption of appropriate industrial policies, the creation of dynamic comparative advantages, knowledge coordination between public and private sectors in law-making and the use of state action to identify growth sectors and enhance the private sector's competitiveness. Both state and market are understood to play a key role in the successful implementation of the proposed measures. In this context, regional development is also believed to include a political component, with a particular accent being placed on self-reliance and autonomy which are considered as a precondition for the success of regional schemes in Africa. These various considerations constitute the main components of the concept of regional developmentalism through law, which is developed throughout the monograph.

VII. Conclusion

This chapter was used to develop the concept of regional developmentalism through law, which constitutes the conceptual framework within which this study is developed. The chapter provided for the different components of the general structure of the study, placing a strong emphasis on the various ways and the various areas in which law can be used to promote development in the context of regionalism. The chapter also examined the theoretical considerations underlying the correlation between the main topics analysed throughout the monograph, namely law, regionalism and development, using these correlations to explain the choice of the concept of *regional developmentalism through law* as a suitable theoretical framework to study the crucial role that law can play to support the achievement of the objectives of the Treaty of Abuja.

In particular, while a brief historical background and a general overview of regional integration efforts were used to situate the study within the literature and to provide the general context in which it is developed, the switch from old regionalism to new regionalism allowed us to distinguish different approaches and mechanisms within which law is expected to play a key role to support regional initiatives. While under old regionalism a particular emphasis was placed on the crucial role played by the state to promote development through regional cooperation, as well as interventionist and protectionist measures; new regionalism focused more on the role of the market and the promotion of freer trade through legal and economic integration.

Both analyses were used to identify the key aspects that law can take in the context of regionalism. These include the economic component, which provides for the main strategy adopted to promote regional development, taking into account the particular circumstances of the participating countries; and the political component, which focuses on the institutional and legal aspects of regionalism and the various mechanisms needed to ensure the successful achievement of the regional objectives. In light of these considerations, the last section of the chapter was used to introduce the concept of *regional developmentalism through law*, which emphasises the need to adopt a conceptual structure in which the various regional schemes under the banner of the AEC are analysed in light of their ability to adopt regulatory and institutional frameworks that are adapted to the circumstances and particular needs of the African economies.

Notes

1. The concept was developed in Cappelletti, M., Seccombe, M. and Weiler, J. (1986), *Integration Through Law: Europe and the American Federal Experience—Vol. 1: Methods, Tools and Institutions, Bk 2: Political Organs, Integration Techniques and Judicial Process*, Berlin; New York: W. de Gruyter, p. 42.
2. Ibid.
3. This distinction between rules and mechanisms has been developed in Toohey, L. (2011) 'When "failure" Indicates Success: Understanding Trade Disputes

Between ASEAN Members' in Buckley, R.P., Hu, R.W. and Arner, D.W. (eds) *East Asian Economic Integration: Law, Trade and Finance*, Cheltenham; Northampton: Edward Elgar, p. 150.
4. See Davidson, P. (2004) 'The ASEAN Way and the Role of Law in ASEAN Economic Cooperation' *Singapore Year Book of International Law* 8, p. 167.
5. See Porges, A. (2011) 'Dispute Settlement' in Chauffour, J-P. and Mau, J-C. (eds) *Preferential Trade Agreement Policies for Development: A Handbook*, Washington, DC: The World Bank, p. 467.
6. Schwarzenberger, G. (1962) *The Frontiers of International Law*, London: Steven and Sons Limited, p. 14.
7. Hurrell, A. (2001) 'The Politics of Regional Integration in MERCOSUR' in Bulmer-Thomas, V. (ed.) *Regional Integration in Latin America and the Caribbean: The Political Economy of Open Regionalism*, London: University of London, Institute of Latin American Studies, p. 200.
8. Carreau, D., Juillard, P. and Flory, T. (1980) *Droit international économique*, 2nd ed., Paris: Librairie Générale de droit et de jurisprudence; Fox, H. (1992) 'The Definition and Sources of International Economic Law' in Fox, H. (ed.) *International Economic Law and Developing States: An Introduction*, London: British Institute of International and Comparative Law, p. xxi; Ver Loren van Themaat, P. (1981) *The Changing Structure of International Economic Law: A Contribution of Legal History, of Comparative Law and of General Legal Theory to the Debate on a New International Economic Order*, The Hague; Boston; London: Martinus Nijhoff Publishers.
9. See, generally, Schwarzenberger (1970).
10. De Waart, P., Peters, P. and Denters, E. (1988) *International Law and Development*, Dordrecht; Boston; London: Martinus Nijhoff Publishers, p. xxiii.
11. See Bach, D. (1998) 'Régionalisme et mondialisation en Afrique subsaharienne: le retournement d'un paradigme' in Bach, D. (ed.) *Régionalisation, mondialisation et fragmentation en Afrique subsaharienne*, Paris: Karthala, p. 18. Original colonial territories members of the Federation included Senegal, French Sudan (currently Mali), French Guinea (currently Guinea) and Cote d'Ivoire.
12. See Peters, W.C. (2010), *The Quest for an African Economic Community: Regional Integration and Its Role in Achieving African Unity: The Case of SADC*, Frankfurt am Main: Peter Lang, p. 67. The foundations of SACU were laid as early as 1889. Its founding members included South Africa, Lesotho, Botswana and Swaziland.
13. See Robson, P. (1968) *Economic Integration in Africa*, London: Allen and Unwin, p. 97. The framework for regional cooperation in the region was developed during the colonial period through the establishment of a Customs Union between Kenya and Uganda, later joined by the then Tanganyika.
14. See, generally, Merry, S.E. (1991) 'Law and Colonialism' 25(4) *Law and Society Review* 890, p. 891.
15. See, generally, Lugard, F. (1922) *The Dual Mandate in Tropical Africa*, Edinburgh; London: W. Blackwood and Sons. See also Betts, R.F. (2004) *Decolonization*, London; New York: Routledge and Darby, P. (1987) *The Three Faces of Imperialism*, New Haven, CT: Yale University Press, p. 31.
16. See, generally, Frank, A.G. (1966) *The Development of Underdevelopment*, New York: Monthly Review Press, p. 5. See also Merry (1991), p. 891 and Radice, H. (2008) 'The Developmental State Under Global Neoliberalism' 29(6) *Third World Quarterly* 1153, p. 1159.

The capitalist system is understood here as a system based on an economy controlled and developed by a private ownership driven by the need to exploit and commodify resources, including labour, to increase its profit.

17. See, generally, Merry (1991), p. 896.
18. See Freund, B. (1988) *The Making of Contemporary Africa*, Houndmills: Palgrave Macmillan and Boone, C. (2003) *Political Topographies of the African State: Rural Authority and Institutional Choice*, Cambridge: Cambridge University Press.
19. See Rodney, W. (1974) *How Europe Underdeveloped Africa*, Cape Town; Dakar; Nairobi; Oxford: Pambazuka Press (originally published in 1972 by Bogle-L'Ouverture Publications), pp. 155–157. These transnational trading companies included, *inter alia*, French-controlled *Compagnie Française d'Afrique Occidentale (CFAO), Société Commerciale Ouest Africaine* (SCOA) and British-controlled United Africa Company (UAC) in West Africa. These companies specialised in the export of various goods such as cocoa from Cote d'Ivoire and the Gold Coast (currently Ghana) or groundnut, coffee and bananas from Guinea.
20. See Ninsin, K.A. (2008) 'West Africa's Integration: The Logic of History and Culture' in Adejumobi, S. and Olukoshi, A. (eds) *The African Union and New Strategies for Development in Africa*, Amherst, New York: Cambria Press, p. 133.
21. See Rodney (1974), p. 157.
22. See Jones, C.A. (1983) *The North-South Dialogue: A Brief History*, London: Frances Pinter, pp. 1–15. See also Trebilcock, M.J. and Prado, M.M. (2014) *Advanced Introduction to Law and Development*, Cheltenham: Edward Elgar, p. 187.
23. See Holland, R.F. (1985) *European Decolonization 1918–1981: An Introductory Survey*, Basingstoke; London: Palgrave Macmillan, p. 112.
24. See Pahuja, S. (2011) *Decolonising International Law: Development, Economic Growth and the Politics of Universality*, Cambridge: Cambridge University Press, p. 38. The author develops this argument with reference to developing countries in general.
25. See Chatterjee, P. (1993) *Nationalist Thought and the Colonial World: A Derivative Discourse*, Tokyo: Zed Books for the United Nations University, p. 30. See also Arndt, H.W. (1987) *Economic Development: The History of an Idea*, Chicago; London: University of Chicago Press. Here the author argues that the acceptance by developing countries of their *backwardness* was made possible by the separation of the political and the economic spheres at the international level, leading them to strive for equality at the political level and to accept their putative inferiority at the economic level.
26. See, generally, Rist, G. (1997) *The History of Development: From Western Origin to Global Faith*, London: Zed Books.
27. See Trebilcock and Prado (2014), p. 15.
28. Wealth being measured here by a country's gross domestic product (GDP) or its gross national income (GNI).
29. Trubek, D.M. and Santos, A. (2006) 'Introduction: The Third Moment in Law and Development Theory and the Emergence of a New Critical Practice' in Trubek, D.M. and Santos, A. (eds) *The New Law and Economic Development: A Critical Appraisal*, Cambridge: Cambridge University Press, p. 17. See also Pahuja (2011), p. 56.
30. See Trebilcock and Prado (2014), p. 4.
31. For the particular use of legal transplants in modernisation processes, see Newton, S. (2006) 'The Dialectics of Law and Development' in Trubek, D.M. and Santos, A. (eds) *The New Law and Economic Development: A Critical Appraisal*, Cambridge: Cambridge University Press, pp. 180–189. See also Sherman, F.C. (2009) 'Law and Development Today: The New Developmentalism' 10(9) *German Law Journal* 1257, p. 1261. This use of legal

transplants provides a first insight into the particular role that law is supposed to promote development, which will be subsequently developed in the particular context of regional integration.

32. See, generally, Schwarzenberger, G. (1970) *Economic World Order? A Basic Problem of International Economic Law*, Manchester: Manchester University Press.
33. See Mkandawire, T. (2001) 'Thinking About Developmental States in Africa' 25 *Cambridge Journal of Economics*, p. 290.
34. Pririe, I. (2013) 'Globalisation and the Decline of the Developmental State' in Fine, B., Saraswati, J. and Tavasci, D. (eds) *Beyond the Developmental State: Industrial Policy Into the Twenty-First Century*, London: Pluto Press, p. 148.
35. This distinction has been provided in Fine, B. (2013) 'Beyond the Developmental State: An Introduction' in Fine, B., Saraswati, J. and Tavasci, D. (eds) *Beyond the Developmental State: Industrial Policy Into the Twenty-First Century*, London: Pluto Press, p. 4.
36. See Trubek, D.M. (2009) 'Developmental States and the Legal Order: Towards a New Political Economy of Development and Law' *Legal Studies Research Paper Series Paper No.1075* (University of Wisconsin Law School), p. 3.
37. See Castells, M. (1992) 'Four Asian Tigers With a Dragon Head: A Comparative Analysis of the State, Economy and Society in the Asian Pacific Rim' in Henderson, R. and Applebaum, J. (eds) *State and Development in the Asian Pacific Rim*, London: Sage Publications, p. 55. See also Fine (2013), p. 4.
38. See Mkandawire (2001), p. 291.
39. See Stubbs, R. (2009) 'Whatever Happened to the East Asian Developmental State? The Unfolding Debate' 22(1) *Pacific Review*, pp. 1–22. See also Evans, P., Rueschemeyer, D. and Skocpol, T. (eds) (1985) *Bringing the State Back In*, Cambridge: Cambridge University Press.
40. See Fine (2013), p. 4. See also Khondker, H. (2008) 'Globalisation and State Autonomy in Singapore' 36(1) *Asian Journal of Social Science*, p. 36.
41. See Kufuor, K.O. (2006) *The Institutional Transformation of the Economic Community of West African States*, Aldershot: Ashgate, p. xii.
42. See Chang, H-J. (2015) 'Is Industrial Policy Necessary and Feasible in Africa? Theoretical Considerations and Historical Lessons' in Noman, A. and Stiglitz, J.E. (eds) *Industrial Policy and Economic Transformation in Africa*, New York: Columbia University Press, p. 44.
43. See, generally, Shapiro, H. (2007) 'Industrial Policy and Growth' *DESA Working Paper No. 53*, p. 1. See also Trubek and Santos (2006).
44. See Trebilcock and Prado (2014), p. 19. The concentration on the production of raw materials and primary commodities was considered as detrimental to these countries' long-term developmental goals, given the particularly deteriorating terms of trade of these products compared to manufactured goods produced by industrialised countries.
45. See in particular Frank (1966).
46. See, generally, Tamanaha, B. (1995) 'Lessons of Law-and-Development Studies' 89(2) *American Journal of International Law*, p. 478 and Coastworth, J. (2005) 'Structures, Endowments and Institutions in the Economic History of Latin America' 40(3) *Latin America Research Review*, p. 126.
47. The classical theory of international trade was developed in Smith, A. (1904) *The Wealth of Nations*, 5th ed. (first published in 1776), London: Methuen & Co Ltd. And Ricardo, D. (1817) *On the Principles of Political Economy*, London: John Murray. While Smith focused on specialisation in international trade, Ricardo developed the theory of comparative advantage in international trade.

48. See Riedel, J. (1986) 'Myths and Reality of External Constraints on Development' *Thames Essays No.47*, London: Trade Policy Research Centre, p. 11.
49. Smith (1904), Book IV. See also Lowenfeld, A.F. (2008) *International Economic Law*, 2nd ed. Oxford; New York: Oxford University Press, p. 5.
50. See Mensah, J. (ed.) (2008) *Neoliberalism and Globalization in Africa: Contestations From the Embattled Continent*, New York: Palgrave Macmillan, p. 3. See also Balassa, B. (1989) *Comparative Advantage, Trade Policy and Economic Development*, London: Harvester Wheatsheaf, p. 3.
51. See Pitelis, C.N. (2011) 'Foreign Direct Investment and Economic Integration' in Jovanovic, M.N. (ed.) *International Handbook on the Economics of Integration, Vol. III: Factor Mobility, Agriculture, Environment and Quantitative Studies*, Cheltenham; Northampton: Edward Elgar, p. 21.
52. Ibid. See also Jomo, K.S., Chung, C.Y., Folk, B.C., ul-Haque, I., Phongpaichit, P., Simatupang, B. and Tateishi, M. (1997) *Southeast Asia's Misunderstood Miracle: Industrial Policy and Economic Development in Thailand, Malaysia and Indonesia*, Boulder (USA) and Oxford: Westview Press.
53. See Kowalski, P. (2011) 'Comparative Advantage and Trade Performance: Policy Implications' *OECD Trade Policy Paper No 121,* OECD Publishing, p. 8. See also generally Helpman, E. (2010) 'Labor Market Frictions as a Source of Comparative Advantage, with Implications for Unemployment and Inequality' *NBER Working Paper* No. 15764.
54. See Harrison, G. (2000) *Neoliberal Africa: The Impact of Social Engineering*, London; New York: Zed Books, p. 5.
55. Cammack, P. (2002) 'Neoliberalism, the World Bank and the New Politics of Development' in Khotari, U. and Minogue, M. (eds) *Development Theory and Practice: Critical Perspectives*, Basingstoke: Palgrave, p. 159.
56. See Radice (2008), p. 1155.
57. Harvey, D. (2007) 'Neoliberlism as Creative Destruction' *The Annals of the American Academy of Political and Social Science*, Vol. 610 NAFTA and Beyond: Alternative Perspectives in the Study of Global Trade and Development, p. 22.
58. This process has been referred to either as *neoliberal globalisation*—in analyses presenting neoliberalism as being the inherent nature of globalisation—or *globalised neoliberalism*—which considers neoliberalism as one of the various theories which are being spread through globalisation, in the same way that capitalism was spread to the rest of the world through colonisation. This aspect of globalisation is analysed in more detail in Chapter 5, which focuses on the political economy of regional integration in Africa. For further details on the rise to prominence of neoliberalism, see, among others, Hayashi, S. (2010) 'The Developmental State in the Era of Globalisation: Beyond the Northeast Asian model of Political Economy' 23(1) *The Pacific Review*, pp. 45–69; Peck, J. and Tickell, A. (2002) 'Neoliberalizing Space' 34(3) *Antipode*; and Radice (2008).
59. See Comaroff, J. and Comaroff, J.L. (2000) 'Millennial Capitalism: First Thoughts on a Second Coming' 12(2) *Public Culture*, p. 305. See also
60. See Cammack (2002), p. 5.
61. See Kufuor (2006), p. xiii.
62. See, generally, Ferguson, J. (2006) *Global Shadows: Africa in the Neoliberal World Order*, Durham and London: Duke University Press. See also Khotari, U. and Minogue, M. (eds) (2002) *Development Theory and Practice: Critical Perspectives*, Basingstoke: Palgrave and Cooke, B. (2003) 'A New Continuity with Colonial Administration: Participation in Development Management' 24(1) *Third World Quarterly*, pp. 47–61.

63. See Trebilcock and Prado (2014), p. 19.
64. See Biswaro, J.M. (2012) *The Quest for Regional Integration in the Twenty First Century: Rhetoric Versus Reality: A Comparative Study*, Dar Es Salaam: Mkuki na Nyota, p. xx.
65. See Kyambalesa, H. and Houngnikpo, M. (2006) *Economic Integration and Development in Africa*, Aldershot: Ashgate, p. xxv. See also United Nations Economic Commission for Africa (hereinafter UNECA) (2010) *Assessing Regional Integration in Africa IV: Enhancing Intra-African Trade*, Addis Ababa: UNECA, p. xix
66. See Kennes, W. (1999) 'Africa Regional Economic Integration and the European Union' in Bach, D. (ed.) *Regionalisation in Africa: Integration and Disintegration,* Oxford: James Curry. See also Omilola, B. (2011) 'To What Extent Are Regional Trade Agreements in Africa Fulfilling the Conditions for Successful RTAs?' 3(6) *Journal of African Studies and Development* 105.
67. This approach was developed by Jacob Viner in his Viner, J. (1950) *The Customs Union Issue,* London; Lancaster, PA: Stevens and Sons. The approach was further developed in Balassa, B. (1962) *The Theory of Economic Integration*, London: Allen and Unwin.
68. This is the approach adopted by the Treaty of Abuja, which provides in its article 6 for the gradual establishment of an AEC in six stages, which include the gradual abolition of tariff and non-tariff barriers. As will be highlighted in the following section, the same approach is followed by the various RECs which constitute the pillars of the AEC.
69. See Mattli, W. (1999) *The Logic of Regional Integration: Europe and Beyond*, Cambridge: Cambridge University Press, pp. 31–32.
70. See Pelkmans, J. (1986) *Completing the Internal Market for Industrial Products*, Luxembourg: Office for Official Publications of the European Communities, p. 318.
71. For more details, see Balassa (1962) and Kyambalesa and Houngnikpo (2006), p. 1.
72. Ibid. The Eurozone, which includes 19 of the 28 members of the European Union, falls in this category.
73. See, generally, Hansen, J.D. and Nielsen, J.W. (1997) *An Economic Analysis of the European Union*, 2nd ed., London: The McGraw-Hill Companies, p. 4.
74. See Biswaro (2012), p. 32.
75. See, for example, Peters (2010), p. 60 and Gambari, J.A. (1991) *Political and Comparative Dimensions of Regional Integration: The Case of ECOWAS*, Atlantic Highlands, NJ; London: Humanities Press International, p. 13.
76. See in particular Draper, P. (2010) 'Rethinking The (European) Foundations of Sub-Saharan African Regional Economic Integration: A Political Economy Essay' *OECD Development Centre Working Papers*, No. 293, OECD Publishing, Paris.
77. Ibid.
78. See Robson, P. (1997) 'Integration in Sub-Saharan Africa' in El-Agraa, A.M. (ed.) *Economic Integration Worldwide,* Basingstoke: Palgrave Macmillan, pp. 268–295.
79. The theoretical framework on which this approach is based was developed in Mitrany, D. (1944) *A Working Peace System* (version published in 1966 by Quadrangle Books).
80. This theoretical framework is used as a basis for the analysis of cases of sectoral integration, which is included as one of the key aspects of the regional developmentalism.
81. Neo-functionalism has been described in Haas, E. (1964) *Beyond the Nation-State: Functionalism and International Organization*, Stanford, CA: Stanford University Press.

82. See Biswaro (2012), p. 20 and Mattli (1999), p. 24. These aspects are analysed in the monograph when discussing particular cases such as the European Economic Community or the East African Community.
83. This theory is developed in Keohane, R.O. (2003) 'Political Authority After Intervention—Gradation in Sovereignty' in Holzrefe, J.K. and Keohane, R.O. (eds) *Humanitarian Intervention: Ethical, Legal and Political Dilemmas,* Cambridge: Cambridge University Press.
84. See Biswaro, J.M. (2005) *Perspectives on Africa's Integration and Cooperation: From OAU to AU: Old Wine in New Bottle?* Dar-es-Salaam: Tanzania Publishing House.
85. This aspect of supranationalism is analysed in more detail when discussing the principles of direct effect and supremacy of regional law.
86. Sweet, A.S. and Brunell, T.L. (1998) 'Constructing a Supranational Constitution: Dispute resolution and governance in the European Community' 92 (1) *The American Political Science Review*, p. 63.
87. This particular approach was developed in Moravcisk, A. and Schimmerlfenning, F. (2009) 'Liberal Intergovernmentalism' in Wiener, A. and Diez, T. (eds) *European Integration*, Oxford: Oxford University Press, pp. 67–87.
88. See Kennes (1999), p. 32.
89. See Simon, D. (2003) 'Regional Development-Environment Discourses, Policies and Practices in Post-Apartheid Southern Africa' in Grant, A. and Soderbaum, F. (eds) *The New Regionalism in Africa*, Aldershot, England: Ashgate, p. 71.
90. Absolute sovereignty here includes the formal maintenance of state borders and the principle of non-interference in domestic affairs.
91. See, generally, Clapham, C. (1996) *Africa and the International System: The Politics of State Survival*, Cambridge: Cambridge University Press. See also Soderbaum, F. (2004) 'Modes of Regional Governance in Africa: Neoliberalism, Sovereignty Boosting, and Shadow Networks' 10(4) *Global Governance* 419, p. 426.
92. See Kouassi, R.N. (2007) 'The Itinerary of the African Integration Process: An Overview of Historical Landmarks' 1 *African Integration Review*, p. 1. See also Kennes (1999), p. 27.
93. All but one (Morocco) of the 53 independent states of Africa eventually became OAU members.
94. These were among the objectives that were provided in article II(1) of the Charter of the Organisation of African Unity (hereinafter OAU Charter).
95. OAU Charter article II(2). Other critical fields included, inter alia, transport and communications, education and culture, and scientific and technological cooperation.
96. See Mahiou, A. (1993) *La Communauté Economique Africaine,* 39(1) *Annuaire français de droit international,* p. 799. The author also highlights the fact that economic integration was not included in the objectives of the early efforts towards regionalisation.
97. See Onwuka, R. and Sesay, A. (1985), *The Future of Regionalism in Africa*, London: Palgrave Macmillan, p. 59.
98. See Peters (2010), p. 26.
99. See UNECA (2008) *Assessing Economic Integration in Africa III: Towards Financial and Monetary Integration in Africa*, p. 1.
100. See Article 4(2) of the AEC Treaty.
101. See www.au.int/
102. See Oppong, R.F. (2011) *Legal Aspects of Economic Integration in Africa*, Cambridge: Cambridge University Press, p. 19.
103. See article 4(1)(d) of the AEC Treaty.

104. See Malewezi, J. (2001) 'Regional Integration: The Path to Prosperity?' in Clapham, C., Mills, G., Morner, A. and Sidiropoulos, E. (eds) *Regional Integration in Southern Africa: Comparative International Perspectives*, Johannesburg: SAIIA, p. 19.
105. See UNECA (2013) *Assessing Regional Integration in Africa VI: Harmonising Policies to Transform the Trading Environment*, Addis Ababa: UNECA.
106. See Gathii (2011), p. 2 and Bhagwati, J.N. and Krueger, A.O. (1995) *The Dangerous Drift to Preferential Trade Agreements*, Washington, DC: AEI Press, p. 2. According to the United Nations Economic Commission for Africa (UNECA) in 2006, out of the 53 Member States of the African Union (former OAU), 26 belonged to at least two regional organisations, 20 belonged to three and one country belonged to four.
107. See UNECA (2006), p. xiii. See also Oppong (2011), p. 75, and Mevel, S., Karingi, S. (2013) 'Towards a Continental Free Trade Area in Africa—A CGE Modelling Assessment with a focus on Agriculture' in Cheong, D., Jansen, M. and Peters, R. (eds) *Shared Harvests: Agriculture, Trade and Employment*, ILO & UNCTAD, p. 281.
108. See Malewezi (2001); Peters (2010), p. 60; and Draper (2010).
109. See Malewezi (2001), p. 21.
110. Mattli (1999), p. 44.
111. This particular approach towards regionalism in Africa is prescribed in Gathii (2011), p. xxix.
112. The promotion of development is provided in article 4(1)(a) of the AEC Treaty as well as in all the Treaties which established the various RECs. This particular aspect of regional integration in the African context has also been analysed in Kufuor (2006), p. ix.
113. The new developmental state paradigm highlights the need for development policies to be adapted to the particular circumstances of different countries and regions and rejects the idea of one-size-fits-all strategies originating from the belief of the existence of universal models and concepts of development. This paradigm argues for the adoption by the state of policies that are not directed to the entire economy but are rather designed for specific sectors and intended to vary across geographic locations. This paradigm has been analysed in Sherman (2009) and Trubek (2009).
114. Further details on the distinction between regional integration and regional cooperation are provided in Langhammer, R. and Hiemenz, U. (1990) *Regional Integration Among Developing Countries: Opportunities, Obstacles, and Options*, Tübingen: JCB Mohr, p. 2.

3 Political Economy of Regionalism in Africa

I. Introduction

As discussed in the previous chapter, the Treaty of Abuja, signed in 1991 by the Member States of the former Organisation of African Unity (OAU), has provided for the achievement of a continental Common Market in Africa by 2028.[1] The Common Market is expected to be established gradually in six stages, of which four involve the establishment and further development of Free Trade Areas and Customs Unions at the level of each Regional Economic Community (REC) listed by the African Union as one of the pillars of the African Economic Community (AEC). This approach to regional integration, which is rooted in the Vinerian (linear) model of economic integration, places a particular emphasis on trade liberalisation and the establishment of sub-regional markets across the continent.

However, the analyses provided in the previous chapter highlighted the need for legal frameworks to be adapted both to regional objectives and to participating countries' particular circumstances for regional integration processes to be successful. Taking this into consideration, the analysis conducted in this chapter focuses on the substantive rules provided by the various integration initiatives which are the subject of experimentation within the continent so far and reconsiders their theoretical foundations and relevance given the particular context of Africa.

In an attempt to both distinguish and understand the particular model of regionalism adopted by the Treaty of Abuja and to further explore the different concepts introduced in the previous chapter, the analysis in this chapter focuses on the different factors that have influenced the different waves of regionalism on the continent, which have been referred to as the move from *old regionalism* to *new regionalism*.[2] In light of the different constraints and challenges still faced by the continent today, the chapter questions the policy process which has shaped regionalism schemes in Africa to date, highlighting the particular emphasis on regional economic integration. In light of this trend, the chapter argues for the need of a different approach to regionalism based on regional developmentalism which, rather than focusing primarily on trade liberalisation and market integration, would be used to promote key sectors in the

RECs economies and to improve specific capabilities more likely to promote sustained economic growth and development across the continent.[3]

In the particular context of Africa, regional integration has often been associated with economic growth and development, as the former is believed to support the achievement of the latter.[4] As discussed in a previous chapter, comparative advantage and economies of scale have often been used as rationale for regional integration in Africa, as it is believed that the African economies, being too small to be viable and to benefit from global economy, would benefit from the integration of their different national markets, economies of scale as well as the pooling of their means of production.[5] Regional integration has therefore been included in the development discourse and listed as one of the key points in the development policies articulated at the continental level.

In order to clearly identify the key factors that have influenced the development discourse in Africa and their correlation with regional integration, the chapter is divided into four key periods which have been affected by different approaches to and/or theories of development and have subsequently produced various sets of different development policies: the period of self-reliance and state-led developmentalism (1960s to early 1980s), which followed the independence of a majority of African countries and influenced the adoption of the Charter of the OAU and the Lagos Plan of Action (LPA); the period of structural adjustment, the Washington Consensus and the subsequent focus on trade liberalisation (1980s to 1990s), which witnessed the significant reduction in the role of the state and the adoption of the Treaty of Abuja; the Post-Washington Consensus (1990s to 2000s) with the adoption of the New Partnership for Africa's Development (NEPAD) Framework; and recent developments, including the Continental Free Trade Area (CFTA), the Tripartite Free Trade Area (TFTA), the Action Plan for Boosting Intra-African Trade (BIAT) and the Programme for Infrastructure Development in Africa (PIDA).

Despite five decades of various programmes and initiatives designed to promote development, Africa remains the least developed continent in the world.[6] The question of efficient allocation of African countries' resources and the integration of their economies into the global system continues to be well debated. Given the fact that the continent's economy continues to be significantly characterised by the production and subsequent export of similar commodities predominantly based on primary products[7] and consequently by situations in which the economies of most neighbouring countries do not complement each other and therefore are not suitable for intra-African trade,[8] several authors have questioned the foundations of African regional integration in Africa and have called for the adoption of a new approach which would not be based solely on trade liberalisation.[9]

Taking into account the different periods in the development discourse in Africa and highlighting the various constraints identified in the literature on regional integration, the chapter argues for the adoption of a new approach to regionalism on the continent, an approach that would provide for rules focusing on trade facilitation, infrastructure and capacity-building, industrialisation, as well as measures that would need to be adapted to each region's needs and particular circumstances.[10] The analysis conducted in the following sections, which reflects the various points mentioned above, is therefore intended to provide a political economy of regionalism in Africa through the application of the various theoretical arguments developed in the previous chapter, with a view to identifying the most efficient way in which law could be used to strengthen the efforts towards regional development across the continent. It is against such backdrop that the analysis provided in the next chapters is developed.

II. The 1960s to 1980s: The First Attempt Towards Self-Reliance and State-Led Developmentalism

After their accession to independence, the majority of Sub-Saharan African countries (hereinafter SSA countries) sought to extend their newly acquired political autonomy to their economic activities and adopted a series of measures and policies which constitute what has been coined as *state-led developmentalism*.[11] Motivated by the desire to overcome their economic dependence on the former colonial powers,[12] most SSA countries opted for state interventionism and protectionism, which included the concentration of government intervention in economic activities and sectors which were considered as more profitable than others. In most countries, this approach involved a policy of import substitution industrialisation, given that most of their economies were characterised by the production and export of raw material and primary commodities and the import of manufactured good.[13] Import substitution industrialisation was therefore designed to create and promote national industries supposed to produce manufactured products intended specifically to replace similar products imported from developed countries.[14]

As discussed in previous chapters, this approach was based on the developmental state paradigm, in which the states consider the promotion of sustained economic development and the allocation of a country's resources as their primary responsibility.[15] During this period, the state's responsibility was thought to include the elaboration of economic policies and the adoption of various measures to promote economic growth, such as the use of tariffs and quantitative restrictions to protect infant industries from foreign influence.[16] This was achieved by measures such as the control of inward investments to ensure that foreign capital was used to promote the countries' national interest, focusing on priorities such as the development of viable manufactures and infrastructures.[17]

It is in this context that in May 1963, the African states signed the Charter establishing the OAU, an institution which was supposed to complement and promote their national development programmes.

II.1. Regional Cooperation and Self-Reliance in the Charter of the Organisation of African Unity (OAU) and the Lagos Plan of Action (LPA)

The objectives of the OAU were, *inter alia*, to "coordinate and intensify [its Member States'] cooperation and efforts to achieve a better life for the peoples of Africa".[18] The focus under the OAU was on the *regional cooperation* among its Member States rather than *regional integration*, as during this period, a stronger emphasis was placed on the role of the state, which was supposed to retain its prerogatives in the planning of its economic activities and the adoption of policies adapted to its own development objectives.[19] The Charter provided for economic cooperation and the harmonisation of the Member States' policies targeting the promotion of specific sectors likely to promote economic growth, such as transportation and communication.[20] This approach, which was also adopted by several RECs created during the same period,[21] reflected the desire for the concerned states to protect their newly acquired independence and to retain control over their own development processes while also avoiding foreign interferences in their internal affairs.[22]

However, after almost two decades, the strategy promoted by the OAU did not seem to produce the expected results, as most countries had failed to advance economically.[23] This situation was further exacerbated by the oil crises in the 1970s, which revealed the still strong dependence of African economies on primary commodities and the failure both to industrialise and to diversify their exports.[24] Several reasons have been proposed to explain the failure of state-led developmentalism in Africa during that period. On the one hand, this situation was considered as the result of the strong reliance of the African economies on a few primary commodities and their subsequent vulnerability to price changes and the depreciation of their terms of trade.[25] On the other hand, the failure was believed to be the result of a lack of institutions and administrative mechanisms supposed to provide the African economies with the capacity to implement their development programmes.

To address this issue and find a collective solution to a set of economic problems which affected the entire continent, the OAU Member States (in collaboration with the United Nations Economic Commission for Africa, which provided economic analysis to inform the Member States' decision) adopted the Lagos Plan of Action for the Economic Development of Africa 1980–2000 in April 1980.[26] The LPA was adopted to correct the mistakes of the OAU Charter which had not provided its Member States with enough insight on an Africa-specific approach to economic development and proper guidance on the type of policies which could help them achieve their development goals.[27] The LPA, therefore, proposed an approach to economic development that was regional rather than national and put a particular emphasis on external support and collective self-reliance.[28] The LPA constituted a further step toward a closer cooperation among the OAU Member States and a promotion of regional and sub-regional integration, a new strategy which was evidenced by the wording of the document itself.[29]

Blaming the deterioration of economic conditions in most African countries on structural problems (consequences of colonisation), the "over-dependence of the continent's economy on the export of basic raw materials and minerals", in short, "external economic dependence",[30] the LPA provided for several measures which included, inter alia, the

> realis[ation] [of] sub-regional and regional internally located industrial development; co-operat[ion] in the field of natural resources control, exploration, extraction and use for the development of [their] economies for the benefit of [their] peoples; the set[ting] up of . . . appropriate institutions to achieve these purposes; and the develop[ment] [of] indigenous entrepreneurship.[31]

To achieve its objectives of collective self-reliance and regional interdependence, the LPA identified specific sectors which required a closer cooperation among the OAU Member States.[32] These sectors included agriculture, science, and technology, with a particular emphasis on industry, which was expected to play a major role at both the national and sub-regional levels.[33]

In contrast with the OAU Charter, which focused primarily on (individual) self-reliance, ISI and limited cooperation among OAU Member States, the LPA approach was based on a combination of collective self-reliance, industrialisation and closer sub-regional and regional integration.[34] This approach was subsequently incorporated in the Final Act of Lagos, which, for the first time, envisaged the creation of an AEC which would be aimed at "promot[ing collective, accelerated, self-reliant and self-sustaining development of [the] Member States".[35]

However, this project and the various accompanying measures were heavily criticised and subsequently frustrated by the Bretton Woods institutions (World Bank and International Monetary Fund, hereinafter referred to as Bretton Woods System) and the structural adjustment programmes which initiated the rise of the Washington Consensus as the most prominent approach to development in Africa.

III. The 1980s to 1990s: The SAPs, the Washington Consensus and the Subsequent Focus on Trade Liberalisation

III.1. The Berg Report and Policy-Lending Through the Structural Adjustment Programmes

In response to the LPA, the World Bank published a report entitled "Accelerated Developed in Sub-Saharan Africa: A Plan for Action"[36] intended to provide policy recommendations designed to help the African countries face the type of economic crises that they experienced in the 1970s and the early 1980s.[37] In contrast with the LPA, the Berg Report identified the domestic policies followed by African states rather than external factors as the main reason for their poor economic performance.[38] In particular, the Berg Report noted the failure of African countries to industrialise through import substitution and their increased dependence on exports of a few commodities and imports of capital goods.[39] Rather than advocating for an approach similar to that of the LPA strategy, which was based on collective self-reliance and industrialisation, the Berg Report proposed an economic strategy driven by the market, therefore requiring a significant reduction of the role of the state in economic development.[40]

The approach proposed by the Berg Report served as a precursor for the Structural Adjustment Programmes (SAPs) which impacted the course of the development policy adopted by the continent in the following decades.[41] The SAPs provided for a set of neoliberal policies which focused on privatisation, liberalisation and fiscal austerity.[42] The SAPs also advocated a reduction in the size of governments, more particularly of state's intervention in the economy.[43] This approach, which constituted a shift in global development discourse, was developed into a set of specific policies later coined as the *Washington Consensus*.[44]

The new approach advocated for free trade and placed a particular emphasis on markets rather than states as institutions with the capacity to allocate economic resources more efficiently and thereby promote sustained economic growth.[45] The proponents of this approach, which is based on the principle of comparative advantage, justify its use in the context of Africa by noting the fact that through the export of primary commodities and mineral resources African countries would earn enough foreign exchange and resources necessary for their industrialisation. Their industrialisation was expected to allow them to diversify their exports and thereby promote economic growth.[46]

To achieve this goal, this approach, therefore, advocated for the adoption of an outward-oriented philosophy by developing countries, focusing on exports, trade liberalisation and the organisation through both national and regional markets.[47] These policies were expected to help these countries integrate the world economy from which they were expected to benefit. SSA countries were therefore expected to gradually remove all barriers to trade across-borders in order to promote the production of wealth and benefit among others from foreign investment.[48] Foreign investment was believed to benefit the concerned countries by bringing more factors of production and thereby increasing and diversifying their export base.

Over the years, the Washington Consensus managed to become the norm or paradigm in the global development discourse. Through conditionality imposed by the Bretton Woods System in the structural adjustment programmes, as well as the influence of various development agencies on the choice of policies implemented by aid recipients, market-based ideology quickly became ever-present in the international development discourse and influenced the economic policies of most SSA countries over the years.[49] This new paradigm promoted by the Bretton Woods System and other development agencies was believed to represent a "universal convergence" in the approach towards development and consisted of an economic ideology expected to promote economic development regardless of the national circumstances of the countries supposed to implement it.[50] By adopting this approach, developing countries were therefore expected to conform to international standards by applying an "idealised . . . economic model" which would enable them to catch up with the "developed world".[51]

However, while trade liberalisation and the implementation of market-based policies were expected to promote sustained economic growth and thereby an improvement of the standards of living in those countries, most countries failed to achieve this goal and instead experienced a further deterioration of their economic conditions.[52]

In this particular context of trade liberalisation and market-based reforms, regional integration was expected to focus on freer trade and to involve the removal of tariff and non-tariff barriers to trade among African countries of the same region, thereby promoting the free movement of goods, services and factors of production. This strategy was believed to benefit SSA countries as it would allow them to gain access to regional markets in which they could exchange the products in which they have comparative advantage for those in which they do not.[53] Regional integration was also meant to help them integrate the world economy and therefore to gain access to industrial markets from which they could potentially acquire the technology and resources necessary to upgrade their own local firms and promote the industrialisation of their economy.[54] It is against such background that the AEC was introduced in the Treaty of Abuja adopted in 1994.

III.2. Impact on the Treaty of Abuja and African RECs

Although it was expected to emulate the LPA, the Treaty of Abuja reflected the recent shift of paradigm in the global development discourse. Article 4 of the Treaty of Abuja provided for the objectives of the AEC, which included, *inter alia*, the

> establish[ment] on a continental scale, [of] a framework for the development, mobilisation and utilisation of the human and material resources of Africa in der to achieve a self-reliant development; to promote co-operation in all fields of human endeavour . . . [and] to coordinate and harmonise policies among existing and future economic communities in order to foster the gradual establishment of the Community.

These objectives were rhetorically in line with the vision provided in the LPA, a vision which was meant to be adapted to the specific needs and circumstances of the African continent.

However, the main strategies chosen to achieve these objectives, which were inspired from the market-based reforms conducted across the continent, are likely to be problematic, given all the shortcomings and the adverse effects which have resulted from similar measures.[55] These strategies include, *inter alia*:

III.2.1. Trade Liberalisation

Regional trade liberalisation is provided in article 4.2 of the Treaty of Abuja.[56] Despite the various benefits presented to SSA countries by the proponents of the SAPs, evidence has shown that the policies promoted by the Bretton Woods System and development agencies are unlikely to be adapted to the specific needs and circumstances of the African economies and are therefore not likely to produce the expected results. Complete trade liberalisation, in particular, would not be suitable to most African economies as their exports are not diversified enough and therefore do not have real comparative advantage in the global market.[57]

As was the case during the period of state-led developmentalism, the majority of African economies still depend on the production of a few primary commodities and a significant import of manufactured goods. In the few cases where it has happened, industrialisation has been very slow, given the negative impact resulting from the access to national markets by foreign competitors, often better resourced and producing more attractive commodities. This situation is likely to affect these countries' infant industries, often not able to cope with foreign competition.[58] As a consequence, rather than promoting the industrialisation of these African economies, trade liberalisation has instead increased their dependence on the export of primary commodities, as countries have been unable to promote the growth of their national industries. This situation is unlikely to promote sustained economic growth in most SSA countries, given that the prices of primary commodities tend to decrease compared to the price of manufactured goods imported by SSA countries.[59]

In addition, the promotion of foreign investment, which was expected to provide African economies with new capital and new technologies for their industrialisation, has focused predominantly on the extraction of minerals and the production of a few primary commodities with no equivalent investment in local industries, therefore hindering these countries' goal of diversifying their exports.[60] Moreover, foreign firms in developing countries often turn out to be subsidiaries operating for the benefit of bigger corporations often based in developed countries. These subsidiaries are therefore more likely to transfer any profit made from their activities in these countries to their parent companies in industrialised countries, thereby undermining the economy of the developing state in which they have invested.[61]

Furthermore, exports of most SSA countries continue to be based on similar commodities, which consist mainly of primary commodities and mineral resources.[62] These exports are mostly destined for markets in developed countries which, in turn, provide for the manufactured products imported by SSA countries.[63] Given that most SSA countries do not have industries with the capacity to convert their primary products into processed goods their economies barely complement each other, as they produce goods which are not needed for trade at the regional level.[64]

Sectoral integration, as well as the creation of regional value chains, could constitute viable alternative to complete trade liberalisation as promoted by in SSA countries. As analysed in the context of the European Coal and Steel Community (ECSC) and the Association of Southeast Asian Nations (ASEAN), various sectoral integration initiative could be conducted by taking into consideration the particular circumstances of the participating countries and by targeting key economic sectors which are more likely to promote export diversification and sustained economic growth in the concerned SSA countries. This would allow the SSA countries to proceed to a gradual liberalisation while taking time to organise their economies by improving and strengthening their infant industries' international competitiveness.[65] SSA countries could also draw from the ASEAN model which focuses on establishment of a regional production network through the improvement of regional value chains among the ASEAN countries.[66]

III.2.2. Harmonisation of National Policies[67]

As a consequence of policy-lending through the SAPs and the associated market-based reforms which advocated for a reduction of the size of governments especially in the economic sector, most SSA countries have been deprived of the ability to develop their own development policies and to allocate their domestic resources in order to achieve their development goals, as it was the case in the period of post-independence.[68] The various reforms and structural adjustments required by the Bretton Woods System and different development agencies have resulted in the substitution of the SSA countries by the former as the main actors in policy formulation for development.[69] Over the years, the decision-making powers of the Bretton Woods System and aid agencies regarding the economic policies of Sub-Saharan states have increased to such an extent that these countries have experienced a partial loss of sovereignty, and national governments in those countries have been turned into simple recipients responsible for implementing policies that are elaborated on their behalf.[70]

However, as discussed in the following chapters, policy autonomy is crucial in the context of regional integration. The ASEAN Charter, for instance, has provided for specific measures aimed at preserving the ASEAN countries' policy autonomy as well as preventing any interference in their internal affairs.[71] Moreover, in the context of the European Community, despite the fact that the European Union (EU) has adopted a liberal (free market) approach to regional integration,[72] EU countries initially retained their autonomy to develop their own economic policies.[73] Although the Community has evolved over the years to now include supranational policy and decision making, the EU countries have retained a relative control over their economic and development policies through both supranational and intergovernmental institutions.[74] This arrangement has allowed the EU countries to develop a set of economic policies at the regional level which are intended to both complement and harmonise their national policies.

In this context, regional integration efforts in Africa are not likely to be successful in achieving their objectives, given the inability for SSA countries to set their own development goals and develop their national economic policies. This situation is further aggravated by the rules governing the world trading system, which further restrain the SSA countries' policy autonomy. These rules are analysed in the following section which focuses on GATT/WTO.

III.3. Further Trade Liberalisation Through GATT and the WTO

The World Trade Organization (WTO) was established in January 1995 to regulate and promote international trade.[75] Similar to the Bretton Woods System, the WTO system was developed within market-based discourse that promotes trade liberalisation as the most appropriate method to promote economic growth and development. The WTO system is expected to promote the free movement of goods across the globe by providing a set of coercive rules and principles against any governmental interventions likely to affect free competition and a market-based international economy.[76] To achieve this goal, the WTO provides for a set of rules and principles aimed at setting international standards which are not always adapted to the needs and circumstances of most developing countries.[77] These principles include, inter alia, National Treatment and the Most-Favoured-Nation rule, which are aimed at promoting a freer trade, fair competition and reciprocity among the WTO Member States.[78]

Rules governing regional integration are found in GATT 94 article XXIV, which provides for the establishment of Free Trade Areas and Customs Unions which are expected to promote trade liberalisation through regional trade agreements providing for closer integration between the economies of countries involved in such processes.[79] For this purpose, countries parties to such agreements are expected to eliminate any customs duties or other restrictive measures of trade "with respect to substantially all trade" between them.[80]

However, as discussed earlier, complete trade liberalisation does not seem adequate in the Sub-Saharan context, given that most SSA countries' economies are based on the production and subsequent export of a few unprocessed products, including agricultural commodities and mineral resources which do not constitute a viable source of revenue given their price fluctuation. To benefit from international trade and thereby promote their sustainable economic growth, trade policies in SSA countries could instead focus on industrialisation and structural transformation, which would, in turn, support the production of processed and manufactured goods and thereby promote export diversification.[81]

For this purpose, SSA countries are expected to opt for an approach to regional integration which could be considered as non-WTO-compliant. This approach is to be based on targeting and selectivity, and to include sectoral integration initiatives as well as the adoption of interventionist measures aimed at promoting trade facilitation, while also strengthening key sectors and industries likely to help these countries achieve their development goals. However, such an approach to regional integration could be accommodated under the WTO Enabling Clause adopted in 1979,[82] which constitutes an exception to GATT 94 article I:1 (most-favoured-nation obligation) targets regional trade agreements involving less-developed countries. In particular, the Enabling Clause provides for a series of exceptions to the MFN rule[83] that are particularly "designed to facilitate and promote the trade of developing countries" in light of their particular circumstances.[84] These provisions under the Enabling Clause, therefore, seem to indicate that safeguard measures and mechanisms that are particularly designed to promote trade and economic growth while being tailored to the needs of developing countries could be allowed under the WTO rules, even in case they are not consistent with the provisions of GATT 94 article XXIV.[85]

In addition to the safeguard measures provided under the Enabling Clause, SSA countries may also invoke GATT 94 article XVIII, which provides for special measures designed for the protection and the nurturing of infant industries in poor developing countries and countries with balance-of-payment issues, with a view to developing their economies.[86] This provision can be used to justify punctual state intervention within the African RECs to support the establishment and the growth of regional industries which have the capacity to promote regional development.

The analysis conducted in this section was used to highlight the particular way in which the coercive rules and principles provided by the various WTO agreements have also placed a stronger emphasis on the promotion of free trade as a goal to be achieved by SSA countries. This approach has been reflected in trade agreements both among SSA countries and with their external partners, which tend to place a particular accent on the promotion of trade liberalisation rather than focusing on more urgent development priorities.[87]

IV. The Late 1990s to 2000s: The Post-Washington Consensus and NEPAD

IV.1. Re-Introduction of the State Through Good Governance and the Rule of Law

The year 1990 experienced another shift in international ideology which influenced the reconsideration of the role of the state in the development discourse. Given the apparent failure of the SAPs and the subsequent debates on the role that states should play in economic development, the Bretton Woods System proceeded to a re-conceptualisation of the concept of development.[88]

It is in this context that the state was reintroduced in the development discourse through what has been coined as the *Post-Washington Consensus* and the corollary concepts of *good governance* and *rule of law*.[89]

Good governance and rule of law were introduced in an attempt to improve the SAPs, which were believed to have been unsuccessful given their failure to handle the economic structures and the institutional frameworks of the recipient countries.[90] The new Consensus, therefore, reintroduced the state in the development discourse, limiting its role to that of an *enabling state* expected to provide a favourable environment in which a market can both be established and function properly.[91]

A well-functioning market is believed to require *good* governance and the adoption and subsequent enforcement of *appropriate* policies, which include property rights and product liability rules, bankruptcy legislation, and well-functioning bureaucratic and court systems to help coordinate various market activities.[92] New concepts have therefore been included in the development discourse, including *institution-building*, to provide states with the appropriate political framework intended to build confidence around market security as well as *law reform*, aimed at improving predictability by providing a set of new and efficient legal rules.[93] Law reform, in particular, is expected to promote economic growth by providing the market with a rules-based coordination mechanism which is likely to promote the rule of law, increase predictability and lower transaction costs, thereby ensuring the proper functioning of the market.[94] As pointed out in Chapter 2, law in this context is expected to stem from a specific model of rules which is deemed to be *ideal* or *global*, and therefore to provide for a set of *international* standards which countries are encouraged to follow through harmonisation and legal convergence in order to achieve economic growth and development.[95]

With this new paradigm, which is based on the liberal democracy theory, the focus is no longer on reducing the role of the state but rather on capacity building and the creation of an *effective state*.[96] However, despite the re-conceptualisation of the role of the state in development under the Post-Washington Consensus, the economic approach promoted under the first Washington Consensus remains virtually the same. Good governance and rule of law reforms, which are intended to help countries improve both their institutional and legal frameworks, are conceived and developed as market-enhancing instruments rather than engines promoting sustained economic growth.[97]

This new approach has also been reflected in various regional reforms conducted across the continent, including by the strengthening of regional institutional and legal frameworks (ECOWAS) and the promotion of legal reforms aimed at providing appropriate rules-based mechanisms deemed necessary to promote intra-regional trade (OHADA, for instance). However, as argued in previous sections, these various reforms, which are meant to conform to international standards, are not always suitable in the context of Sub-Saharan Africa. Given the SSA countries' economic conditions, the emphasis should rather be on concepts such as *developmental* governance and the implementation of special rules targeting specific sectors and aimed at enhancing key governance capabilities needed to support sustained economic growth and the development of their economies.[98]

IV.2. Second Attempt Towards Regional Developmentalism Through NEPAD

The NEPAD Framework was adopted by the Member States of the African Union in October 2001.[99] Similar to the LPA, NEPAD is a policy document aimed at providing the African Union with a programme promoting sustainable economic growth and development across the continent. Taking into account the various shifts in global development discourse, the NEPAD Framework is intended to provide a new approach in addressing Africa's economic challenges which is supposed to be adapted to the SSA countries' particular circumstances. For this purpose, NEPAD is intended to provide a "common vision . . . [in order] to place [African countries], both individually and collectively, on a path for sustainable growth and development and, at the same time, to participate actively in the world economy".[100]

Acknowledging the particular situation of African economies (including the over-dependence on the production of a few commodities, the inability to properly compete in the world economy and the consequent marginalisation created by this situation),[101] NEPAD provides a new strategy and a set of new policies that place a particular emphasis on economic and corporate governance. This new strategy also advocates for regional and sub-regional approaches to development[102] and focuses in particular on regional capacity-building and a greater use of the state to promote economic growth and development in Africa. This strategy, which is expected to result from empowerment and self-reliance, is supposed to provide for a new and more appropriate paradigm to address the perpetuation of poverty in SSA and to foster sustainable development across the continent.[103]

The new strategy introduced by NEPAD, therefore, provides a new approach towards regional integration that is rhetorically based on regional developmentalism and is supposed to correspond to the continent's specific conditions.[104] This new approach provides a set of key propositions that are supposed to help the SSA countries achieve their economic goals, including a re-conceptualisation of the role played by the state in regional integration (to ensure, *inter alia*, the effective ownership of development programmes), the adoption of regional and sub-regional priorities and a particular focus on popular participation. Through these various measures, regional integration efforts are expected to move from trade liberalisation and a market-based focus to a stronger emphasis on sustainable development and the improvement of SSA countries' international competitiveness.[105]

IV.2.1. Re-Conceptualisation of the Role of the State

To ensure the effectiveness of policy-making and the implementation of economic policies which are adapted to the particular needs of the continent, the role of the state, as well as state interventionism, are redefined in the development discourse, focusing on capacity-building and collective self-reliance.[106] The state is expected to be used in this context to identify regional and sub-regional development priorities and to help create a strong regional production base which is intended to focus on the strengthening of national industries within specific regions.[107]

This focus on the role of the state also highlights the need for development programmes and initiatives to be primarily set by the SSA countries according to their regional needs rather than being strongly influenced by external factors.[108]

IV.2.2. Increased Popular Participation

This proposition focuses more particularly on the need to establish new economic and political structures which would be more adapted to regional needs and priorities, promoting popular participation in the policy-making process and ensuring that both industries and local businesses' inputs are taken into account in development-related policy-making. This strategy is used to promote a people-based development and to ensure the adoption of new policies which are adapted to each region's needs and priorities, thereby ensuring the effective implementation of these policies.[109]

IV.2.3. Identification of Both Sectoral and Regional Priorities

The goal of this measure is to enhance regional development and economic integration in the view to improve the international competitiveness of the SSA countries' economies. This goal is meant to be achieved through the pooling of neighbouring countries' resources to enhance regional development as well as through the identification of common projects compatible with integrated country and regional development programmes. This also involves the harmonisation at the regional level of economic and investment policies on matters of common interest.[110]

This strategy also includes the identification of a set of measures aimed at supporting local production in key sectors which are more likely to promote a sustainable development across the continent's regions and sub-regions.[111] Moving on from the focus on trade liberalisation and the economic growth expected to result from such process, this new approach is aimed at promoting economic transformation and industrialisation.[112] These economic priorities include, inter alia, the promotion of agriculture, the building of regional and continental infrastructure, skills development and access to the markets of developed countries for African exports.[113]

However, it should be noted that, unlike the LPA, which was taken into in the elaboration of the Treaty of Abuja, NEPAD's policies have not been translated into any Treaty or Convention at either continental or regional levels. In addition, neither the Treaty of Abuja nor the Treaties establishing the various RECs have been amended to include the various recommendations which have been made by NEPAD. Furthermore, NEPAD was intended to provide a separate framework promoting economic cooperation among its participating countries and therefore has not provided for either a rules-based or an institutional mechanism to support the effective implementation of its various recommendations.[114] The lack of both a clear strategy and adequate regulatory and institutional frameworks has therefore prevented the effective implementation of the new paradigm provided through NEPAD.[115]

V. Recent Developments: CFTA, TFTA, BIAT and PIDA

In the same vein as that of NEPAD, the African Union has launched recent initiatives which are, inter alia, aimed at advancing regional integration at the continental level. These initiatives include the African Union Agenda 2063, which constitutes a strategic framework document adopted by the African Union in 2013 providing for actions and measures aimed at boosting the socio-economic transformation of the continent in the next 50 years.[116] The Agenda aspires to, inter alia, a "prosperous Africa based on inclusive growth and sustainable development" and an "integrated continent, politically united and based on the ideals of Pan-Africanism and the vision of Africa's Renaissance".[117]

In particular, the goal of integrating the continent is expected to be achieved through the creation of a CFTA, which is supposed to be the first major step towards the establishment of the AEC.[118] The negotiations for the establishment of the CFTA were launched by the AU Assembly at the 25th Summit of Heads of State and Government on 15 June 2015 in Johannesburg, with the aim of reaching agreements on trade in goods and services, while resolving the main issues hindering regional integration efforts in Africa, including multiple and overlapping memberships, RECs progressing at different pace, and insufficient competitiveness, economic transformation, industrialisation and production diversification.[119]

The TFTA launched on 10 June 2015 by the Heads of State and Government of the Common Market for Eastern and Southern Africa (COMESA), East African Community (EAC) and Southern African Development Community (SADC) constitutes yet another recent initiative aimed at launching a third wave in regional integration efforts in Africa, moving from RECs to continent-wide groupings.[120] The TFTA, which will include 26 countries with a combined population of 530 million and a GDP of 630 billion US dollars, could potentially give the impetus for more interregional groupings and, thereby, boost the establishment of the CFTA.[121]

Alongside the CFTA and the TFTA, other regional initiatives have been launched with the aim of solving the issues of the lack of sufficient production capacity and industrialisation faced by most African economies. This is particularly the case of the Action Plan for BIAT adopted by the African Union

Heads of State and Government in January 2012 to tackle supply constraints through trade facilitation, productive capacity enhancement, trade finance, trade-related infrastructure improvement etc.[122] Similar to BIAT, PIDA, a joint initiative headed by the African Union Commission, NEPAD's Development Planning and Coordination Agency and the African Development Bank, was endorsed by the African Union Heads of State and Government in January 2012 with a view to developing a strategic framework for the building and development of regional infrastructure meant to boost the productive capacity of the African economies.[123]

Similar to the various measures advocated by NEPAD, these recent initiatives reflect various aspects of the regional developmentalism approach proposed throughout this study and reaffirm the need for regional frameworks to be adapted to local circumstances and realities. In the particular context of the AEC, alongside rules aimed at promoting economic integration and market access (demand), there is a more urgent need for appropriate regulatory arrangements targeting trade facilitation, productive capacity building and economic transformation.[124]

VI. Conclusion

This chapter was aimed at providing a clear understanding of the particular circumstances within which the AEC introduced by the Treaty of Abuja is expected to be established. The analysis conducted in the chapter highlighted the particular constraints and challenges faced by SSA countries and the various ways in which regional integration has been employed to address them. In addition, the study of the different shifts in both global and continental development discourses has allowed us to understand the specific model of regional integration adopted by the Treaty of Abuja, and more particularly its focus on market-led integration and the establishment of a continental Common Market.

As in the previous chapter, this chapter was used more particularly to highlight the need for regional integration efforts to be adapted to the particular circumstances and specific needs of countries involved in such processes. Through different sections which concentrated on various strategies adopted by African regional integration processes, the analysis conducted in this chapter was used to demonstrate that focusing on trade liberalisation and market-led integration alone is not sufficient to promote sustainable economic growth and thereby foster development across the continent.

A particular emphasis was therefore placed on the various attempts made over the years to re-conceptualise the foundations of regional integration in Africa and the need to reconsider the role of regionalism in the development discourse. NEPAD, CFTA, TFTA, BIAT and PIDA, which are the latest of such initiatives, were used to provide a new approach based on regional developmentalism through law, which advocates for the adoption of a set of frameworks that need to be adapted to regional and sub-regional needs and priorities.

The various aspects of the study conducted in this chapter are used in the last chapters of the monograph, which provide a critical analysis of various regional processes conducted across the continent, focusing on the legal framework provided by these schemes and assessing their suitability based on the particular circumstances within which their objectives are supposed to be achieved.

Notes

1. Article 6 of the Treaty of Abuja provides for the establishment of the AEC "in 6 stages of variable duration over a transitional period [which should not exceed] thirty-four years".
2. This distinction has been provided, among others, in Kufuor, K.O. (2006) *The Institutional Transformation of the Economic Community of West African States (ECOWAS)*, Aldershot: Ashgate. See also Mansfield, E.D. and Milner, H.V. (1999) 'The New Wave of Regionalism' 53 *International Organization* 589 and Krueger, A. (1995) *Trade Policies and Developing Nations*, Washington, DC: Brookings Institution. The authors note the general trend followed by countries involved in *old regionalism* schemes (the 1950s to 1990s), which mostly adopted import-substitution and protectionist measures, while *new regionalism* initiatives (post-1990s) focus more on market-led integration and the establishment of Monetary and Economic Unions.
3. The concept of regional developmentalism has been discussed and developed in chapter two of the monograph.
4. Bobo, B.H. and Sintin-Aboagye, H. (eds) (2012), *Neo-Liberalism, Interventionism and the Developmental State: Implementing the New Partnership for Africa's Development*, Trenton, New Jersey; London: African World Press, p. ix.
5. See Hope, R.K. (2002) 'From Crisis to Renewal: Towards a Successful Implementation of the New Partnership for Africa's Development' 101 *African Affairs*, pp. 387–402.
6. United Nations Development Programme (2014), *Human Development Report*, p. 163. Of the six regions of the world (which also include the Arab States, East Asia and the Pacific, Europe and Central Asia, Latin America and the Caribbean and South Asia), SSA has the lowest Human Development Index. For further discussions on the apparent lack of impact of the various development programmes and initiatives in Africa, see Bobo and Sintin-Aboagye (2012); Mbaku, J.M. (2004) 'NEPAD and Prospects for Development in Africa' 41(4) *International Studies* 387–409; and Mills, G. and Oppenheimer, J. (2002) 'Partners, Not Beggars' 160 (2) *Time Europe*, p. 35.
7. As it will be explained later, most of most of these commodities being destined for the industrialised countries in the north, which, in turn, provide most of Africa's imports in manufactured goods.
8. To have economies that complement one another, the neighbouring countries would need to produce and exchange commodities that are more diversified and are needed in their respective national markets.
9. On the unsuitability of neighbouring economies for intra-African trade see Ilorah, R. (2012) 'The Realities of Regional Integration: The NEPAD Perspective' in Bobo and Sintin-Aboagye (eds), p. 187. See also Jebuni, C.D. et al. (1999) 'A Case Study of the Economic Community of West African States (ECOWAS)' in Oyejide, A., Elbadawi, I. and Yao, S. (eds) *Regional Integration and Trade Liberalisation in Sub-Saharan Africa*, Vol.3: Regional

Case Studies, London: Houndmills, p. 38 and pp. 24–65. On the need for a new approach to regional integration see Draper, P. (2010) 'Rethinking The (European) Foundations of Sub-Saharan African Regional Economic Integration: A Political Economy Essay' *OECD Development Centre Working Papers*, No. 293, OECD Publishing, Paris

10. See Kaplinsky, R. (2005) *Globalisation, Poverty and Inequality: Between a Rock and a Hard Place*, Cambridge: Polity, p. 240.
11. See Meyns, P. and Musamba, C. (2010) 'Introduction: Recent Debates on the Developmental State in Africa' in Meyns, P. and Musamba, C. (eds) *The Developmental State in Africa: Problems and Prospects*, Institute for Development and Peace, University of Duisburg-Essen (INEF-Report, 101/2010), p. 7 and Rapley, J. (1996) *Understanding Development: Theory and Practice in the Third World*, Boulder, CO; London: Lynne Rienner, pp. 27–44. This situation has also been discussed in Mkandawire, T. (2001) 'Thinking about Developmental States in Africa' 25 *Cambridge Journal of Economics*, p. 291. Various studies have been conducted on specific countries, including in Edge, W.A. (1998) 'Botswana, A Developmental State' in Edge, W.A. and Lekorwe, M.H. (eds) *Botswana: Politics and Society*, Pretoria: J.L. van Schaik, pp. 333–348 and Meisenhelder, T. (1997) 'The Developmental State in Mauritius' 35(2) *Journal of Modern African Studies*, pp. 279–297.
12. Gunder Frank, A. (1970) 'The Development of Underdevelopment' in Rhodes, R. (ed.) *Imperialism and Underdevelopment*, New York, London: Monthly Review Press, pp. 4–17.
13. See, in general, Chang, H-J. and Rowthorn, R. (eds) (1995) *Role of the State in Economic Change*, Oxford: Clarendon Press; New York: Oxford University Press.
14. See Rapley (1996), pp. 27–44.
15. See Castells, M. (1992) "Four Asian Tigers with Dragon Head: A Comparative Analysis of the State, Economy and Society in the Asian Pacific Rim' in Henderson, R. and Applebaum, J. (eds) *State and Development in the Asian Pacific Rim*, London: Sage, p. 55 and Mkandawire (2001), p. 290. See also Prempeh, H.K. (2006) 'Marbury in Africa: Judicial Review and the Challenge of Constitutionalism in Contemporary Africa' 80(4) *Tulane Law Review*, p. 1262 and Salacuse, J.W. (1999) 'From Developing Countries to Emerging Markets: A Changing Role for Law in the Third World' 33 *International Law*, 875, p. 876.
16. These measures were part of the Import Substitution Industrialisation (ISI) strategy adopted by several countries in the 1960s, including Ghana, Madagascar, Nigeria, Tanzania and Zambia. For more details, see Chang, H. (2004) 'Institutional Foundations for Effective Design and Implementation of Trade and Industrial Policies in Least Developed Economies' in Soludo, C., Ogbu, O. and Chan, H. (eds) *The Politics of Trade and Industrial Policy in Africa: Forced Consensus?* Trenton, NJ: Africa World Press, p. 135.
17. Kapur, D. et al. (1997) *The World Bank: Its First Half Century*, Washington, DC: Brookings Institution, pp. 537–547. See also Vandervelde, K.J. (1998) 'The Political Economy of a Bilateral Investment Treaty' 92(4) *The American Journal of International Law* 621, p. 622.
18. Charter of the OAU, article II (1)(b).
19. See Ngugi, J.M. (2005) 'Policing Neo-Liberal Reforms: The Rule of Law as an Enabling and Restrictive Discourse' 26 *U.Pa.J.Int'l Econ. L.* 513, p. 526. This strategy is similar to the approach that was adopted by the ASEAN countries in the 1967 ASEAN Declaration.
20. See Charter of the OAU, article II (2).

21. This vision was adopted by the Members of the Southern Africa Development Coordination Conference (SADCC) and inspired its Project Coordination Approach (PCA) to regionalism. A similar vision was adopted in the 1975 ECOWAS Treaty, which provided for the "promotion of cooperation and development" among its Member States.
22. See Barkan, J.D. (1994) 'Resurrecting Modernisation Theory and the Emergence of Civil Society in Kenya and Nigeria' in Apter, D.E. and Rosberg, C.G. (eds) *Political Development and the New Realism in Sub-Saharan Africa*, Charlottesville; London: University Press of Virginia, p. 87.This was enshrined in article III of the Charter of the OAU, which lists the "Non-interference in the internal affairs of each state and the respect of the sovereignty and territorial integrity of each State" as principles to be observed scrupulously by all Member States.
23. Tamanaha, B.Z. (1995) 'The Lessons of Law and—Development Studies' 89 *Am. J. Int'l. L.* 470, p. 472.
24. Nyang'oro, J.E. and Shaw, T.M. (1992) *Beyond Structural Adjustment in Africa: The Political Economy of Sustainable and Democratic Development*, New York; London: Praeger, p. 5.
25. See Cardoso, F.H. and Faletto, E. (1978) *Dependency and Development in Latin America*, Berkeley; London: University of California Press, p. xxii.
26. Nyang'oro, J.E. (1992) 'The Evolving Role of the African State Under Structural Adjustment' in Nyang'oro, and Shaw (eds), p. 11.
27. Cummings, R.J. (1992) 'A Historical Perspective on the Lagos Plan of Action' in Nyang'oro, J.E. and Shaw, T.M. (eds) *Beyond Structural Adjustment in Africa: The Political Economy of Sustainable and Democratic Development*, p. 33.
28. OAU (1980) *Lagos Plan of Action for Economic the Development of Africa 1980–2000* (hereinafter LPA), article 1. See also Nyang'oro and Shaw (1992), p. 4.
29. The document included provisions with statements such as "we commit ourselves individually *and collectively*" or "we hold firmly to the view that these commitments will lead to the creation, at the national, *sub-regional* and *regional* levels, of a dynamic and *interdependent* African economy" (LPA, article 3. Emphasis added).
30. See Gathii, J.T. (2000) 'Retelling Good Governance Narratives on Africa's Economic and Political Predicaments: Continuities and Discontinuities in Legal Outcomes Between Markets and States' 45 *Vill.L.Rev.*971, p. 1009.
31. LPA, article 3.
32. See Usman, M.T. 'NEPAD and the Economic Integration Agenda in Africa—Reflection on the Prospect and Constraints' in Boko, S.H. and Seck, D. (eds) (2008) *NEPAD and the Future of Economic Policy in Africa*, Trenton, New Jersey; London: Africa World Press, p. 308.
33. These sectors are provided for in chapters I, II and V of the LPA. Industrialisation is provided in articles 52 and 66a of the LPA. See also Gattamorta, M.E. (2005) 'The Evolution of Development Strategies for Africa: From the Lagos Plan of Action to the Report of the Commission for Africa' *CeMiSS Quarterly*, p. 81.
34. As discussed later in this chapter, this approach adopted by the LPA constitute one aspect of the concept of regional developmentalism, which emulates the ideological component "developmental state" paradigm and argues for the establishment of regional cooperation initiatives primarily aimed at promoting economic development in the participating countries. As highlighted in the context of the "developmental state", *self-reliance* is a key issue in this context,

as it is used to ensure the autonomy of the overall process from any interferences or external influences likely to disrupt the achievement of the objectives assigned to the process.

35. Final Act of Lagos, article II. The Final Act provided for the creation of the AEC as well as the different stages of its implementation.
36. Word Bank (1981) *Accelerated Development in Sub-Saharan Africa: An Agenda for Action.* The report was prepared by Elliott Berg (hereinafter Berg Report).
37. These crises resulted from the oil shocks which occurred in the 1973 and 1979, the subsequent rise and fall in commodity prices (a major part of these commodities being part of Africa's primary exports) and the recourse by African governments to a significant amount of external borrowing from banks in developed countries, which left them in a vulnerable position. The 1973–1975 world recession that caused a decline in exports earnings and the inability for African governments to adopt appropriate measures to respond adequately to the adverse circumstances resulted in the deterioration of economic conditions in SSA and increased indebtedness for most SSA countries. For a more detailed analysis of the 1970s crises, see Clark, J.M. Jr (1992) 'The Sovereign Debt Crisis: A Lawyer's Perspective' in Fox, H. (ed.) *International Economic Law and Developing States: An Introduction*, London: British Institute of International and Comparative Law. See also Law. Krumm, K.L. (1985) 'The External Debt of Sub-Saharan Africa: Origins, Magnitude and Implications for Action' *Staff Working Paper No SWP 741*, Washington, DC: The World Bank.
38. Berg Report, p. 3.
39. Fullbrook, E. (2007) *Real World Economics: A Post-Autistic Economics Reader*, London: Athem Press, p. 275.
40. Bobo and Sintin-Aboagye (2012), p. 13.
41. Nyang'oro and Shaw, (1992), p. 1.
42. Stiglitz, J.E. (2002) *Globalisation and Its Discontents*, New York: W.W. Norton & Co, p. 53.
43. World Bank (1991) *World Development Report 1991: The Challenge of Development*, p. 9.
44. The concept was introduced in Williamson, J. (1990) 'What Washington Means by Policy Reform' in Williamson, J. (ed.) *Latin American Adjustment: How Much Has Happened?* Washington, DC: Institute for International Economics, pp. 7–20. Referring to structural adjustment programmes in Latin America, which were aimed at substituting market-based economic systems for traditional statist systems, the author coined as "Washington Consensus" a set of ten policy reforms recommended by three Washington, DC-based institutions (World Bank, International Monetary Fund and US Treasury Department), which included among others trade liberalisation, deregulation and the promotion of foreign direct investment.
45. See Marangos, J. (2009) 'What Happened to the Washington Consensus? The Evolution of International Development Policy' 38 *The Journal of Socio-Economics* 197, p. 198.
46. See Mkandawire, (2001), p. 305. See also Jackson, J.H. (1997) *The World Trading System: Law and Policy of International Economic Relations*, 2nd ed., Cambridge, MA: MIT Press.
47. See Peet, R. (ed.) (2003) *Unholy Trinity: The IMF, World Bank and WTO*, London & New York: Zed Books, p. 14.
48. Vandervelde (1998), p. 625.
49. A situation sometimes referred to as "policy-lending". See Van Waeyenberge, E. (2006) 'From Washington to Post-Washington Consensus: Illusions of

Development' in Fine, B. and Jomo, K.S. (eds) *The New Development Economics: After the Washington Consensus*, New Delhi: Tulika Books; London: Zed Books, p. 24. See also Boughton, J.M. (2006) 'Who's in Charge? Ownership and Conditionality in IMF-supported Programs' in Ranis, G., Vreeland, J.R. and Kosack, S. (eds) *Globalisation of the Nation State: The Impact of the IMF and the World Bank*, London: Routledge, pp. 19–33.

50. See Williamson, J. (1993) 'Democracy and the "Washington Consensus"' 21(8) *World Development*, p. 1334. See also Peet (2003), p. 14. See also Gibbon, P. (1993) 'The World Bank and the New Politics of Aid' 5(1) *European Journal of Development Research* 35. Killick, T. and Hewitt, A. (1996) 'Bilateral Aid Conditionality and Policy Leverage' in Stokke, O. (ed.) *Foreign Aid Towards the Year 2000: Experiences and Challenges*, London: Frank Cass, pp. 130–167. The authors argue that, over the years, international aid programmes were increasingly shaped after the Bideas and the Washington Consensus.
51. See Pahuja, S. (2011) *Decolonising International Law: Development, Economic Growth and the Politics of Universality*, Cambridge University Press, pp. 3, 38 and 46. The author questions the claim of "universality" shared by the proponents of the new paradigm (universality that the author considers as putative) and argues that the new discourse was adopted to maintain the exemplarity of the West (what was implied by in the term "developed world") and its proven ability to master economic development.
52. Countries like Ghana, for instance, while it was able to relatively increase in its exports as a result of market-based reforms, also experienced a significant decrease in its manufacture production in the early 1990s, hence failing to promote a sustained economic growth—see Shefaeddin, S.M. (2005) 'Trade Liberalisation and Economic Reform in Developing Countries: Structural Change of De-Industrialisation?' *UNCTAD Discussion Paper No.179*. The author argues, inter alia, that liberalisation as an economic policy was only appropriate for countries with industries that were near the stage of maturity (as it had been in the case of the Brazilian aerospace industry) and was likely to have adverse effects developing countries trying to promote their infant industries. See also Bond, P. and Dor, G. (2003) 'Neoliberalism and Poverty Reduction Strategies in Africa' *Discussion Paper for the Regional Network for Equity in Health in Southern Africa (EQUINET)*, p. 8. Here the authors highlight the adverse effects of the reforms on social conditions (standards of living) in Southern African countries, including Malawi, Zambia and Zimbabwe.
53. See Kapur et al. (1997), p. 512.
54. See Bobo and Sintin-Aboagye (2012), p. 214.
55. See Shefaeddin (2005).
56. Article 4.2 of the Treaty of Abuja provides for the "liberalisation of trade through the abolition, among Member States, of Customs Duties levied on imports and exports and the abolition, among Member States of Non-Tariff Barriers in order to establish a free trade area at the level of each regional economic community"
57. See UNECA (1990) *African Alternative Framework to Structural Adjustment Programmes for Socio-Economic Recovery and Transformation*, Addis Ababa: United Nations, p. 19. See also UNCTAD (2000 & 2002) *Trade and Development Report*, New York; Geneva: United Nations. It is argued that, although trade liberalisation might result in a significant increase of exports, it might not constitute the most appropriate measure to help developing countries diversify their exports and shift their production system out of primary commodities and thereby, thereby promoting sustained economic growth. The report argues for trade policies that take into account local circumstances

and maximise a sustained domestic growth, including policies that might not involve the reduction of trade barriers.

58. UNECA (1989), p. 19.
59. See Paul, J.R. (2003) 'Do International Trade Institutions Contribute to Economic Growth and Development?' 44(1) *Virginia Journal of International Law*, p. 30.
60. Alves, P., Draper, P. and Khumalo, N. (2009) 'Africa's Challenges in International Trade and Regional Integration: What Role for Europe?' *SAIIA Occasional Paper No 32*, p. 5.
61. See Vandervelde (1998), p. 626.
62. Ilorah (2012), p. 187.
63. Browne, R.S. (1996) 'How Africa Can Prosper' in Balaam, D.N. and Veseth, M. (eds) *Readings in International Political Economy*, Upper Saddle River, NJ: Prentice Hall; London: Prentice-Hall International, pp. 281–282.
64. Draper (2010), p. 16.
65. Lall, S. (2004) 'Selective Industrial and Trade Policies in Developing Countries: Theoretical and Empirical Issues' in Soludo, Ogbu and Chan (eds). See also Amsden, A.H. (1989) *Asia's Next Giant: South-Korea and Late Industrialisation*, Oxford; New York: Oxford University Press. See also Chang, H. (2002) *Globalization, Economic Development and the Role of the State*. See also Rodrik (2009), p. 217.
66. See Kaplinsky (2005), p. 236. The author discusses the case of China which managed to "source raw materials and capital goods as inputs into its manufacturing processes" from ASEAN countries, including Thailand and Singapore.
67. Article 4.2. (e) of the Treaty of Abuja provides for "the harmonisation of national policies in order to promote Community activities, particularly in the fields of agriculture, industry, transport and communications, energy, natural resources, money and finance, human resources, education, culture, science and technology".
68. Olukoshi, A.O. (2004) 'Democratisation, Globalisation an Effective Policy Making in Africa' in Soludo, Ogbu and Chan (eds), p. 59.
69. van de Walle, N. (2001) *African Economies and the Politics of Permanent Crisis, 1979–1999*, Cambridge: Cambridge University Press, p. 276. As discussed in Peet (2003), this was justified by the fact that international financial institutions were (and are still) considered as the most appropriate actors able to both access and promote the ideal set of economic policies that developing countries need in order to promote economic growth and catch up with developed nations. A similar argument is developed in Boughton (2006).
70. Soludo, Ogbu and Chan (2004), p. 135. See also Collier, P. and Gunning, J.W. (1999) 'Why Has Africa Grown Slowly?' 13(3) *The Journal of Economic Perspectives* 3, p. 13.
71. See ASEAN Charter preamble, para 2(e). See also Okamoto (2011), p. 291, where the author argues that ASEAN was considered by its participating countries as an instrument against external interference in their domestic policies.
72. Kelly, D. (2005) 'Trade, Security and Globalisation' in Kelly, D. and Grant, D. (eds) *The Politics of International Trade in the Twenty-First Century: Actors, Issues and Regional Dynamics*, Houndmills, Basingstoke, Hampshire; New York: Palgrave Macmillan, pp. 75–77. The author argues that the European Union was built on three types of liberalism: democracy or "regulatory liberalism"; commerce and trade or "commercial liberalism"; and institutions or "regulatory liberalism".
73. See Ruggie, J. (1982) 'International Regimes, Transactions, and Change: Embedded Liberalism in the Postwar Economic Order' 36(2) *International*

Organization. Here the author argues that the strategy chosen by the EU was an "embedded liberalism" compromise, which was established gradually.

74. See Giplin, R. (2000) *Global Political Economy: Understanding the International Economic Order*, Princeton, NJ: Princeton University Press, p. 357. See also Draper (2010), p. 11.
75. The creation of the WTO was preceded by the adoption of the General Agreement on Tariffs and Trade in 1947, which provided for the first set of rules aimed at governing international trade. The WTO was established as an intergovernmental organisation in 1995 by the Marrakech Agreement, which also included GATT 47 (in its 1994 amended version). For more details on the various aspects of the WTO, see Jackson (1997). See also Gupta, K.R. (2007) 'Objectives of GATT and Developing Countries' 35(2) *South African Journal of Economics* 126.
76. See Peet (2003), p. 146. See also Hoekman, B.; Mattoo, A. and English, P. (eds) (2002) *Development, Trade and the WTO: A Handbook*, Washington, DC: World Bank, p. 43 and Jackson (1997), p. 49.
77. See Khor, M. (2008) 'The World Trading System and Development Concerns' in Serra, N. and Stiglitz, J. (eds) *The Washington Consensus Reconsidered: Towards A New Global Governance*, Oxford: Oxford University Press.
78. These principles are provided in articles 1 and 3 of GATT 47. While National Treatment obliges WTO Member States to treat imported and locally-produced goods equally, the MFN rule prevents WTO Member States from discriminating between their trading partners and requires them to grant special favours (including lower customs duties applied to foreign goods) to all WTO Members equally.
79. See GATT 94 article XXIV para 4.
80. GATT 94, article XXIV para 8.
81. Noman, A., Botchwey, K., Stein, H. and Stiglitz, J.E. (2012) *Good Growth and Governance in Africa: Rethinking Development Strategies*, Oxford: Oxford University Press.
82. Decision of 28 December 1979 (L/4903), (hereinafter Enabling Clause).
83. Article 2 (c) of Decision L/4903 provides that the contracting parties of the GATT may accord differential treatment to "regional or global arrangements entered into among less-developed contracting parties for the mutual reduction or elimination of tariffs". These provisions provide countries signatories of such agreements with more flexibility than the provisions of GATT 47 article XXIV.
84. Article 3 (a) of Decision L/4903 especially provides that "any differential and more favourable treatment provided under [the Enabling Clause] shall be designed to facilitate and promote the trade of developing countries and not to raise barriers to or create undue difficulties for the trade of any other contracting parties".
85. See WTO, Committee on Trade and Development, Legal note on regional trade arrangements under the Enabling Clause, WT/COMTD/W/114, (13 May 2003), para. 5. For further details on the exceptions provided under the Enabling Clause, see also Alavi, J.S. (2011) 'Regional Trade Agreements among Developing Countries: Enabling Clause Re-visited', *SSRN Electronic Journal*.
86. GATT 94 article XVIII provides that "[t]he contracting parties recognize that the attainment of the objectives of this Agreement will be facilitated by the progressive development of their economies, particularly of those contracting parties the economies of which can only support low standards of living and are in the early stages of development".

87. See Narlikar, A. (2004) 'Developing Countries and the WTO' in Hooking, B. and McGuire, S. (eds) *Trade Politics*, 2nd ed., London; New York: Routledge, p. 137. See also Hoekman, B. and Kostecki, M.M. (2001) *The Political Economy of the World Trading System: The WTO and Beyond*, 2nd ed., Oxford: Oxford University Press and Finger, J.M and Schuler, P. (2002) 'Implementation of WTO Commitments: The Development Challenge' in Hoekman, Mattoo and English (2002). The authors argue that both the WTO rules and principles and the cost incurred by developing countries to implement them have managed to switch these countries' attention from their development goals to the promotion of international free trade.
88. Pierson, C. (1992) 'Democracy, Market and Capital: Are There Necessary Economic Limits to Democracy?' 40 *Political Studies*, Special Issue, p. 83.
89. The concept of "Post-Washington Consensus" was developed by Joseph Stiglitz in various papers and books, including 'Towards a new paradigm for development: Strategies, policies and processes' a paper presented at The Prebisch Lecture at UNCTAD, October 1998.
90. See Stiglitz (1998), p. 25.
91. See Craig, D. and Porter, D. (2006) *Development Beyond Neoliberalism? Governance, Poverty Reduction and Political Economy*, London and New York: Routledge, p. 13.
92. See World Bank (1997) *World Development Report 1997: The State in a Changing World*, Washington DC: World Bank, pp. iii–iv. See also See Saitoti, G. (2002) *The Challenges of Economic and Institutional Reforms in Africa*, Aldershot: Ashgate. See also Khan, M. (2012) 'Beyond Good Governance: An Agenda for Developmental Governance' in Sundaram, J.K. and Chowdhury, A. (eds) *Is Good Governance Good for Development*, London: Bloomsbury Academic, p. 153. The author argues that this type of governance should be referred to as *market-enhancing* governance instead of *good* governance, as it consists of policies which, although they could be *appropriate* for market enhancement might prove to be inadequate for sustained economic growth.
93. See Craig and Porter (2006), p. 6.
94. The process conducted by OHADA provides an example of such law reform which is conducted at a regional level.
95. Thomas, C. (2008) 'Re-Reading Weber in Law and Development: A Critical Intellectual History of "Good Governance" Reform' *Cornell Law Faculty Publications*, Paper 118, pp. 99–100. Here the author criticises the tendency of the "good governance" and "rule of law" paradigm to follow a one-size-fits-all approach through the development of global standards which are believed to be most appropriate to promote economic growth in countries irrespective of their particular circumstances. This particular issue is analysed in the context of the Organisation for Harmonisation of Business Law in Africa in order to evaluate the approach followed by the organisation.
96. World Bank (1997), pp. iii–iv. See also Saitoti (2002).
97. Mbaku (2004), p. 390. See also Ngugi, J.M. (2005) 'Policing Neo-Liberal Reforms: The Rule of Law as An Enabling and Restrictive Discourse' 26 *U.Pa.J.Int'l Econ. L.* 513, p. 517 and Przeworski, A. (1991) *Democracy and the Market: Political and Economic Reforms in Eastern Europe and Latin America*, Cambridge: Cambridge University Press, p. 183.
98. The concept of *developmental* governance is developed in Khan (2012).
99. The NEPAD Framework was adopted in Abuja in October 2001The African Union was established in May 2001 and launched in July 2002 to replace the OAU. For a historical background of the African Union, see ww.au.int
100. NEPAD Framework, article 1.

101. Ibid, article 33.
102. Ibid, articles 86–95. This strategy is intended to address the shortcomings of previous programmes which tended to promote a set of policies designed to support economic growth regardless of SSA countries' particular circumstances. The new strategy is therefore aimed at providing an approach supposed to correspond to the needs of specific countries and regions.
103. Ibid, article 27. See also Djuidje Kouam, R. (2008) 'APRM and the Challenges of the Implementation of Economic Governance Standards in Africa: A Critical Assessment' in Boko, S.H. and Seck, D. (eds) (2008) *NEPAD and the Future of Economic Policy in Africa*, Trenton, New Jersey; London: Africa World Press, pp. 113 & 126 and Aka, P.C. (2012) 'Political Analysis of the Genesis of NEPAD' in Bobo and Sintin-Aboagye (eds), p. 56.
104. Although it provides for various measures which are apparently based on regional developmentalism, NEPAD's strategy also places a strong emphasis on the promotion of private enterprise and the establishment of well-functioning market as key factors for the promotion of sustainable development in Africa. This aspect of NEPAD is discussed in more details in Nnadozie, E. (2008) 'NEPAD, APRM, and Institutional Change in Africa' in Adejumobi, S. and Olukoshi, A. (eds) *The African Union and New Strategies for Development in Africa*, Amherst; New York: Cambria Press, p. 209 and Adejumobi and Olukoshi (2008), p. 4.
105. NEPAD Framework, section 20. See also Mbaku (2004), p. 408. Regional integration is expected to provide African infant industries with a safe and protected environment within which they could be developed and matured to become globally competitive.
106. See Olukoshi (2004), p. 66. These two concepts were also included in the Lagos Plan of Action which represented one of the first attempts towards regional developmentalism.
107. See Bobo and Sintin-Aboagye (2012), p. 14.
108. Ibid, article 27. See also Odularu, G.O. (2008) 'The Challenges of Globalisation and Regional Integration: Lessons From Africa' in Boko, S.H. and Seck, D. (eds) (2008) *NEPAD and the Future of Economic Policy in Africa*, Trenton, NJ; London: Africa World Press, p. 297.
109. NEPAD Framework, section 10. See also Odularu (2008), p. 300.
110. NEPAD Framework, section 92.
111. See Oladuru (2008), p. 296.
112. This approach is considered as necessary to help SSA countries upgrade from their role of suppliers of cheap labour and raw materials to a status of countries able to develop a broader capital goods sector, through economic diversification and the development of regional value chains. See NEPAD Framework, section 5 and Noman, Botchwey, Stein, and Stiglitz (2012).
113. NEPAD Framework, section 94.
114. To ensure the achievement of NEPAD's objectives, an African Peer Review Mechanism (APRM) was established at the 2002 Durban African Union's Summit. The APRM operates through the assessment of Member countries' progress towards the achievement of NEPAD's goals. This assessment is conducted on a voluntary basis by a set of institutions controlled by the NEPAD signatories' heads of state and government.
115. See Mbaku (2004), p. 394. See also Maluwa, T. (2006) 'The Move From Institutions? Examining the Phenomenon in Africa' 100 *Proceedings of the Annual Meeting (American Society of International Law)*, p. 295.
116. DeGhetto, K., Gray, J.R., and Kiggundu, M.N. (2016) 'The African Union's Agenda 2063: Aspirations, Challenges, and Opportunities for Management Research' 2 *African Journal of Management* 1, p. 1.

117. See African Union's Agenda 2063, www.un.org/en/africa/osaa/pdf/au/agenda2063.pdf, accessed on 12/12/2017.
118. UNECA, Friedrich-Elbert-Stiftung (2017) 'The Continental Free Trade Area (CFTA) in Africa—a Human Rights Perspective' UNECA, p. 3.
119. See www.au.int/web/en/ti/cfta/about, accessed on 12/12/2017. These negotiations, which were supposed to lead to the establishment of the Continental Free Trade Area in 2017, are yet to be concluded. See also Soininen, I. (2014) 'The Continental Free Trade Area: Current State of Play' *Policy Brief* 01, Saana Institute; and Mevel and Karingi (2013), pp. 281 and 285.
120. UNECA, Friedrich-Elbert-Stiftung (2017), p. 24.
121. Ibid.
122. See www.au.int/en/ti/biat/about, accessed on 12/12/2017.
123. See www.au.int/en/ti/pida/about, accessed on 12/12/2017. PIDA includes the development of infrastructures in various sectors, including energy, ICT, transport and transboundary water.
124. UNECA, Friedrich-Elbert-Stiftung (2017), p. 27.

4 Contextualising the Concept of Integration Through Law

I. Introduction

Following on from the initial insights developed in the first chapter, which focused on the general conceptual framework used throughout the study, this chapter is aimed at providing a more detailed analysis on the critical role played by law in the particular context of regional integration, thus offering further details on the concept of integration through law and giving grounds for its use in the remaining chapters of this study. The primary goal of this chapter is to go beyond law itself and provide a comprehensive analysis by highlighting the various factors that influence the form that law takes in the context of regional integration. This analysis focuses more particularly on the reasons that motivate countries to adopt various Regional Trade Agreements (hereinafter RTAs), the different goals that regional integration is expected to achieve and the circumstances of the participating countries combined with the specific opportunities which are presented to them.[1] Throughout this analysis, a special emphasis will also be placed on the particular frameworks and legal instruments adopted to mirror the special circumstances of the participating countries, as well as the set of specific activities that are supposed to be coordinated by the RTAs in order to achieve their objectives.[2] These instruments are considered in light of their eventual application in the context of the various regional processes conducted under the banner of the African Economic Community (AEC).

RTAs can be distinguished by the approach that they adopt towards regional integration, which can be, on the one hand, *minimalist*—i.e. providing for a number of rules and provisions which are supposed to be exhaustive, therefore not requiring further development; or, on the other hand, *interventionist*—requiring a set of various coordination mechanisms and special institutions to support the effective implementation of the RTA.[3] These approaches are often determined by the level of integration sought by countries involved in regional integration initiatives.

On the one hand, initiatives which are limited to the simple removal of trade barriers and to the early stages of economic integration between countries seem to adopt the minimalist approach. Under this approach, countries are likely to adopt a minimal legal framework, which includes a light regulatory architecture and weak institutions, as well as a dispute settlement mechanism relying on consultations between participating countries, aimed at finding unique solutions to specific problems which might arise.[4] In addition, countries that adopt this approach tend to be motivated by the desire to retain their sovereignty and preserve the discretion to manage the evolution of their integration endeavours.[5]

On the other hand, some RTAs—often the ones with more ambitious objectives including deeper economic integration among the participating countries—do not produce their effects automatically and require specific mechanisms in order to be implemented effectively.[6] As highlighted by several authors, most RTAs are "incomplete contracts", which simply provide for general objectives to be achieved, and therefore need to be "managed" in order to produce their full effects.[7] Special institutions can be created to this effect, with increased powers and the responsibility to support the implementation of the RTA by unpacking the general principles that it provides, hence guiding the behaviour of the different stakeholders as their circumstances change.[8] In the same vein, the responsibility to settle disputes likely to arise regarding the meaning and the interpretation of the RTAs' provisions might be entrusted to a special institution operating under a set of specific rules and procedures. This mechanism, which is based on a legalistic approach, is deemed to increase the level of compliance with, and ensure the effective implementation of regional rules through prompt and impartial rulings over potential violations of the RTAs' provisions.[9]

In addition, this chapter also gives further overview on the central role occupied by the concept of integration through law in the overall research, a concept that encompasses, on the one hand, the multiple roles that law can play in the context of regional integration and, on the other hand, the particular way in which legal rules, norms and mechanisms come to shape the development of regional trade agreements. This is expected to be achieved by placing a particular emphasis on the rules that are produced by specific RTAs in light of the special circumstances of each region, as well as the various mechanisms established to meet the RTAs normative expectations and to coordinate and monitor the set of activities that are supposed to result from the implementation of the RTAs.[10]

Regional integration initiatives around the world vary in terms of approach, size, functional scope, set of objectives and targeted sectors and institutional design, each of which requires a particular type of mechanisms for their implementation. In order to contextualise the concept of integration through law and highlight the various roles that law can play to support regional integration, the following sections will be dedicated to the analysis of the North American Free Trade Agreement (NAFTA), the Common Market of the Southern Cone (MERCOSUR) and the Association of Southeast Asian Nations (ASEAN), with a particular emphasis on each region's particular circumstances and the various coordination mechanisms provided to support the achievement of their respective RTAs.

This analysis proves particularly important, as it identifies the role that law can play at various levels of integration, hence highlighting the fact that the shapes and forms that regional frameworks can take are dependent on the status and the depth of their corresponding regional processes. Rather than indicating an apparent similarity between the particular circumstances of these RTAs and those in the African context, the choice of these particular RTAs can be explained by the fact that they provide various types of legal processes which could be used to advance the regional initiatives in the context of the AEC. The particular focus will be on the different approaches adopted by these initiatives (minimalist under NAFTA and more interventionist under MERCOSUR and ASEAN), assessing their effectiveness given the particular circumstances and opportunities available to their participating countries. This analysis is used to highlight the various processes chosen by these initiatives—including market access, trade liberalisation, trade facilitation and the establishment of a regional production base—to achieve their goal of increasing regional economic growth, as well as the corresponding coordination arrangements provided by their RTAs. This to consider their potential application at various stages of the regional processes conducted in the context of the AEC.

This approach is important as, rather than focusing solely on the model provided by the European Union, which is believed to constitute both the most advanced case of regional integration in the world and one in which law has been used to a full extent, the chapter also covers other models which, given the great diversity and disparity that characterises African economies, could also prove appropriate in the AEC context. A greater emphasis will be placed on the coordination mechanisms used to ensure the effective application and enforcement of regional rules, highlighting the distinction between, on the one hand, intergovernmental and supranational governance arrangements, and, on the other hand, interstate and transnational dispute resolution mechanisms.[11] This analysis is aimed at investigating the merits of each arrangement and their various effects on regional integration.

II. Market Access and Trade Liberalisation Under NAFTA

NAFTA,[12] which was signed in December 1992 between the United States, Mexico and Canada, entered into force on 1 January 1994 and established the largest single marketplace in the world.[13] The signature of the Agreement, which was first of its kind as it took place between two wealthy countries (Canada and the United States) and a developing country (Mexico), followed a series of initiatives which determined the particular approach to regional integration adopted by the three countries.

On the one hand, it succeeded the 1989 U.S.-Canada Free Trade Agreement, which was aimed at precluding protectionist economic measures[14] in both countries, thereby securing access to large markets for their exports.[15] NAFTA was therefore considered by the two countries as a continuation of their previous Agreement, adding Mexico in order to ensure that the promotion of political stability and economic growth in their direct neighbour. On the other hand, Mexico had been reforming its trade and investment policies since the 1980s, changing its economic strategy from a restrictive and protectionist trade regime to economic liberalisation, which was expected to promote economic growth in the country.[16] Mexico, therefore, considered NAFTA as an opportunity to consolidate its new economic strategy as well as increase its credibility, including by furthering its trade and investment liberalisation, as well as gain more access to the U.S. market for its exports.[17] Moreover, the Canadian and Mexican economies were both already significantly dependent on their trade with the United States, thereby using NAFTA as an instrument to both regulate and consolidate trade relations between the three countries.

As a result, the objectives set by the Agreement focused on the elimination of barriers to trade and the facilitation of cross-border movement of goods and services between participating countries; the promotion of conditions of fair competition in the Free Trade Area; the increase of investment opportunities in the Member States; the adequate and effective protection and enforcement of intellectual property rights in each Member State; and the creation of effective procedures for the implementation, application and joint administration of the Agreement and for the resolution of disputes.[18] These measures were adopted with the view to enhance the welfare of the three countries and raise the living standards of their populations.[19] Two separate agreements—the North American Agreement on Labour Cooperation (NAALC) and the North American Agreement on Environmental Cooperation (NAAEC)—was adopted alongside the main RTA as a compromise between the three participating countries, with a view to improving working conditions and living standards as well as fostering the protection and improvement of the environment in the territories of the participating counties.[20]

In the context of NAFTA, which focuses chiefly on the removal of barriers to trade in goods[21] and services[22] between the three Member States and provides neither for an external tariff common to all three Member States nor for the removal of obstacles to the free movement of persons and capital, regional integration efforts are limited and are not expected to progress to the establishment of a Common Market.[23] Consequently, NAFTA has adopted a minimalist approach to regional integration, providing for a vast number of definitional and normative notions. Moreover, the Agreement seems very detailed, precise and relatively comprehensive,[24] covering various matters ranging from removal of trade barriers[25] to issues of environment and intellectual property, therefore leaving very little to interpretative discretion. Beyond its goal to create a Free Trade Area, the Agreement also includes detailed rules for other matters such as the treatment of foreign investment; government procurement; and trade in services, including financial and transportation services.[26] The approach adopted under NAFTA, therefore, differs from other types of RTAs which provide general objectives to be achieved[27] and require the establishment of special institutions for the coordination of regional efforts. In contrast, NAFTA has provided for a rules-based coordination mechanism, which will be analysed in the next section.

II.1. Rules-Based Coordination Mechanism

In light of the above comments, it can be noted that NAFTA has been designed on a rules-based approach which does not require a significant amount of coordination and monitoring by special institutions, but has rather provides for a full set of rules covering matters ranging from market access for goods and customs procedures to standards-related measures and government procurement.[28]

Moreover, in the context of NAFTA, there is no formal need for a full-fledged harmonisation of the Member States laws and policies, given that the Agreement is aimed at governing the relations between three participating countries rather than issuing common policies and coordinating common actions between the three countries as well as vis-à-vis third countries.[29] This mechanism, which is based on a very strong intergovernmental rather than a supranational approach to regional integration, is influenced by a *laissez-faire* approach popular with a number of large export-oriented firms in the U.S. and Canada, which would prefer to rely on the dynamics of the market (supply/demand) rather than a new set of rules which would require a significant amount of changes in their way of doing business.[30] A similar rules-based mechanism could be used in the context of the African regional schemes in the early stages of integration, as well as to regulate specific sectors and areas that are considered as crucial to achieve regional development. This would also allow accommodating the sovereignty concerns of the African countries while also ensuring the smooth progression of the overall regional processes.

This approach has strongly influenced the institutional framework[31] and enforcement mechanisms established by NAFTA, which are characterised by the predominant role played by the Member States' governments.[32]

As a consequence of its strong intergovernmental design and the relative comprehensiveness[33] of the Agreement, NAFTA has only provided for the creation of two common institutions, namely the Free Trade Commission (the Commission) and the Secretariat, which have limited powers and are either directly controlled by the participating countries (Commission) or used to provide administrative support (Secretariat).[34] The Commission is composed of cabinet-level representatives of the participating countries and was created to supervise the implementation of the Agreement, oversee its further elaboration and resolve any disputes that could potentially arise regarding the implementation or the application of the Agreement.[35] The Secretariat, a unique institution consisting of three national sections in each participating country, was established to provide assistance to the Commission, administer the dispute resolution process, as well as provide administrative support to panels and committees.[36]

This institutional arrangement seems to meet the needs of the participating countries, given the rule-based approach adopted in the Agreement, which provides for the various stages of implementation, and therefore does not seem to require the establishment of supranational institutions to coordinate their common actions. However, it should be highlighted here that this arrangement seems to be suitable in a region with a country which strong both economically and politically like the United States, therefore able to provide the impetus necessary for the regional initiative to progress.

II.2. Interstate Dispute Resolution and Arbitration

In contrast with its strongly rule-based coordination mechanism, NAFTA has provided for a dispute resolution system that is rather reactionary, relying primarily on consultation and conciliation between the participating countries, which are aimed at finding unique solutions to specific problems as they arise.[37]

Chapter 20, Section B of the Agreement therefore provides for a dispute resolution mechanism which applies "with respect to the avoidance or settlement of all disputes between the Parties regarding the interpretation or application of th[e] Agreement or wherever a Party considers that an actual or proposed measure of another Party is or would be inconsistent with the obligations of th[e] Agreement or cause nullification or impairment".[38] As highlighted in a previous section, this approach might also have been chosen to accommodate the sovereignty concerns of the participating countries, to ensure that they retain control on the overall process and keep their respective legal and judiciary systems relatively unchanged.[39]

Several options are provided for disputes which might arise between the three participating countries in the context of NAFTA: a party may resort either to the General Agreement on Tariffs and Trade (GATT) dispute settlement mechanism[40] or to the NAFTA dispute resolution procedure.[41] The NAFTA dispute resolution system, in particular, has several stages, which include firstly an attempt for consultations between the concerned parties as well as a conciliation procedure managed by the Free Trade Commission.[42]

In case the consultation and conciliation arrangements are inconclusive, the Agreement has also provided for the establishment by the Commission of an arbitral panel to decide the issue.[43] The arbitration panel issues its decision in the form of a report which, however, is not binding and parties to the dispute are left to "agree on the resolution of the dispute, which normally shall conform to the determinations and recommendations of the panel ".[44] In case the parties do not reach an agreement regarding the resolution of the dispute, retaliation could constitute the last option available to the prevailing party, which may use it to force the other party to comply with the decision of the panel 30 days after it has been issued.[45] In a like manner, arbitration is also the preferred medium to settle commercial disputes between private parties within the Free Trade Area and between investors and the participating countries.[46]

The existing NAFTA dispute settlement mechanism, which involves the intervention of state actors (Free Trade Commission and bi-national panels) and the adjudication of quasi-judicial like institutions (arbitral tribunals), does not in itself guarantee the enforcement of NAFTA rules, as it results in the issuance of decisions that are not binding in nature.[47] Under this procedure, compliance with the NAFTA rules is therefore left to the discretion of the participating countries, which have the capacity to resort to retaliation as the only means to force other parties to comply with a specific rule.

II.3. Impact of the NAFTA Model on Economic Development

In light of the objectives provided in the Agreement, NAFTA's impact on the three participating countries can be considered to be relatively positive, as trade and investment flow among the three participating countries increased significantly after the entry into force of the Agreement.[48]

Of the three participating countries, Mexico requires a particular attention, given the positive impact that NAFTA was expected to have on the country's development strategy and economic performance, an expectation similar to those of most African countries involved in regional integration initiatives.[49]

NAFTA's impact on the Mexican's economy was relatively positive, as the preferential access to the larger market enabled the country to expand its exports exponentially,[50] while, by supporting and furthering the various economic reforms initiated by the Mexican government, the Agreement also allowed the country to enhance its productivity (especially in the manufacturing sector) and to attract more foreign direct investment (mostly from the United States).[51] A few adverse effects also resulted from the establishment of NAFTA, including the concentration of foreign investment in sectors which manufacturing operations requiring a large amount of imported components, hence increasing the country's dependence on imports, and thereby causing the loss of a number of local industries.[52] The strong emphasis on free trade under NAFTA has, therefore, influenced the adoption of several measures which, despite being adequate to increase trade levels, could potentially distort the economic goals of a developing country.[53]

The rather limited impact that NAFTA appears to have had on Mexico's economic performance suggests that, although the free trade and minimalist approaches adopted in the Agreement could be used to promote economic growth and boost a country's trade activities, more coordination measures and state intervention might be required to convert economic growth and increased productivity into improved domestic competitiveness and economic development.[54] NAFTA's approach to regional integration could potentially be detrimental or significantly limited in the African context, given the low level of industrialisation in the majority of countries and the critical need for economic transformation, which require more interventionist measures in order to be successful.

III. Trade Liberalisation and Economic Integration Through MERCOSUR

MERCOSUR, which constitutes the largest economic bloc in Latin America,[55] was established by the Treaty of Asunción (hereinafter ToA) signed by Argentina, Brazil, Paraguay and Uruguay on 26 March 1991.[56] Similar to the case of Mexico, most Latin American nations pursued a wave of economic reforms in the early 1980s, abandoning their import substitution industrialisation (ISI) strategies and adopting trade liberalisation as a means to support their economic growth.[57]

Reforms in Argentina and Brazil, in particular, were instrumental in laying the foundation for integration efforts in the region. The two countries adopted the Programme for Integration and Economic Cooperation (PICE) in 1986, an instrument which was aimed at pursuing unilateral trade liberalisation programmes and structural adjustment measures, while also inciting economic integration between them.[58] Several other instruments were adopted by the two countries to boost the integration of their respective economies,[59] leading eventually to the incorporation of Paraguay and Uruguay to the initiative and the signing of the ToA, which was expected to both expand and further institutionalise the integration efforts in the region.[60]

III.1. Treaty of Asunción, Economic Growth and Expansion of Domestic Markets

Unlike the case of NAFTA, MERCOSUR was considered by its participating countries as an instrument to promote economic exchange and enhance intra-regional trade instead of simply coordinating and improving substantial pre-existing cross-border trade.[61] The ToA was therefore intended, among other things, to foster trade among the participating countries by going beyond the simple expansion of their respective domestic markets and eventually establishing a Common Market among them.[62] This model of integration was expected to consolidate their economic strategies and accelerate economic development in the region.[63] A similar approach has been adopted by the Treaty of Abuja and the majority of African RTAs, which consider economic integration as a means to boost intra-regional trade and promote economic transformation in the participating countries.

To achieve its objectives, the ToA provided for four key measures, including the adoption of a trade liberalisation programme (TLP), the coordination of the participating countries' macroeconomic policies, the establishment of a Common External Tariff, and the adoption of sectoral agreements to optimise the use and mobility of factors of productions.[64] The TLP, in particular, was aimed at establishing a Free Trade Area in the region, through automatic reduction of customs duties as well as the elimination of non-tariff restrictions on the free movement of goods between the participating countries.[65]

The ToA differs from NAFTA in various ways. Rather than providing for a set of detailed provisions for the coordination of the integration process, including rules for the various stages of the implementation and the decision-making process, as it is the case under NAFTA, the Treaty of Asunción is a short and open-ended document (with only 24 articles), which provides for general principles and objectives to achieve, leaving room for further and deeper integration at a later point in time.[66] At its adoption, the ToA was therefore aimed at providing a broad and flexible framework for economic integration among its Member States and the establishment of a Common Market among the signatories by 1994.[67]

In addition, MERCOSUR was intended to constitute a step forward from NAFTA, as it provided for measures going beyond the establishment of a Free Trade Area, including the adoption of a Common External Tariff and the coordination of the participating countries' macroeconomic policies. These measures, which are aimed at establishing a more advanced model of regional integration, were likely to require a more sophisticated legal and institutional framework to coordinate the progress of the integration process towards the establishment of a Common Market.[68]

III.2. Establishment of the Customs Union and the Adoption of the Protocol of Ouro Preto

MERCOSUR countries negotiated and adopted a Common External Tariff (CET) in December 1994, formally transforming the organisation into the Customs Union.[69] As provided in article 5 of the ToA, the CET was intended to increase the international competitiveness of the participating countries, using tariffs to regulate their trade with third countries, thereby increasing their participation in the world economy.[70] To ensure a smooth and effective coordination of the Customs Union, MERCOSUR countries also adopted the Protocol of Ouro Preto (hereinafter POP) in 1994, providing for a regulatory and institutional framework intended to be more advanced than the arrangement under NAFTA and aimed at regulating more complex issues such as the reduction of regional disparities among MERCOSUR countries as well as redistributional policies.[71]

The POP, therefore, provided for several intergovernmental institutions with decision-making powers of which the main ones are the Council of the Common Market (CMC, a Spanish acronym for *Consejo del Mercado Común*) and the Common Market Group (GMC, a Spanish acronym for *Grupo Mercado Común*). Whereas the CMC is responsible for the "political leadership of the integration process and for making the decisions[72] necessary to ensure the achievement of the objectives defined by the Treaty of Asunción", the GMC was established as the executive organ of the Community, responsible for the good functioning of the organisation. Alongside the two main institutions, the MERCOSUR Trade Commission (CCM, Spanish acronym for *Comisión de Comercio del MERCOSUR*) was created to assist the CMG with specialised economic issues (such as competition, customs and procurement) and the production and application of common trade policy instruments in connection with the operation of the Customs Union.[73]

Besides the three intergovernmental institutions, the POP also provided for two institutions with a consultative role—the Joint Parliamentary Commission and the Economic-Social Consultative Forum; as well as an Administrative Secretariat to provide operational support to the other institutions.[74] Under this structure, the institutions with decision-making powers are expected to play a major role in the coordination of the organisation's efforts towards a deeper economic integration. However, being essentially intergovernmental (with most decision-making powers remaining with the participating countries' governments) in the likes of the institutional framework under NAFTA, this arrangement might not constitute an adequate coordination mechanism, given the ambitious objectives set by the ToA and the various issues likely to arise in this context.[75] As discussed earlier, such an institutional framework might be appropriate for models such as NAFTA, which focuses on the removal of tariff and non-tariff barriers but does not provide for the adoption of a CET and common trade policies.

The effectiveness of the coordination mechanism provided by the ToA may be questioned particularly with regard to the implementation of the instruments adopted by the MERCOSUR institutions to support the establishment of a Common Market. In this regard, article 42 of the POP provides that "[t]he decisions adopted by the MERCOSUR organs provided for in Article 2 of this Protocol shall be binding and, when necessary, must be incorporated in the domestic legal systems in accordance with the procedures provided for in each country's legislation". Moreover, article 38 of the same Protocol provides that "[t]he States Parties undertake to take all the measures necessary to ensure, in their respective territories, compliance with the decisions adopted by the MERCOSUR organs provided for in Article 2 of this Protocol".

Consequently, the Decisions of the CMC, the Resolutions of the GMC and the Directives of the CCM are all supposed to be binding upon the participating countries, which are responsible for their application in their respective territories. However, the fact that the application of MERCOSUR primary (ToA) and secondary (institutions' instruments) rules are subject to each country's legislation is likely to pose a problem and delay the establishment of the Common Market, given the different implementation rules followed by MERCOSUR countries.[76] Whereas countries like Paraguay and Argentina recognise the supremacy of the international order over their domestic legal systems (and thereby follow a monist system towards international law),[77] Brazil and Uruguay require the adoption of subsequent legal instruments to *internalise* international norms (following a dualist system).[78] This situation highlights the need to address the issue of the implementation of regional rules, to ensure that the regional process can progress smoothly and produce its expected effects.

This arrangement adopted by MERCOSUR seems quite limited and therefore likely to affect the transformation of the regional group into a Common Market. The adoption of a robust dispute settlement mechanism might be appropriate to address this issue, to ensure the effective implementation and enforcement of MERCOSUR rules.

III.3. Quasi-Judicial Dispute Settlement Mechanism

The Protocol of Brasilia (hereinafter PB) of 17 December 1991 has provided for a hybrid dispute settlement mechanism (DSM) over matters of interpretation, implementation and violation of rules emanating from the ToA and any related legal instrument.[79] This mechanism, which is relatively more rules-based and institutionalised than the arrangement under NAFTA, is intended to ensure the effective implementation of the different instruments adopted by the Community.

This DSM is conducted in three stages, which include direct negotiations by the Member States concerned,[80] the submission of a claim to the GMC[81] and recourse to arbitration as the last option.[82] The initial stages of this mechanism are therefore characterised by the direct involvement of state actors whereas the last stage of the process, namely the arbitral proceedings, has been delegated to the adjudication of ad hoc arbitral tribunals.[83]

The arbitration procedure under MERCOSUR distinguishes itself from the one provided under NAFTA by the fact that decisions made by ad hoc tribunals can be appealed to a Permanent Review Tribunal (PRT), which was established by the Olivos Protocol in 2002.[84] The PRT's decisions are supposed to have the effect of *res judicata*, i.e. they are both binding and enforceable in the participating countries.[85] Moreover, the PRT also presented the opportunity to promote the use of precedents in arbitration proceedings, which is likely to somehow contribute to the establishment of a regional legal system. The establishment of permanent quasi-judicial institution[86] was therefore intended to improve compliance with the rules produced by the MERCOSUR institutions.

The Olivos Protocol also provides a special procedure for claims filed by private parties (individuals or corporations) which are affected by any legal or administrative measure or act by a participating country that they consider in violation of MERCOSUR rules.[87] These claims can only be filed to the National Section of the Common Market Group where the private party has its habitual place of residence or place of business[88] and are resolved in a process which involves consultations between the National Sections of the two participating countries involved[89] and the intervention of the GMC.[90] In case the dispute is not resolved through this procedure, the same claim may be submitted to the general DSM by the participating country in which the claim was initially filed on behalf of the concerned private party.[91]

However, even though MERCOSUR has provided for a relatively more advanced dispute settlement and enforcement mechanism to ensure compliance with regional rules, including through the establishment of a permanent tribunal, this arrangement may prove to be inadequate to support the establishment of a Common Market. Concerns have been raised regarding disputes filed in the Member States' national jurisdictions, in particular, prompting the participating countries to consider the establishment of a MERCOSUR Court.[92] Establishing a MERCOSUR Court is considered as a more effective method to support the successful establishment of a Common Market in the region, by ensuring that the various rules issued by the MERCOSUR institutions (decisions, resolutions and directives) are applied uniformly across the region.[93]

III.4. Effect of MERCOSUR

MERCOSUR seems to be a more advanced form of economic integration than NAFTA, to the extent that it has achieved the Customs Union, not only by eliminating barriers to intra-regional trade and ensuring the free movement of goods and services among its participating countries but also by an increased coverage of the CET and the reduction of non-tariff barriers.[94] As highlighted by several reports, these measures have been instrumental in the significant increase of intra-regional trade, which has mostly concentrated in manufactured goods.[95] Moreover, through the adoption of several Protocols and other legal instruments by its decision-making institutions, MERCOSUR has also managed to unpack the general principles provided in the ToA and somehow ensured a continued evolution of economic integration efforts in the region.

However, despite a strong impetus in its early years,[96] in light of the ambitious objectives set in the ToA, regional integration under MERCOSUR has only been partially successful. The CET, for example, has been riddled with several exceptions, preventing the participating countries from using it as an effective development tool.[97] Moreover, the strong intergovernmental character of the coordination mechanism provided by MERCOSUR seems limited to further the integration efforts in the region and consequently to address key issues which could potentially delay the establishment of a Common Market within MERCOSUR.[98] It is believed that the achievement of a deeper and more complex level of integration such as a Common Market might require the establishment of supranational institutions dedicated to regional matters, with enough autonomy and independence to coordinate the integration process and address issues such as the reduction of regional economic disparities, the enhancement of international competitiveness and the harmonisation of macroeconomic policies.[99] These actions prove important to the promotion of regional development, which is the main objective in the context of the AEC.

IV. Regional Production Base and Trade Facilitation Through ASEAN

ASEAN is a regional group that was originally created on 8 August 1967 by Indonesia, Malaysia, the Philippines, Singapore and Thailand.[100] The case of

ASEAN proves particularly important to analyse, as it offers a model of regionalism which differs from that of NAFTA and MERCOSUR in its focus and its main objectives. Under ASEAN, a greater emphasis is placed on economic cooperation, trade facilitation and the establishment of a regional production base, rather than focusing primarily on trade liberalisation (free trade) and the elimination of tariff and non-tariff barriers between participating countries.[101]

Moreover, regional integration in the context of ASEAN has been driven by external rather than internal demand over the years, following the outward-oriented economic strategy adopted by most countries in the region which are more concerned about enhancing their capacity to supply markets outside the region (such as the United States and the European Union).[102] As will be discussed and highlighted in the following sections, the approach adopted by ASEAN towards regional integration has been strongly influenced by the dynamics of its regional market and the particular circumstances in which it was established. This section focuses particularly on the singular way in which the regional market stemmed from the economic policies adopted by the participating countries before it was institutionalised under ASEAN.[103]

IV.1. ASEAN Declaration and De Facto Economic Integration[104]

ASEAN, as provided in the 1967 Declaration signed by its original members, was originally created as an organisation intended at preserving political stability in the region through the promotion of mutual assistance and collaboration among the participating countries.[105] Although it was included among the objectives of the region, economic development was nevertheless considered as the primary responsibility of each national government, with ASEAN being used as a political forum for collaboration on matters of common interest. These included, *inter alia*, the expansion of their trade, the improvement of their transportation and communication infrastructures, and the consensual resolution of disputes.[106] Moreover, regional cooperation through ASEAN was also considered by the participating countries as an effective means against any external interference in their domestic affairs, thereby ensuring their policy autonomy and national independence.[107] These various considerations, as well as the initial strong political nature of the organisation, are the crucial factors which determined the shape and pace of integration efforts in the region.

By the early 1980s, most countries in the region adopted export-oriented economic strategies which consisted of various state interventions in the form of policies aimed at enhancing the competitiveness and increasing the exports of specific industries or firms.[108] These policies, which included significant tariff reductions, combined with the improvement of infrastructures (including transport and communication) facilitated the scattering of economic activities within the region, thereby creating a *de facto* economic integration.[109] Regional value chains (RVCs) were established in these circumstances, through the relocation of various industries from newly industrialised countries to countries with cheaper labour, as well as the specialisation of each country in the production of specific components of the production chains.[110] Over the years, these RVCs developed into a regional division of labour and the establishment of a robust production network which, given its rapid growth and the desire from countries in the region to further their cooperation, seemed to require the support of a regional institution-building process.[111]

IV.2. Move to a Rules-Based Integration Through AFTA

ASEAN underwent several changes over the years, the most significant of which was the signing of the Agreement on the Common Effective Preferential Tariff (CEPT) Scheme on 28 January 1992.[112] The agreement, which established the ASEAN Free Trade Area (AFTA), marked the shift by ASEAN from a political association to a rules-based organisation.[113] AFTA was established to support the efforts towards regional integration by ensuring the free flow of the goods produced in each ASEAN country within the regional production network.

Moreover, AFTA is believed to have been established in response to the surge in North America and Europe towards preferential trade agreements and to be aimed at furthering the region's efforts towards economic integration by improving its attractiveness for foreign direct investment through the establishment of a free trade area.[114] Furthering their efforts towards regional integration was therefore considered by ASEAN countries as a means to support their national development strategies, as the increased foreign direct investment could potentially enhance the international competitiveness of private firms in the region and thereby increase their participation in international trade.[115]

The CEPT Scheme, therefore, provided for a set of various rules aimed at coordinating tariff reductions between ASEAN countries,[116] as well as listing the type of products covered by the agreement, which included manufactured products, including capital goods and processed agricultural products.[117] However, even though it established a Free Trade Area similar to other models analysed in previous sections, the CEPT distinguished itself from the NAFTA model for example by including measures aimed at regulating trade and investment flows to ensure that these did not affect the participating countries' development goals.[118]

In addition to the CEPT, which focused on intra-regional trade of goods, ASEAN countries also adopted a number of other legal instruments to regulate the other matters falling under the ASEAN framework: on the one hand, the 1995 ASEAN Framework Agreement on Services (AFAS), aimed at enhancing the cooperation among participating countries regarding services, including through measures such as the mutual recognition of the professional certifications granted to a service supplier by one of the ASEAN countries; on the other hand, the 1998 Framework Agreement on the ASEAN Investment Area (AIA Agreement), which was aimed at regulating both foreign and local investment in the region. As discussed above, the AIA Agreement reflected the ASEAN countries' determination to use regional integration as a means to further their economic development, including through the regulation of foreign investment in the region.[119]

IV.3. Establishment of a Legal and Institutional Framework Through the ASEAN Charter

The early 2000s marked yet another important step in the transformation of ASEAN into a more formalised and more institutionalised form of regionalism. This included the adoption of a set of additional legal instruments aimed at furthering the efforts towards regional integration. These legal instruments included, among others, the ASEAN Framework Agreement for the Integration of Priority Sectors (AFAIP), signed in November 2004, which was aimed at combining the participating countries' strengths in specific sectors considered as necessary to improve their international competitiveness.[120]

Another key instrument adopted was the 2007 ASEAN Charter (hereinafter "the Charter") which created an organisation relatively more similar to the European Community, the ASEAN Community, which is to be established on three pillars: the ASEAN Security Community, the ASEAN Socio-Cultural Community and the ASEAN Economic Community (hereinafter ASEAN EC).[121] The ASEAN EC, in particular, is expected to be created through the establishment of a single market and production network for the free flow of goods, services, investment and skilled labour, as well as a freer flow of capital.[122] The Charter has also provided for special legal and institutional frameworks which are intended to help the organisation achieve its objectives.[123]

IV.3.1. Enhanced Regulatory Framework

Several legal instruments constitute the regulatory framework used by ASEAN to achieve its new objectives: the ASEAN Trade in Goods Agreement (ATIGA), signed in February 2009, replaced the CEPT Scheme and is aimed at furthering the free flow of goods by addressing issues such as customs integration and the elimination of non-tariff barriers;[124] the ASEAN Comprehensive Investment Agreement (ACIA), also adopted in February 2009 to replace the AIA, is expected to create a "free and open investment regime in order to achieve the end goal of economic integration under the [ASEAN EC]";[125] and the ASEAN Framework Agreement on Services (AFAS), which was already used under AFTA. It should be noted, however, that the Charter has not provided for the adoption of a Common External Tariff for imports into the ASEAN countries, a matter which continues to be regulated by each participating country.[126]

Through these various regulatory instruments, ASEAN has successfully managed to switch to a rules-based and more coordinated approach to regional integration, however, remaining highly intergovernmental.

IV.3.2. Soft Institutional Framework

The Charter has provided for an institutional structure intended to monitor the organisation and coordinate the establishment of the ASEAN EC. The ASEAN Summit (hereinafter "the Summit"), composed of the heads of state and government, is the supreme policy-making body and is expected to provide the general direction of the organisation. Several legal instruments which constitute the regulatory framework of the organisation, including ATIGA and ACIA, have been produced by the Summit accordingly.

Other institutions include the ASEAN Coordinating Council, the ASEAN Community Councils and the ASEAN Sectoral Ministerial Bodies, which are composed of representatives from ASEAN countries and were established to support the work of the Summit.[127] The Charter also provides for the establishment of a Secretariat, headed by a Secretary-General, which serves as the administrative organ of the organisation and also monitors the progress in the implementation of the various Agreements adopted within ASEAN.[128] National Secretariats have been established in each participating country to serve as focal points and support the Secretariat in its tasks.[129] The Charter, however, has not provided the Secretariat with any authority or any mechanism to encourage the participating countries to implement the Agreements adopted by the Summit or to compel any country in breach with its obligations to align its policies with the interests of the Community.

IV.3.3. Dispute Settlement Under the ASEAN Charter

Dispute settlement within ASEAN is governed by two legal instruments: The Protocol to the ASEAN Charter on Dispute Settlement Mechanisms (hereinafter "the DSM Protocol") as well as the Agreement Comprehensive Investment Agreement (ACIA).

The DSM Protocol was adopted by the ASEAN countries in April 2010[130] and provides for a mechanism to settle disputes among the Member States regarding the application and interpretation of the ASEAN Charter or any other Agreement which falls within the remits of the organisation.[131] The procedure provided by the Protocol includes various mechanisms, including consultation between the two opposing parties with the administrative support of the Secretary-General; good offices, mediation or conciliation conducted by a third party; as well as arbitration.[132] This procedure, although is it intended to evidence ASEAN countries' commitment to transforming ASEAN into a rules-based organisation,[133] remains, however, highly politicised and closely controlled by the participating countries.[134] This questions the effectiveness of the ASEAN Dispute Settlement Mechanism (DSM), which seems to lack both the certainty and coercive power that could have been provided by a stronger judicial institution such as the MERCOSUR Permanent Review Tribunal, and which could ensure a more effective enforcement of ASEAN regulatory instruments.[135]

However, it should be pointed out that the ASEAN DSM is in line with the fundamental principles agreed upon by the ASEAN countries, which include amity, cooperation, non-interference and consensus.[136] Through this approach, which is referred to as the "ASEAN Way", ASEAN countries seek to promote a peaceful rather than confrontational method of dispute settlement. This mechanism, which is believed to be inspired from the culture in the region, is deemed to support the progress of the organisation more effectively, by increasing mutual confidence among the participating countries and thereby improving their cooperation.[137]

In addition to the DSM Protocol, disputes involving private parties are governed by ACIA.[138] ACIA article 29 provides that the Agreement applies to investment disputes between a Member State and an investor of another Member State who has incurred any damage or loss resulting from the breach of the Member State's obligations under the Agreement. Similar to the procedure under the DSM Protocol, ACIA provides for several mechanisms to settle disputes between investors and the Member States, including conciliation, consultation, adjudication by local courts and arbitration.[139]

The institutional arrangement provided by the ASEAN Charter, which is characterised by a strong intergovernmental approach, reflects the ASEAN countries' concerns about their national independence and sovereignty and "great attachment to national sovereignty and long-standing non-intervention policy".[140] By providing for the establishment of a strong intergovernmental institution, the Summit, and the creation of various weak institutions controlled by the Summit intended to provide technical and administrative support, ASEAN countries have chosen to retain much of their power, thereby making the progress of the integration process depend solely on the goodwill of their governments rather than common supranational institutions.

Even though the institutional framework provided by the ASEAN Charter might prove limited when envisioning a deeper level of integration such as MERCOSUR or the European Union, it could nevertheless be adapted to the needs and circumstances of the ASEAN countries, which have opted for a rather different model of regional integration. Although the ASEAN Charter has provided for the establishment of a single market,[141] which includes measures for trade and investment facilitation as well as the free flow of goods, services, and capital, the participating countries are expected to retain a significant level of autonomy in their economic policies.[142]

V. Conclusion

This chapter has accounted for a general overview of the diversity of regional integration models and the various ways in which law can be used to support countries involved in integration processes in achieving their objectives. The various sections were used to highlight the fact that each integration model requires a specific set of legal frameworks which are supposed to reflect the particular circumstances of the region and designed to help the regions achieve the objectives contained in their RTAs. In particular, and in light of the analysis conducted in the previous chapter, this chapter was used to identify different uses of law in a regional context, which included the abolition of tariff and non-tariff barriers to promote market access and trade liberalisation, the regulation of regional trade and the attraction of investment to increase the participating countries' international competitiveness, as well as the establishment of an appropriate dispute settlement to ensure the smooth progression of the regional processes.

For this purpose, several legal instruments were identified as means used by countries to achieve their regional objectives and address specific issues that they are likely to face.

On the one hand, the minimalist approach adopted by NAFTA, which provides for a rules-based coordination framework and a political dispute settlement mechanism, has proved to be adapted to processes in which market access and trade liberalisation are sought in order to regulate and eventually increase a pre-existing cross-border trade. In this context, the main agreement signed by the participating countries, which includes rules of origin as well as the various measures to be adopted by each country for the gradual implementation of the RTA, seems sufficient to achieve the region's objectives, as well as address issues such as the abolition of protectionist measures and the liberalisation of the participating countries' investment regimes.

This is also reflected in the rather reactionary dispute settlement mechanism established under NAFTA, which relies primarily on the participating countries' national judiciary systems and, at the regional level, provides for an interstate system with conciliatory mechanisms such as consultation and arbitration. This section was also used to highlight the limitations that the market-led minimalist approach offered under NAFTA could face in the African context, especially given the need for African states to undertake actions designed to regulate their economic growth and to promote the transformation of their economies.

On the other hand, the interventionist approach adopted under both MERCOSUR and ASEAN seems to be more suitable for the African Economic Community, which aims to foster economic transformation and sustainable development within its Member States.

MERCOSUR, for example, has provided for the adoption of a CET and the coordination of its participating countries' macroeconomic policies as important tools to support the region's economic growth and development. These measures, which require a greater commitment from the participating countries in order to achieve deeper integration and thereby increased economic growth, include the adoption of common rules to address new issues such as regional economic disparity and the elaboration and enforcement of common legal instruments. MERCOSUR has also provided for a hybrid dispute settlement mechanism which is aimed at ensuring the effective implementation of the legal instruments issued by the regional institutions. For this purpose, beyond the conciliatory options provided under the Protocol of

Brasilia—which include arbitration, the Olivos Protocol has also established a Permanent Review Tribunal to review the arbitral decisions and strengthen the regional judiciary system.

The regulatory framework provided under ASEAN—which includes legal instruments such as ACIA, the ASEAN Trade in Goods Agreement (ATIGA) and the Framework for Integration of Priority Sectors—offers a nuanced approach to regionalism which focuses more on trade facilitation, the establishment of a regional production base and the regulation of investments in the region. This model of regionalism, which does not include the adoption of a Common External Tariff, seems particularly adapted to the needs of the ASEAN countries and adequate to help them achieve their regional development goals, placing a particular emphasis on the enhancement of their international competitiveness. Moreover, the intergovernmental dispute settlement system currently used by ASEAN seems appropriate to the needs of the participating countries, as it is believed to reflect the particular circumstances of a region in which amity, consensus and non-interference are considered as fundamental principles.

The model of regionalism followed by ASEAN proves particularly important, given that it presents a different approach in which instead of constituting the ultimate objectives pursued by the participating countries, economic integration and trade liberalisation are considered as options within their overall regional strategy. Similar to the recent trends adopted by the African Union through the BIAT and PIDA, in its early years, the process conducted through ASEAN placed a greater emphasis on supply side constraints (production) rather than demand (market access). This particular approach constitutes one of the key components of the notion of regional developmentalism through law used throughout the monograph, in particular when considering its application in the context of the African RECs.

The analysis of these three models of regional integration was also used to highlight the various economic and political factors that influence the approaches adopted in specific Regional Trade Agreements, with a particular emphasis placed on the correlation between these factors and their resulting legal approaches. These various considerations constitute the analytical framework used in the remaining chapters of the monograph, which is aimed at identifying the various ways in which law could be used to support the establishment of an AEC which reflects the needs and opportunities of its Member States.

Notes

1. Duina, F. (2013) *Social Construction of Free Trade: The European Union, NAFTA and MERCOSUR*, Princeton and Oxford: Princeton University Press, p. 3.
2. This aspect of the discussion is inspired by Matsuyama, K. (1998) 'Economic Development as Coordination Problems' in Aoki, M., Kim, H-K. and Okuno-Fujiwara, M. (eds) *The Role of Government in East Asian Economic*

Development: Comparative Institutional Analysis, Oxford: Clarendon Press. The author discusses this notion in reference to the particular role played by governments in East Asian economic development, which consisted in the adoption of special policies to promote specific sectors in East Asian countries.
3. This distinction between minimalist and interventionist approaches has been provided in Duina (2013), p. 5.
4. See Hart, M. (1990) 'A North American Free Trade Agreement—The Strategic Implications for Canada' *Centre for Trade Policy and Law and the Institute for Research on Public Policy*, p. 15. See also Duina (2013), p. 4.
5. Downs, G.W. and Rocke, D.M. (1995) *Optimal Imperfection? Domestic Uncertainty and Institutions in International Relations*, Princeton, NJ: Princeton University Press, p. 77.
6. See Smith, J.M. (2000) 'The Politics of Dispute Settlement Design: Explaining Legalism in Regional Trade Pacts' 54(1) *International Organization* 137, p. 148. See also Snidal, D. (1985) 'Coordination Versus Prisoners' Dilemma: Implications for International Cooperation and Regimes' 79 *American Political Science Review*.
7. This "incomplete" aspect of RTAs been discussed in Laursen, F. (2010) 'Regional Integration: Some Introductory Reflections' in Laursen, F. (ed.) *Comparative Regional Integration: Europe and Beyond*, Surrey: Ashgate. See also Belanger, L. (2009) 'Incompleteness and Maintenance of International Cooperation: The Ex-post Politics of MERCOSUR and NAFTA' Paper presented at the 2009 ABRI-ISA Meeting, Rio de Janeiro, 21–24 July and Cooley, A. and Spruyt, H. (2009) *Contracting States: Sovereign Transfers in International Relations*, Princeton, NJ; Woodstock: Princeton University Press.
8. This is achieved in order to ensure a successful and continued cooperation among countries involved in regional integration and thereby support the effective establishment and development of regional integration initiatives by ensuring the compliance of states taking part in these initiatives. For a more detailed discussion on this aspect of RTAs, see Bouzas, R. and Soltz, H. (2001) 'Institutions and Regional Integration: The Case of MERCOSUR' in Bulmer-Thomas, V. (ed.) *Regional Integration in Latin America and the Caribbean: The Political Economy of Open Regionalism*, London: ILAS, p. 115. See also Ajulo, S.B. (2001) 'Sources of Law of the Economic Community of West African States (ECOWAS)' 45(1) *Journal of African Law* 73, p. 74.
9. See Abott, K.W. et al. (2000) 'The Concept of Legalisation' 54(3) *International Organization* 401. See also Malanczuk, P. (1997) *Akehurst's Modern Introduction to International Law*, 7th ed., New York: Routledge, pp. 273–305 and Shapiro, M.M. (1981) *Courts: A Comparative and Political Analysis*, Chicago: University of Chicago Press.
10. Abbott, K.W., Snidal, D. (2000) 'Hard and Soft Law in International Governance' 54(3) *International Organization* 421, p. 430.
11. This terminology—interstate vs. transnational dispute resolution—has been used in Keohane, R.O., Moravcsik, A., Slaughter, A.M. (2000) 'Legalized Dispute Resolution: Interstate and Transnational'54(3) *International Organization* 457, p. 458. As will be discussed in subsequent sections, interstate dispute resolution mechanisms seem to be more appropriate for intergovernmental arrangements, while transnational mechanisms appear to be the preference in supranational frameworks.
12. Throughout the chapter, "the Agreement" and NAFTA will be used interchangeably, with "the Agreement" used more to refer to the legal instrument signed by the three countries, whereas "NAFTA" is used when referring to the economic aspects of the Agreement and the Free Trade Area that it established.

13. See Abbott, F.M. (2000) 'NAFTA and the Legalisation of World Politics: A Case Study' 54(3) *International Organization* 519, pp. 543–546. The author highlights the fact that NAFTA has a combined GDP of $11 trillion.
14. Protectionist measures were used by these countries to restrict imports into their respective markets.
15. For more details on initiatives from both countries which culminated in the signing of the 1989 U.S.-Canada Free Trade Agreement, see Lipsey, R.G. and Smith, M.G. (1987) *Global Imbalances and US Policy Responses*, Toronto: C.D. Howe Institute.
16. Villarreal, M.A. and Fergusson, I.F. (2015) 'The North American Trade Agreement' *United State Congressional Research Service Report*, p. 3. See also Blecker, R.A. (2009) 'External Shocks, Structural Change, and Economic Growth in Mexico, 1979–2007' 37(7) *World Development* 1274.
17. Smith, M.G. (2011) 'The North American Free Trade Agreement: *fait accompli?*' in Jovanovic, M.N. (ed.) *International Handbook on the Economics of Integration, Volume I: General Issues and Regional Groups*, Cheltenham; Northampton: Edward Elgar, p. 353. See also Abbott and Snidal (2000), p. 426.
18. NAFTA, Article 102.
19. See also Glick, L.A. (1994) *Understanding the North American Free Trade Agreement: Legal and Business Consequences of NAFTA*, 2nd ed., Alphen aan den Rijn; London: Kluwer Law International, p. 3.
20. See Duina (2013), p. 72. See also NAALC article 1 and NAAEC article 1. Both NAALC and NAAEC are considered to be a compromise between the three participating countries as Canada and (particularly) the U.S. were looking to avoid unfair competition from a poorer country with lower labour costs and lower environmental restrictions.
21. These measures were aimed at specific industries, including the textiles, apparel, automotive and agricultural industries.
22. Services covered by NAFTA included, inter alia, financial services and telecommunication services (with some restrictions). More details on services can be found in Haufbauer, G.C. and Schott, J.J. (2005) *NAFTA Revisited: Achievements and Challenges*, Washington, DC: Institute for International Economics.
23. As discussed earlier, a Common Market involves the free movement of goods, services, capital and persons. For more details on the limitations and the particularities of NAFTA, see Glick, L.A. (1994), p. 4 and Gantz, D.A. (2009) *Regional Trade Agreements: Law, Policy and Practice*, Durham, NC: Carolina Academic Press, p. 110.
24. See Laursen (2010), p. 7.
25. These include the NAFTA Rules of Origin, which are used as a distinctive commercial policy instrument. For more details on this aspect of the Agreement, see Estevadeordal, A. (1999) 'Negotiating Preferential Market Access: The Case of NAFTA' Working Paper 3, Institute for the Integration of Latin America and the Caribbean, Inter-American Development Bank.
26. Gantz (2009), p. 108.
27. These RTAs have been referred to as "incomplete contracts".
28. The Agreement provides very detailed rules covering these matters, an approach which seems appropriate in this particular context, given that NAFTA is aimed at governing the relations between three participating countries rather than issuing common policies and coordinating common actions between the three countries. For more details on this aspect of the Agreement, see Bouzas and Soltz (2001), p. 95.
29. See Gantz (2009), p. 110 and Estevadeordal (1999). Rules of Origin, which are directly related to both tariffs and customs, combined with the other set of

rules, are here expected to be used as adjustment instruments facilitating the gradual implementation of the Agreement.

30. See Duina (2013). In the U.S., for example, firms would rely more on corporate associations for industry standards.
31. The Agreement has provided for the establishment of a light institutional framework, with limited powers, which is in clear contrast with the complex institutional infrastructure developed by the European Union. See Inama, S. and Sim, E.W. (2015) *The Foundation of the ASEAN Economic Community: An Institutional and Legal Profile*, Cambridge: Cambridge University Press, p. 41.
32. As described in a previous chapter, the intergovernmental approach considers states as the driving forces behind integration. Under this approach, the focus is on Member States' governments and there is no need for regional legislation as each member state fully exercises its own policies and, as a consequence, regional institutions are deprived of any independent power. The supranationalist approach, on the contrary, argues that regional integration can be achieved by the establishment of regional institutions with more autonomy and stronger powers and through the adoption of a regional legislation which prevails over national legislation.
33. This refers to the fact that the Agreement seems to have provided for most measures required from the participating countries in order to achieve their objectives.
34. See articles 2001 and 2002 of the Agreement. Several panels and committees were also established to support the work of the Commission.
35. See article 2001 of the Agreement.
36. See article articles 2002 and 1908 of the Agreement.
37. The choice of this approach might have been influenced by the level of precision of the rules-based coordination mechanism, as well as the fact that NAFTA is not expected to progress towards a deeper form of integration such as a Common Market. In these circumstances, the establishment of a supranational judicial institution to monitor the application and interpretation of the Agreement would seem both cumbersome and unnecessary.
38. Article 2004 of the Agreement.
39. See Smith (2011), p. 366 and Duina (2013), p. 100.
40. The Agreement offers this option only in case the concerned dispute arises under both GATT (and any subsequent agreement, currently the WTO) and NAFTA rules.
41. Article 2005 of the Agreement.
42. Articles 2006 and 2007 of the Agreement.
43. Article 2008 of the Agreement.
44. Article 2018 (1) of the Agreement.
45. An option discussed in Gantz (2009), p. 140.
46. Article 2022 of the Agreement provides that participating countries should encourage the use of arbitration to settle commercial disputes while articles 1115 to 1137 provide for the use of arbitration under the ICSID Convention or the UNCITRAL Arbitral rules for disputes between an investor and a participating country. Chapter 19 of the Agreement also provides for a review mechanism for antidumping and countervailing duty determinations, which is to be conducted by a bi-national panel composed of members appointed by the concerned participating countries.
47. McRae, D. and Siwiec, J. (2010) 'NAFTA Dispute Settlement: Success or Failure?' available at http://biblio.juridicas.unam.mx/libros/6/2904/21.pdf (accessed on 20/08/2015). The authors discuss the long delays in the

implementation of panel reports and arbitral decisions under the NAFTA dispute settlement mechanism and highlight the more effective use of the WTO dispute settlement system by the participating countries.

48. Blecker, R.A. (2005) 'The North American Economies After NAFTA: A Critical Appraisal' 33(3) *International of Political Economy* 5, p. 7.
49. This is evidenced in article 4 of the Treaty of Abuja which lists economic development as the main objective behind the establishment of an AEC. It must be noted, however, that in contrast with Mexico, the African context does not provide the example of regional initiatives where one of two large industrialised economies are linked with other less developed economies.
50. See Zepeda, E., Wise, T.A. and Gallagher, K.P. (2009) 'Rethinking Trade Policy for Development: Lessons from Mexico under NAFTA' Carnegie Endowment for International Peace Policy Outlook, p. 4. The author notes that the country experienced an exponential growth in manufacturing, while agricultural exports have nearly doubled between 1993 and 2007.
51. On the liberalisation of investment and its impact of the Mexican economy, see Ten Kate, A. (1992) 'Trade Liberalisation and Economic Stabilisation in Mexico: Lessons of Experience' 20(5) *World Development* 659. See also Moreno-Brid, J.C. (2007) 'Economic Development and Industrial Performance in Mexico post-NAFTA' Paper presented at the Taller Nacional sobre 'Migracion interna y destrallos en Mexico: diagnostico, perspectivas y politicas' Mexico City, 16 April, p. 2.
52. See Zepeda et al. (2009), p. 4 and Pacheco-Lopez, P. and Thirlwall, A.P. (2004) 'Trade Liberalisation in Mexico: Rhetoric and Reality' *Department of Economics Discussion Paper No. 04, 03,* University of Kent, p. 16.
53. These measures include, *inter alia*, the prohibition of performance requirements and preference given to the purchase of local products and services in investment operations (as provided in NAFTA article 1106). Performance requirements may be used in particular by countries willing to channel investments towards specific sectors and industries which are expected to benefit their economies.
54. Moreno-Brid (2007), p. 3.
55. See ASEAN Studies Centre (2009) *Mercosur Economic Integration: Lessons for ASEAN,* Singapore: Institute of Southeast Asian Studies (Report requested by the ISEAS to UN Economic Commission for Latin America), p. 7 and See Vaillant, M. (2005) 'MERCOSUR: Southern Integration under Construction' *Internationale Politik und Gesellschaft* 2, p. 63. MERCOSUR Member States gather more than 50% of Latin America's GDP, 43% of its population and more than 50% of its industrial production.
56. Venezuela joined MERCOSUR in 2012 to become its fifth full Member State. Bolivia, Chile, Colombia, Ecuador and Peru are considered as *associate* members of the organisation.
57. See Vaillant (2005), p. 55. As in the case of Mexico, these various reforms were also strongly recommended by international financial institutions such as the IMF and the World Bank.
58. Hirst, M. (1992) *Avances y desafios en la formacion del Mercosur*, Buenos Aires: FLASCO, p. 5. PICE measures targeted specific sectors and covered various areas such as capital goods, food and technological cooperation.
59. The two countries adopted the Treaty on Integration, Cooperation and Development in 1988 and the Buenos Aires Act in 1990, both being aimed at establishing a Common Market between Argentina and Brazil.
60. See Manzetti, L. (1992) 'Economic Integration in the Southern Cone' *North South Focus*, p. 1.

61. See Hurrell, A. (1995) 'Regionalism in the Americas' in Fawcett, L. and Hurrell, A. (eds) *Foreign Policy and Regionalism in the Americas*, pp. 258–259. See also Bouzas and Soltz (2001), p. 112.
62. See preamble of the ToA.
63. Ibid.
64. These measures are provided in articles 1 and 5 of the ToA.
65. See article 1 of the ToA. MERCOSUR adopted a strategy similar to that of the European Union, which is mainly based on the free movement of goods, services and factors of production.
66. This is a typical example of what was referred to as an "incomplete contract" which only provides for general objectives to be achieved and therefore require special mechanisms to produce its effects.
67. The ToA only provided for the general principles necessary to conduct the integration process, including the objectives, the instruments to be used, the structure of the organisation, its period of application and the accession by other countries.
68. A similar objective was assigned to the AEC in article 4 of the Treaty of Abuja.
69. See Olarreaga, M., Soloaga, I. and Winters, A. (1999) 'What's Behind MERCOSUR's Common External Tariff?' *World Bank Policy Research Paper 2231*, p. 4. See also Vaillant (2005), p. 55.
70. The CET was therefore adopted by MERCOSUR as an additional legal instrument used in the context of regional integration to promote the economic development of the participating countries.
71. As provided in article 18 of the ToA, this institutional framework was provided especially to support the establishment of the Common Market. For a more detailed discussion on the issues that the institutional framework provided by the POP was expected to address, see Leipziger, D.M., Frischtak, C., Kharas, H.M. and Normand, J.F. (1997) 'MERCOSUR: Integration and Industrial Policy' 20(5) *The World Economy*.
72. These decisions include various subject matters including the adoption of the Common External Tariff (Decision 007/1994), the promotion and protection of investments from third parties (Decision 011/1994) and the settlement of disputes (Protocol of Brasilia, Decision 001/1991).
73. These institutions are provided for in articles 3 to 19 of the POP. Both the CMC and the CMG were already established through article 9 of the ToA. The MTC, however, was established in 1994 with the special role of supporting the implementation of the Customs Union.
74. Protocol of Ouro Preto articles 22 to 33.
75. See Kaltenthaler, K. and Mora, F.O. (2002) 'Explaining Latin American Economic Integration: The Case of MERCOSUR' 9(1) *Review of International Political Economy*, p. 75.
76. See Bouzas and Soltz (2001), p. 107.
77. See article 45 of the Paraguayan Constitution, articles 27, 31 and 43 of the Argentinian Constitution as well as Decision 7/7/1992 of the Argentinian Supreme Court (case *Ekmekdjian, Miguel Angel v Sofovich, Gerardo and Others*).
78. Articles 239 and 256 of the Uruguayan Constitution provide for the principle of constitutional supremacy and article 5 paragraph 3 of the Brazilian Constitution provides a dualist system in which international conventions need to be approved in each house of the National Congress in order to be equivalent to constitutional norms. For further details on the monist and dualist systems in general, see Novakovic, M. (2013) *Basic Concepts of Public International Law: Monism and Dualism*, Belgrade: Faculty of Law, University of Belgrade;

in MERCOSUR countries, see Vervaele, J.A.E. (2005) 'MERCOSUR and Regional Integration in South America' 54(2) *The International and Comparative Law Quarterly*, p. 394.

79. Protocol of Brasilia, article 1.
80. Ibid, article 2.
81. Ibid, articles 4 to 6.
82. Ibid, articles 7 to 24.
83. Several integration-related issues have been resolved under this procedure, including various cases between Argentina and Brazil concerning, *inter alia*, non-automatic import licenses imposed by Brazil (1997), export subsidies applied by Brazil in favour of its producers of pork meat (1999) and the application of textile safeguards by Argentina (2000), which was deemed to affect Brazilian textile exports. In most cases, awards rendered by the ad hoc arbitral tribunals contained injunctions for the losing party to adjust its domestic legislation and eliminate any measures which were considered as violations of MERCOSUR's objectives. For more details on arbitration under MERCOSUR, see Vinuesa, R.E. (2005) 'Enforcement of MERCOSUR Arbitration Awards Within the Domestic Legal Orders of Member States' 40 *Texas International Law Journal* 425. See also Bouzas and Soltz (2001), p. 100.
84. See Vinuesa (2005), p. 433. Here the author highlights the use of precedents by ad hoc arbitral tribunals, which, he argues, "reinforce the idea of recognising common patterns in the application and interpretation of MERCOSUR law".
85. Olivos Protocol articles 23, 26 and 29.
86. *Quasi-judicial* refers to the fact that the PRT is not a proper court and is composed of arbitrators instead of judges.
87. Olivos Protocol, article 39. These measures have been provided as a tool to protect and promote business activities within the region with the hope of ensuring increased investment and economic growth in the participating countries.
88. Ibid, article 40.
89. Ibid, article 41.
90. Ibid. Articles 42 to 44.1 provide for the intervention of the CMG, assisted in this matter by a group of experts which provides its opinion on the admissibility of the claim filed to the CMG via a National Section.
91. Ibid, article 44.2.
92. Having MERCOSUR cases decided by the various national jurisdictions without any coordination runs the risk of having different interpretations of MERCOSUR rules across the region, hence the need to establish a regional court to address this issue. Further details on this matter can be found in O'Keefe, T.A. (2007), *Latin American Trade Agreements*, Boston: Brill/Martinus Nijhoff, pp. 7–25 and Gantz (2009), p. 376.
93. A Common Court would be used in this context to regulate the application of regional rules in all participating countries, ensuring that both national and regional institutions interpret the rules uniformly.
94. See Arieti, A. (2006) 'The Role of MERCOSUR as a Vehicle for Latin American Integration' 6 *Chicago Journal of International Law*, p. 764.
95. See in particular ASEAN Studies Centre (2009), p. 3.
96. See Boldorini, M.C. and Zalduendo, S. (1995) 'La estructura juridico-institutional del MERCOSUR despues del Protocolo de Ouro Preto' 283 *Boletin Informativo Techint*, p. 117. See also Gantz (2009), p. 378.

97. See Frischtak, C.R. (2011) 'Integration Efforts and Economic Dynamics in South America' in Jovanovic (ed.), p. 438, where the author argues that the exceptions contained in the CET leave out 67% of the items traded by MERCOSUR countries. See also Leiva, E.G. and Diaz, C.R. (2009) 'The Common External Tariff of MERCOSUR. Is it a Tool For Stimulating the Competitiveness of its Members?' *Working Paper*, Inter-American Development Bank, p. 3. The authors explain this situation by the fact that the CET resulted from a compromise between smaller members (Paraguay and Uruguay), which preferred a CET with low rates, to attract more investment, and bigger members (Argentina and Brazil), which favoured higher rates in order to protect local manufacturing from external competition. Therefore, although those exceptions were intended to protect specific sectors and industries against increased imports likely to affect them (similar to the maintenance of concessions under the ASEAN CEPT), they may also reduce the effectiveness of the CET as an instrument for development. Similar difficulties have been discussed in Andriamananjara, S. (2011) 'Customs Unions' in Chauffour, J-P. and Mau, J-C. (eds) *Preferential Trade Agreement Policies for Development: A Handbook*, Washington, DC: The World Bank, p. 115. The author highlights the difficulty faced by developing countries in agreeing on a CET and distributional measures.
98. This includes the reduction of regional disparities, by ensuring that most of the benefits resulting from intra-regional trade are not concentrated in more dynamic countries such as Brazil and Argentina. For further discussions on the disparities between countries in the region, see Berman, M. and Rikap, C. (2010) 'Regional Integration and Export Diversification in MERCOSUR: The Case of Argentina and Brazil' *CEPAL Review 100.*
99. This particular point will be analysed and further developed in the context of the European Community where the creation of supranational institutions determined the successful establishment of a Common Market between the participating countries.
100. They were later joined by Brunei (1984), Cambodia (1999), Laos (1997), Myanmar (1997) and Vietnam (1995).
101. See Pomfret, R. (2011) 'Regional Integration in Asia' in Jovanovic (ed.) Vol. I, pp. 377 & 388.
102. Fujita, M. and Hamagushi, N. (2011) 'Regional Integration of Production Systems and Spatial Income Disparities in East Asia' in Jovanovic, M.N. (ed.) *International Handbook on the Economics of Integration, Volume II: Competition, Spatial Location of Economic Activity and Financial Issues*, Cheltenham; Northampton: Edward Elgar, p. 249.
103. See Mercurio, B. (2011) 'Bilateral and Regional Trade Agreements in Asia: A Sceptic's View' in Buckley, R.P., Hu, R.W. and Arner, D.W. (eds) *East Asian Economic Integration: Law, Trade and Finance*, Cheltenham; Northampton: Edward Elgar, p. 122.
104. This terminology has been borrowed from Fujita, M., Kuroiwa, I. and Kumagai, S. (eds) (2011) *The Economics of East Asian Integration: A Comprehensive Introduction to Regional Issues*, Cheltenham; Northampton: Edwar Elgar, p. 1.
105. 1967 ASEAN Declaration, article 2, para 3. See also Davidson (2004), p. 172 and Leifer, M. (1989) *ASEAN and the Security of South-East Asia*, London and New York: Routledge, pp. 2–3. The authors argue that ASEAN was established on political and ideological foundations rather than economic considerations.
106. Ibid., article 2, paras 3 and 5. The ASEAN Declaration was therefore intended to be a legal instrument complementing each country individual economic policies, including by fostering the inception of common initiatives

and common projects rather than promoting freer trade among the participating countries.

107. See Okamoto, J. (2011) 'Institution Building For Economic Integration in East Asia: A Brief History' in Fujita, M.; Kuroiwa, I. and Kumagai, S. (eds) *The Economics of East Asian Integration: A Comprehensive Introduction to Regional Issues*, Cheltenham; Northampton: Edward Elgar, p. 291.
108. For further details on the economic strategies adopted by the Southeast Asian countries in the early 1980s, see Amsden, A.H. (2001) *The Rise of 'The Rest': Challenges the West From Late-industrializing Economies*, Oxford: Oxford University Press; Wade, R. (1990) *Governing the Market: Economic Theory and the Role of Government in East Asian Industrialisation*, Princeton: Princeton University Press; and Pitelis, C.N. and Kelmendi, P. (2011) 'European Industrial Policy: Perspectives, Trends and a Sustainability-Focused Framework' in Jovanovic (ed.) (2011).
109. See Fujita, M., Kuroiwa, I. and Kumagai, S. (eds) (2011) *The Economics of East Asian Integration: A Comprehensive Introduction to Regional Issues*, Cheltenham; Northampton: Edward Elgar, p. 1.
110. Pomfret (2011), p. 382.
111. See Hu, R.W. (2011) 'China, the US and Regional Institution Building in East Asia' in Buckley, R.P., Hu, R.W. and Arner, D.W. (2011) *East Asian Economic Integration: Law, Trade and Finance*, Cheltenham; Northampton: Edward Elgar, p. 10. See also Nishikimi, K. and Kuroiwa, I. (2011) 'Analytical Framework for East Asian Integration (1): Industrial Agglomeration and Concentrated Dispersion' in Fujita, M., Kuroiwa, I. and Kumagai, S. (eds) *The Economics of East Asian Integration: A Comprehensive Introduction to Regional Issues*, Cheltenham; Northampton: Edward Elgar, p. 60.
112. The CEPT was preceded by the ASEAN Preferential Trading Agreements in 1977.
113. This also represented a move from economic cooperation to economic integration.
114. See ASEAN Studies Centre (2009), p. vii and Davidson (2004), p. 176.
115. See Parrenas, J.C. (1998) 'ASEAN and Asia-Pacific Economic Cooperation' 11(2) *Pacific Review*, p. 236 and Bowles, P. and MacLean (1996) 'Understanding Trade Bloc Formation: The Case of the ASEAN Free Trade Area' 3(2) *Review of International Political Economy*, pp. 319–348. As highlighted in the previous chapter, this constitutes a key aspect of the concept of regional developmentalism in which regional initiatives in general, and regional economic integration in particular, are used as means to achieve and to further the participating countries' economic development.
116. This objective is similar to that of NAFTA and MERCOSUR, which provided for tariff reductions between Canada, Mexico and the United States.
117. See CEPT, article 3. Agricultural products, which were considered as sensitive goods, were not included in the list until 2010. See also Pomfret (2011), p. 379.
118. For example, Article 5D (1) of the CEPT provided for the maintenance by a participating country of concessions aimed at protecting specific sectors likely to be affected by increased imports from other participating countries.
119. Similar to the CEPT, the AIA Agreement provided for measures aimed at supporting national development goals, including measures to limit national treatment to ASEAN investors for ten years before extending it to investors from outside the region (article 4) and the right for participating countries to submit temporary exclusion or sensitive lists to protect particular industries (article7–2). Regarding article 4 in particular, see Nesadurai, H.E.S. (2003) 'Attempting Developmental Regionalism Through AFTA: The Domestic Sources of Regional Governance' 24(2) *Third World Quarterly* 235. Here

the author discusses the use of the AIA Agreement by the ASEAN countries as a legal instrument to further economic development in the region and presents it as a special approach to regional integration called *developmental regionalism*, which is similar of the concept of regional developmentalism discussed in Chapter 2.

120. See preamble of the ASEAN Framework Agreement for the Integration of Priority Sectors. Several protocols were subsequently adopted in application of the AFAIP, focusing the integration efforts on key sectors, including agro-based products, automotives, textiles and apparel. These Protocols provided for the reduction of tariff and non-tariff measures affecting the cross-border trade of these products among the ASEAN countries. They also referred to article 6 of the CEPT, which provided for the application of emergency measures in case a country's economy was affected by increased imports of the same products.
121. The ASEAN Charter was adopted in November 2007 and provides for the establishment of the ASEAN Community, which is based on three pillars: the ASEAN Security Community, the ASEAN Economic Community and the ASEAN Socio-Cultural Community (see preamble of the Charter). The ASEAN Economic Community is referred to as ASEAN EC instead of AEC throughout the chapter, to avoid any confusion with the AEC.
122. See the 2007 AEC Blueprint, article 9. The AEC Blueprint was adopted on 20 November 2007 and provides for the various steps in the establishment of the ASEA Economic Community.
123. The preamble of the Charter lists the establishment of a legal and institutional framework to support the organisation as one of the objectives of the Charter.
124. See the 2007 AEC Blueprint, articles 10 to 19.
125. ACIA article 1 provides for its objective, which is to be achieved through enhancing the protection of investors and their investments within ASEAN, through the liberalisation of the investment regimes of the Member States, the improvement of transparency and predictability of investment rules and the joint promotion of the region as an integrated investment area.
126. This differs from the case of most African RECs, which all provide for the adoption of a CET. ASEAN, therefore, provides for a different path to achieve integration objectives which does not include the establishment of a Customs Union.
127. ASEAN Charter, articles 3, 7–10. This is an indication that decision-making under ASEAN is predominantly intergovernmental.
128. ASEAN Charter, article 11.
129. ASEAN Charter, article 13.
130. Dispute settlement was previously governed by the 2004 Protocol on Enhanced Dispute Settlement.
131. See DSM Protocol, article 2.
132. See DSM Protocol, article 5 to 8.
133. The preamble of the Protocol provides for the "desire of ASEAN leaders [to transform] ASEAN into a rules-based organisation with practical, efficient and credible mechanisms in place to resolve disputes in an effective and timely manner".
134. See Toohey (2011), p. 150. and Davidson (2004), pp. 165–176.
135. This view was expressed by Walter Woon, the then Attorney-General of Singapore, in his paper "The ASEAN Charter Dispute Settlement Mechanisms" Presented at the 10th General Assembly of the ASEAN Law Association in Hanoi, Vietnam in October 2009.

136. This attitude displayed by the ASEAN Member States is reflected by the wording of the Preamble of the ASEAN Charter, in particular para 2 which provides for the principles governing the Charter, including (a) "[the] respect for the independence, sovereignty, equality, territorial integrity and national identity of all ASEAN Member States" and (e) "[the] non-interference in the internal affairs of ASEAN Member States".
137. See Goh, G. (2000) 'The ASEAN Way: Non-Intervention and ASEAN Role in Conflict Management' *Stanford Journal of East Asian Affairs*, p. 114. See also Toohey (2011), p. 182.
138. This option is intended to promote investments in the region by providing businesses operating in the region with protection against participating countries' actions likely to affect their activities.
139. See ACIA, articles 31–33. Article 33 in particular provides for various options of arbitration regimes, including the International Centre for the Settlement of Investment Disputes (ICSID) Rules (provided that both the investor's country and the disputing Member State are parties to the ICSID Convention), the UNCITRAL Arbitration Rules, any regional centre for arbitration within ASEAN or any other arbitration institution agreed upon by the parties.
140. Hermann, C. and Terhechte, J.P. (2009) *European Yearbook of International Economic Law 2010*, Dordrecht: Springer, p. 337. See also Tan, L.H. (2002) 'Law and Policy in ASEAN Economic Integration' 38 *Asia Business Law Review*, p. 7. As will be discussed in the context of African RTAs, the same concern was expressed in the initial efforts towards regional integration on the continent.
141. This approach, although it is different from the Common Market model adopted by other processes such as MERCOSUR and the European Union, could prove more adapted to the circumstances of the African Economic Community.
142. See Yahuda, M. (2004) *The International Politics of The Asia Pacific since 1945*, London: Routledge. The author argues that ASEAN was never meant to become an Economic Union, but was rather "designed to sustain the independence and sovereignty of member states and to encourage regional and national stability".

5 The Establishment of a Common Market Within the European Community

I. Introduction

Following on from the discussion in the previous chapter, this chapter is aimed at providing a further analysis of the role that law can play in the context of regional integration, here focusing more particularly on the various ways in which law can be used both to support the establishment of a Common Market and to regulate its further development. This analysis proves particularly significant, given that the Treaty of Abuja has listed the establishment of a Common Market as one of the objectives to be pursued by the African Economic Community (AEC).[1]

This analysis is particularly aimed at unpacking the European integration process with a view to understanding the legal framework as well as the legal principles and techniques that it provides within their original context.[2] As in previous chapters, the concept of regional developmentalism through law is used to inform the analysis conducted in this chapter, which focuses on both the economic and political functions that law is expected to play in the context of a Common Market. A strong emphasis is therefore placed on the particular techniques and legal instruments provided under the Common Market model and the particular manner in which these can be used to promote regional development in the context of the AEC.

Moreover, beyond the investigation of the various manners in which law can be used to support different models of regional integration, the previous chapter also highlighted the need for countries to adopt adequate coordination mechanisms likely to help them achieve their objectives. The case of MERCOSUR, in particular, proved important, as it was used to demonstrate that deeper and more complex models of integration are likely to require more robust regulatory and institutional frameworks in order to produce their full effects.

This chapter therefore focuses on the creation of the European Economic Community (hereinafter EEC)[3] and its subsequent transformation into a Common Market. For this purpose, rather than providing for an extensive history of the European integration project up to its current form as the

European Union, a stronger emphasis will be placed on its crucial early years and the initial stages of the transformation into a Common Market, with a view to drawing a useful comparison with the African Economic Community and identifying the specific way in which law can be used to achieve the objectives of the Treaty of Abuja. In particular, the analysis focuses on the interventionist approach adopted by the EEC, which is characterised by a supranational institutional framework to manage the functioning of the EEC, a set of specific regulatory instruments adopted to achieve the objectives of the integration project, as well as special techniques and methods to ensure the implementation and enforcement of Community rules. The chapter argues that these special measures were crucial to ensure the achievement of the objectives of the European integration project and support the establishment of a Common Market.

The concept of integration through law introduced in the previous chapters proves particularly important in the context of the EEC, as it provides a more detailed example of the different ways in which law can be used to coordinate and regulate regional integration efforts. In particular, this chapter investigates on the different mechanisms used to address further issues likely to arise in the context of the AEC, including the stagnation of the integration process and the effective implementation and enforcement of Treaty and Community rules.[4] These mechanisms include the elaboration of rules and specific legal instruments to achieve the objectives assigned to the Common Market, positive and negative integration processes intended to facilitate the participating countries' common actions and the establishment of supranational institutions to ensure the effectiveness of the overall process.

For the sake of consistency and clarity, the chapter is divided into four sections which are aimed at analysing the European integration process in a way which highlights the various aspects of law aforementioned.

The first section focuses on the Treaty of Paris, the sectoral approach that was adopted at the inception of the integration process and the objectives that it was expected to achieve. A particular emphasis is placed on the rationale behind the creation of the European Community and its further development into a Common Market, which is a deeper form of integration.[5] This analysis is used to highlight the various factors and particular circumstances that have influenced the adoption of the Market model of integration within the EEC.

The second section focuses on the expansion of the integration process through the Treaty of Rome,[6] which established the EEC, and places a particular emphasis on both the objectives assigned to the Community and the various instruments provided to achieve them. This section is used in particular to explore the economic aspect of the approach adopted by the EEC Treaty, highlighting the particular manner in which the various legal instruments adopted by the participating countries were expected to promote economic growth within the region, e.g. the promotion of growth through freer trade, economies of scale, and production of exports to larger markets.

The third section analyses the legal integration process conducted within the EEC through the critical analysis of concepts such as *positive integration*—which involves the elaboration of common policies aimed at addressing common issues at the regional level—and *negative integration*—involving the removal of trade barriers between EEC Member states.[7] The section is also used to highlight the key role played by Community institutions—in particular, the Common Court and the Commission—in advancing the integration efforts towards the effective establishment of a Common Market.

The last section focuses on the Single European Act (hereinafter SEA) and highlights the key role that the additional measures provided by the Treaty were instrumental to the completion of a Common Market in Europe.

II. Sectoral Approach and the Inception of the Integration Process Under the Treaty of Paris

Similar to the case of the Association of Southeast Asian Nations (ASEAN), the circumstances that influenced the early efforts towards regional integration in Europe, including the adoption of Treaty of Paris, were primarily based on peace and security considerations. To this effect, the history of European integration dates back to the end of World War II, which can be considered as the "catalyst" that initiated the process which has resulted in the creation of the European Union. Europe had been the scene of successive wars and tensions among nations which had left them economically devastated. The idea of coming together therefore emerged and was seen as a means to achieve peace and stability among European nations, as well as a tool to rebuild their economies. The pursuit of a common goal—their economic recovery—was therefore seen as the strategy which could potentially help prevent wars in the future.[8]

With financial aid from the United States, through the European Recovery Programme (ERP, also known as the Marshall Plan) which was aimed at regenerating the European economy, European governments initiated a plan to rebuild war-devastated regions, remove trade barriers between countries, modernise industry and make the continent prosperous.[9] The need to establish a central entity to coordinate these efforts and manage the recovery plan emerged, given the display by European governments of their incapacity to spare their populations from the atrocities of war.[10] With regard to the EEC, the aim was, therefore, to establish among European countries a central institution which would be used as an effective tool to prevent the resurgence of pan-European armed conflicts in the future by channelling all the efforts in common projects which would benefit all participating countries.

Furthermore, as the fact that these states saw themselves as democracies—with elected governments subject to the rule of law—did not prevent them from going to war with each other, European leaders agreed upon the establishment of a central authority with a significant amount of autonomy and powers which would be used to induce them to work together towards their common welfare.[11] This central institution would be in charge of coordinating specific areas of their economic production and promoting their welfare and development.[12]

It therefore follows that the main objective of the European integration process was to maintain peace and drawing the different European countries together, whereas economic integration and a strong institutional framework were used as the means to achieve this objective.[13] This approach, which resulted from the particular circumstances which prevailed at the time in Europe, was considered as the most adequate to help the participating countries achieve their objectives.[14] This approach has been reflected in the various Treaties, rules and adopted for over half a century by the EEC Member States. These legal instruments were used to lay down the foundations for the establishment of what over the years became a supranational leviathan, ensuring its evolution from the European Coal and Steel Community (ECSC) in 1951 to the current European Union.[15]

II.1. Sectoral Integration

The Treaty of Paris (hereinafter ToP), which established the ECSC, was signed on 18 April 1951. This Treaty, which provided for the initial objectives of the organisation, laid down the foundations upon which European integration was to be built. The ToP provided for the establishment of an organisation which was aimed at conducting a sectoral integration, overseeing the participating countries' coal and steel industries. Given the constant rivalry which existed between France and Germany, this strategy was adopted in order to promote economic cooperation and stabilise the relationship between the two countries, through the establishment the promotion of a "highest level of productivity" and the distribution of production among the participating countries.[16]

This strategy, based on economic integration between the two countries, took a functionalist approach and was originally aimed at integrating the two countries' coal and steel industries. Cooperation in this sector, which was regarded at the time as an important resource for economic growth,[17] would require both sides to work closely together and was expected to have repercussions at the political, social and cultural levels as well.[18] The integration of one particular area of their economies, i.e. the coal and steel industry, was therefore expected to be the first step towards a greater integration and cooperation between the two countries which would, in turn, make war and conflicts inconceivable.[19] As this idea of cooperation between France and Germany could potentially benefit the whole of Europe by promoting peace and security at the continental level, the project was extended to other neighbouring countries (Belgium, Italy, Luxembourg and the

Netherlands) and the ECSC was created by the signing of the Treaty of Paris in 1951.

As provided in Article 1 of the ToP, the ECSC was "founded upon a common market, common objectives and common institutions". These objectives were supposed to be achieved through a strategy consisting in the elimination of import and export duties, and of measures or policies discriminating between stakeholders involved in the operations pertaining to the Common Market, as well as subsidies granted by the participating countries or any other restrictive practices.[20] Very early, the idea of European economic integration was therefore linked to the idea of trade liberalisation and the ECSC was mandated both to promote a multilateral trade liberalisation and to abolish any measures or practices that could potentially restrict the sharing or exploitation of pre-existing national markets.[21] Regional efforts were therefore aimed at expanding national markets in coal and steel, economic necessity being used here as the driving force through which the ECSC was meant to achieve its objective of promoting peace and security.

On the political front, moving away from the more traditional intergovernmental system of cooperation between countries which prevailed at the time, the ECSC was designed as an organisation with supranational powers responsible for the coordination and monitoring of its member states coal and steel industries.[22] It must be pointed out that, although the ECSC was already based on the idea of the establishment of a Common Market among its Member States, the early stages of European integration did not focus on all sectors of the economy, but rather on the promotion and expansion of particular industries (coal and steel).[23]

The creation of the ECSC and the establishment of its original institutional framework laid down the foundations for the building of a supranational constitutional order within which the founding Member States' governments would learn how to work together and be bound by a supranational rule of law.[24] Even though it concentrated only on key industries (coal and steel), the ToP constituted the first attempt toward collective action and integration at the European level and provided for the general trade policies that would characterise the European integration process over the years. Moreover, the Treaty was used both to adopt a market approach towards regional integration and to adopt a coordination mechanism intended to be rules-based, and highly institutionalised.

The apparent success of their first attempts towards regional integration, which included increased trade levels among the participating countries, encouraged the ECSC countries to continue in the path of economic integration and caused the drafting of subsequent treaties inspired from the ToP.[25] These subsequent Treaties were aimed at supporting the progression of the European integration process, to improve the regulatory techniques and implement the various trade policies as necessary. Of all these Treaties, the Treaty of Rome, which is analysed in the following section, constitutes a major milestone as it provides for additional legal instruments specifically intended to further advance the integration process.

III. Deeper Integration Under the Treaty of Rome (EEC Treaty)

Following the ToP, and with the idea of deepening their economic integration and extending their experience to the rest of Europe, the six ECSC countries[26] signed the EEC Treaty on 27 March 1957, which led to the establishment of the EEC on 1 January 1958.[27] Whereas the ToP was an agreement between six countries, focusing on key sectors (coal and steel), the EEC Treaty was more inclusive of other European countries and expanded the scope of European integration to economic activities in general.[28] Moving the focus from merely the safeguard of peace and security in Europe, the EEC Treaty was expected go a step further and "lay the foundations of an *ever closer union* among the peoples of Europe [and] ensure the economic and social progress of [European] countries by common action to eliminate the barriers which divide[d] Europe".[29]

III.1. Trade Liberalisation

As provided in Article 2 of the Treaty, the EEC's main objective was to gradually establish a Common Market in Europe, to "promote throughout the Community a harmonious development of economic activities", the creation of economic wealth and to "rais[e] the standard of living and closer relations between the [participating countries]". In view of the Customs Union theory on which the integration process was based, trade occupied a prominent place in the EEC Treaty, which provided for various measures aimed at eliminating the various barriers hampering import or export of specific goods between the EEC Member States.[30] This cross-border trade was supposed to happen between industrialised countries which were at fairly similar levels of development and involved exchanges of a wide variety of products which concentrated mostly on manufactured goods.[31]

However, unlike other regional integration projects such as the North American Trade Agreement (NAFTA), the rules provided by the EEC Treaty were not restricted to the trade in goods but also involved fundamental principles under which services, capital and labour (people) were also supposed to move freely within the Community.[32] The Common Market[33] was supposed to be established once these four freedoms had been effectively implemented, a process which was expected to promote economic growth and facilitate the distribution of resources within the Community.[34]

To achieve these various objectives and to ensure that the integration process served the common interest, the EEC Treaty provided for the establishment of specific institutional and regulatory frameworks, which are analysed in the following section.

III.2. Rules-Based and Institutionalised Coordination Mechanism

III.2.1. Institutional Framework

The task of coordinating the Community was entrusted to four main institutions to which Member States delegated the power and autonomy necessary for independent action.

Composed of representatives of the Member States' governments, the European Council is responsible for ensuring that the objectives set out in the Treaty are attained through its decision making and its coordination of the Member States' general economic policies.[35] The Council is one of the legislative bodies of the Community, endowed with the important task of determining the general vision of the Community and deciding on which path the Community should take to fulfil its mission. Next, to the Council, the European Parliament (EP), which consists of representatives of the peoples of the Member States, exercises advisory and supervisory powers under the EEC Treaty.[36] As it will be discussed in a subsequent section, the role and powers of the EP were increased and reinforced by the SEA and subsequent Treaties, granting to the EP the status of *co-legislator* with the Council.

In addition, the Community also has an executive body which is composed of members chosen on the ground of their general competence and their independence.[37] The particular role of the Commission is to ensure the application of the Treaty and the measures taken by the other institutions, to formulate recommendations and deliver opinions on matters dealt with in the Treaty, to participate in the shaping of measures taken by the EP and the Council and any other task required by the Council for the implementation of measures taken by the latter.

To ensure that in the interpretation and the application of the Treaty the law was observed, the European Court of Justice (ECJ; later on the Court of Justice of the European Union, CJEU) was established.[38] For this purpose, the Court gives preliminary rulings concerning the interpretation of the Treaty, the validity and interpretation of acts of the institutions of the Community, the interpretation of the statutes of bodies established by an act of the Council, where those statutes thus provide.[39] The Court is also mandated to review the legality of the acts of the Council and the Commission other than recommendations or opinions; it also decides any case brought by the Commission or a Member State against a Member State which would have failed to fulfil an obligation under the Treaty.[40] The critical role played by the Court will be analysed in more details in the following section.

The founding Treaties, therefore, provided for an institutional framework and a system of governance that was somehow based on the national structure of most of the Member States, with a legislative branch to produce the legal arsenal enshrined with the vision necessary to run the Community; an executive branch to implement the vision; and a judicial branch to ensure that the vision and its implementation measures go in line with the spirit of the Treaty.[41] These institutions are supposed to manage the integration process through various acts which constitute the regulatory framework of the Community. However, as it will be analysed in a subsequent section, the mere existence of these institutions and the assignment of specific roles to each one of them were not sufficient to prevent the stagnation of the integration process which occurred in later years. This particular issue is evidenced in the case of several regional schemes in Africa which, although they have provided for a set of common institutions expected to coordinate their efforts towards regional integration, have barely achieved their objectives.[42]

As it will be evidenced in the section focusing on the ECJ (subsequently renamed the CJEU), specific methods and techniques would prove to be necessary to give these institutions the capacity to effectively implement the regulatory framework that they were supposed to build and thereby establish the Common Market.

III.2.2. Regulatory Framework

The founding Treaties, which constituted primary Community law and were used to lay down the foundations upon which European integration could be built, did not provide many details on the particular methods which were to be used to establish a Common Market. It was therefore clear that the provisions of the Treaties would need to be expanded through Community legislation which was expected to set up common rules in the various fields that they were meant to cover.[43] The Treaties, therefore, provided for Community rules to be adopted in the form of *Regulations*, *Directives* and *Decisions*, which constituted the secondary legislation designed to facilitate the achievement of the goals of the Treaty.[44]

Regulations were initially to be adopted by the Council and the Commission (later on in collaboration with the European Parliament), and are designed to establish substantive rights originating from the main Treaty provisions.[45] Regulations are designed to have general application and direct legal effect as soon as they are adopted and thereby become the "law of the land".[46] This ensures the application of specific Treaty provisions directly in the Member States' legal systems and therefore enabled private parties to invoke European law in national courts.[47]

As an illustration, the EEC Treaty provided for the issuance of Regulations by the Council to set out measures regarding matters such as the free movement for workers (article 49) or customs duties (article 27). Important steps towards the establishment of the Common Market were hence taken through the means of Regulations, including the establishment of the Customs Union through Regulation No 950/68[48] or the establishment of the freedom of movement for workers within the Community through Regulation No 1612/68.[49]

Directives are provided to lay down general, substantive guidance as to the meaning of the Treaty provisions.[50] Addressed to the Member States, they are used to compel them to achieve a particular result within a specific deadline. For instance, specific Directives were supposed to be issued by the Council to provide the Member States with a timetable for the abolition of customs duties on imports.[51] Directives are used more in the context of harmonisation, as by providing for standards to be met in national legislation, they promote the approximation of Member States' laws and increase their similarity.[52] Directive 78/660/EEC of 25 July 1978 can be included in this category, as it was aimed at harmonising the accounts of certain types of companies operating in the Member States.[53]

Decisions are instruments used by the Commission to compel specific entities to comply with Treaty provisions. Decisions are therefore expected to be binding in their entirety, but only on the people to whom they were addressed and can, therefore, be enforced in national courts.[54]

The Treaty has therefore provided for a diversified regulatory framework with a set of legal instruments aimed at achieving different goals and at addressing specific issues in order to ensure the effective establishment of a Common Market. Regulations are adopted to address core issues such as the implementation of the Community core principles, whereas directives are used to harmonise the participating countries' legal systems and decisions prescribe actions to be taken by specific entities.

In addition to these instruments, the Community regulatory framework also includes a set of common policies aimed at ensuring the proper functioning of the Common Market.[55] These common policies included, among others, a competition policy, used to regulate the market in order to avoid any abuses of market position and therefore guarantee a level playing field to all firms operating within the Community;[56] and a Regional Policy, through which the Community provided funds to address regional disparities and support economic growth in underdeveloped regions and sectors.[57] In addition, common policies could also be used as protectionist measures, aimed at restricting access to some products from third countries, in order to both protect and promote particular industries and sectors within the Common Market. These policies include, for instance, the Common Agricultural Policy (EEC Treaty, Title II), which consists of a set of various regulations used to protect the agricultural market from competition from third countries, including through import restrictions and export subsidies. Similar measures could be adopted by the AEC countries in order to promote various sectors likely to be affected increased imports from third countries.

Through these various legal instruments, the EEC Treaty therefore provided for a complex coordination mechanism to be used by the common institutions to support the establishment of a Common Market by dictating the different stakeholders' behaviour and regulating the different activities supposed to promote the participating countries' economic growth. The various sources of Community law (the Treaty and secondary sources) were used either as instruments in the context of positive integration (in the law-making process or to harmonise the Member States' legal systems as it was the case with Directives) or as legal bases for negative integration. These two concepts will be discussed in the next section.

IV. Governance Through Legal Integration[58]

IV.1. Positive Integration Through the Approximation (Harmonisation) of Laws

Approximation (harmonisation) of laws is an aspect of the European integration process which requires a particular focus. The EEC Treaty, which laid the foundations for the establishment of a Common Market, provided for different rules to be applied in and by the participating countries in order to promote economic integration (e.g. Common Agricultural Policy, Competition Policy and Regional Policy). However, the Treaty was not the only source of law applicable in the Member States and national rules continued to be applicable alongside Treaty provisions. As this situation could potentially create some disparities among the Member States and therefore prevent the creation of a Common Market, the approximation (harmonisation) of national laws was provided in the EEC Treaty.[59] Harmonisation was therefore expected to produce common rules which were expected to ensure the proper functioning of the Community and to help establish a Common Market.[60]

However, as will be analysed in the following section, which focuses on ECJ jurisprudence, both primary and secondary Community sources to some extent were also used in the context of negative integration. To achieve this integration, Community law was granted a special character by the ECJ which managed to distinguish it from the ordinary international law and allowed it to confer rights and obligations on the participating countries but also on individuals within the participating countries.[61] The Court also ensured the effective application of the provisions of the founding Treaties, as their binding effect required Member States' national courts to apply them. These measures were critical to ensuring the implementation of Community rules and the advancement of the overall integration process.

Given the particular role that it played in the establishment of European integration and subsequent move towards a European Common Market, by ensuring the effecting implementation of Community legislation and by providing the impetus to the other institutions when the integration project experienced a relative stagnation, the next section is going to focus on the ECJ. The section will particularly focus on the different techniques and methods used by the Court to conduct its negative integration, i.e. the striking down of national rules restricting the flow of trade between the Member States. This integration conducted by the Court was critical in the development of European integration and the establishment the Common Market.

IV.2. Negative Integration Through the Jurisprudence of the ECJ

This section focuses on the ECJ[62] originally created by the Treaty of Paris in 1951 which, although it had been created with the vague goal of ensuring that "law was observed" in the functioning of the European Community, grew to become one of the principal architects of the European Union. Through a series of strategic decisions and radical stances, the Court managed to shape European legal integration and to induce European countries to adopt a favourable attitude towards integration, a role that it was never expected to play when the Community was established.[63] Through the work of the Court, several questions and issues were addressed, including the attitude that European countries should have towards European law and which source of law would take precedence in case of a conflict between European law and national law.[64] The following lines will, therefore, be an account of the evolution of the work of the ECJ and the impact that it had on European integration in general.[65]

As provided in article 164 of the EEC Treaty, the Court was established to ensure that in the application and interpretation of the Treaty "the law is observed".[66] The Court would monitor the activities of the other institutions through judicial review of their acts and ensure the enforcement of the Treaty through the settlement of disputes brought to it either directly by the other institutions or a participating country's government or through preliminary reference.[67]

As mentioned above, the ECJ was not expected to play a prominent role in European integration; the participating countries therefore never foresaw the critical role that the Court grew to play in the advancement of the European integration process. Moreover, this was evidenced in the early theories of economic integration, which did not pay much attention to the Court and rather considered it as a support to the work of the other institutions, or a "technical servant".[68] A similar situation can be observed in several African RECs (especially in the context of the Southern African Development Community and the early years of the Economic Community of West African States). The Court was therefore expected, in the context of the EEC, to support the other institutions (mainly the Council and the Commission) in monitoring the Member States' legal systems, ensuring that any variations between them would not be an obstacle to cross-border trade.[69]

However, as the early Treaties did not establish fully formed communities but rather laid the foundations on which these communities were supposed to be built, the framework that they established still needed to be improved and had several gaps which needed to be filled. As discussed in the previous chapter, this situation relates to the *incompleteness* of regional agreements which need to be coordinated in order to produce their effects and adapt to new circumstances arising in the course of the integration process. In response to this situation, in the 1960s the Court conducted what several authors have labelled as a "legal revolution" and assumed the mission to fill some of the gaps left in the early Treaties. As will be analysed in the following sections, through a series of milestone judgments the Court managed to assume the role of the locomotive of the integration process and to turn the EEC Treaty into a contract that was binding on the EU Member States and created both obligations for their governments and rights for their citizens.[70]

Therefore, although it had been ignored by the early integration theories and had probably been established to play the role of a simple agent, the ECJ grew to play a proactive role never played by other international judicial institutions before and later on gave the European integration process the impetus that it needed in order to progress.[71] Through the development of the preliminary reference procedure the Court associated European citizens to the European integration process and made them the "guardians of the integrity of the Community system".[72] Moreover, by the elaboration of two fundamental principles—direct effect and supremacy—through two milestone judgments in the early 1960s, the Court managed to give to the EEC Treaty the qualities of a quasi-constitution.[73] In addition, through the doctrine of mutual recognition created in the late 1970s, the Court significantly contributed to the completion of the Common Market.[74]

Furthermore, through its case law and by ensuring that any implementing acts adopted by the Member States were consistent with the acts of the Community, the ECJ managed to impose its vision of the European Community legal order[75] and, rather than playing the role of a secondary institution whose work was meant to depend on the work of the other main institutions, used the very nature and objectives assigned to the Community to exert pressure on those institutions to further European integration.[76]

In an attempt to understand the particular factors that set the Court to play such an important role in European integration, the next section will focus on the preliminary reference procedure which initiated the Court's legal activism.

IV.2.1. Legal Integration Through Preliminary Reference

The preliminary reference procedure was established by article 177 of the EEC Treaty (subsequently amended to 234 EC and 267 TFEU) which provided that "the Court of Justice [should] have jurisdiction to give preliminary rulings concerning the interpretation of [the] Treaty; the validity and interpretation of acts of the institutions of the Community; the interpretation of the statutes of bodies established by an act of the Council, where those statutes so provide". According to this procedure, any national court dealing with a question of Community law could, before taking its decision on the issue, refer it to the ECJ to receive its guidance in the form of a preliminary ruling. In cases where the national court dealing with the issue was a court of last resort, the said court had to refer the case to the ECJ for its preliminary ruling.[77]

In other words, a reference for a preliminary ruling can be explained as a request from a national court to the ECJ to give its interpretation on a specific provision of the Treaties and to rule on the validity or interpretation of any acts of the Community institutions, including legislative acts such as Regulations or Directives. In the course of this task, the Court would often also rule on the interpretation of Community law in relation to national law.

This procedure, which was initially established by the ToP (in article 41), was later on improved in the EEC Treaty (in article 177), which gave to the ECJ a critical role in the building of the European legal order in its current form.[78] Through a preliminary ruling, the Court was not expected to act as a court of appeal, as it did not decide the case or did not make a judgment on the issue brought to the national court. The Court rather served as an advisory body, ensuring that national courts interpreted Community law correctly when making their final decisions on the issue.[79]

This procedure, therefore, helped to ensure the effective and uniform application of Community law by giving the Court direct access to the Member States' legal systems.[80] The opportunity was thus given to the Court to give its opinion on the application of Community law within the Member States' jurisdictions and to determine the status of Community law within the Member States' legal systems. This was an innovation, as it departed from common practice in other international settings where Member States were the main actors, therefore the only ones allowed to bring a dispute to a Community court. In that case, the application and interpretation of Community law would have to depend on the goodwill of the Member States authorities, thereby running the risk of becoming a dead letter, thus delaying the overall integration process.[81]

Moreover, by giving private litigants direct access to Community law and national courts the opportunity to engage in a direct conversation with a supranational institution, the preliminary ruling procedure managed to "domesticate" the Treaties and give life to legal instruments which were produced at the Community level. In other words, through this procedure, private litigants were able to "use" the supranational rules made available to them and the Court ha[d] a chance to ensure [that] they use them "correctly".[82]

Through the dialogue between national courts and the ECJ, national judges were co-opted into the EU judicial architecture and grew to become key players in European legal integration.[83] This procedure appealed to national judges as it conferred on them a new jurisdiction and powers that they did not previously have under national constitutional law.[84] Throughout the years, this dialogue that was maintained between national and supranational judges managed to ensure the implementation of the Treaty and the law that stemmed from it and to establish some sort of hybrid legal culture made of a mixture of national and supranational legal customs. This legal culture played a critical role in the adoption of Community law in the Member States and created an original new legal order, the European legal order, which was made up of a mixture of national and international legal concepts.[85]

It is worth mentioning that the success of the preliminary reference procedure might be due also to the restrictions that the original Treaties put on the right for individual litigants to challenge any breach of Community law. Indeed, the EEC Treaty did not give individuals the possibility to bring cases directly before the Court. The only procedure that was available to citizens was restricted to the right to submit an action for annulment to the Court in case they had been directly and individually affected by an act of the Community.[86] The preliminary reference procedure, therefore, revealed to be appealing, as it gave natural and legal persons the opportunity to have their cases reviewed by the supranational court which would use Community law to protect them against any abuse by the other Community institutions or any participating countries.[87] By placing individual litigants at the centre of the integration process, giving them the opportunity to invoke Community legislation in legal proceedings in national courts and under the scrutiny of the ECJ, this procedure also managed to ensure the implementation and the effectiveness of Community law.[88]

Throughout the years, the preliminary reference procedure has grown to become one of the most common as people became more acquainted with the role that the ECJ was called to play in the building of the European Community. As soon as the law created by the Community began to penetrate the Member States' legal systems and to affect the way business was conducted in Europe, people resorted to the authority of the Court as it was seen as the only institution which knew the spirit of the Treaty or any legislation emanating from it and which was, therefore, the most capable to handle it. This is another important aspect of the work of the Court as it highlights the need to establish a judicial institution with enough power and authority to ensure that various measures adopted by countries involved in a Common Market are in line with the objectives of the regional agreement.[89]

Through its dialogue with national courts, the Court also managed to get involved in the law-making process, as through its important task of interpreting the Treaty the Court had the opportunity to share its understanding of the Treaty and to spread this vision within its jurisdiction. In the same vein, through national courts, this procedure also gave the Court direct access to each participating country's legal system, an access which allowed the Court to ensure that national provisions were compatible with the spirit of the Treaty.[90] Preliminary references, therefore, played a central role in European integration, as they constituted the "primary interface between national law and [Community] law" and were used to determine their interaction in the construction of the Common Market.[91]

Through its monopoly in the interpretation of the Treaty and in reviewing the legality of the acts of the Community, the ECJ was therefore given the foundations on which it could build its authority and the necessary power to force all stakeholders—from Community's institutions to participating countries' governments—to respect their engagements and abide by the rules that they had created. The Court was thereby able to give life to the provisions of the Treaty and to the other legal instruments which emanated from it. This was based on the vision that, by signing the Treaty and agreeing to establish a

Community with supranational powers, the participating countries had given up part of their sovereignty to allow the creation of a European legal system.

In the same vein and with the support of national courts, the ECJ took it further and, considering that the Treaty was more than a simple agreement between its Member States, also established rights for natural and legal persons to be enforced in their national courts.[92] The preliminary reference procedure, therefore, played a crucial role in the creation, the implementation and the development of European Union law which was achieved through the creation of the most fundamental principles governing the European legal order: direct effect and supremacy.[93]

IV.2.2. Direct Effect and Supremacy of Community Law

As argued by various commentators, direct effect and supremacy are the "Twin Pillars upon which [the] Community rests".[94] Whereas direct effect can be defined as the capacity conferred on a norm of Community law to be enforceable or invokable in participating countries' courts, supremacy is the capacity for Community law to be preferred and applied over conflicting national norms in national legal proceedings. The two principles work in tandem to the extent that one allows Community law to gain access to national legal systems, whereas the other provides it with a prominent position over conflicting national provisions and obliges the participating countries to apply Community law over national law.[95] It is on these two principles developed by the ECJ that the true effectiveness of EU law, which was essential in the creation of a Common Market through binding norms, was founded.

IV.2.2.1. EFFECTIVE APPLICATION OF COMMUNITY LAW THROUGH DIRECT EFFECT

Direct effect was created especially to ensure the application of Community law in the participating countries' domestic legal systems. It was introduced by the ECJ in 1962 in its ground-breaking judgment in Case 26/62 *Van Gend en Loos*.[96] Importing goods from Germany into the Netherlands, Van Gend en Loos (hereinafter Van Gend), a business from the Netherlands was required to pay customs duty imposed by Dutch law. Van Gend challenged the legality of the duty in a Dutch tribunal, claiming that the imposition by the Dutch government was a breach of the provisions of article 12 of the EEC Treaty (now Article 30 TFEU).[97] The Dutch tribunal referred the question to the ECJ under the preliminary reference procedure.

Using this opportunity to establish itself as an engine of European integration, the then Court used a "purposive method of interpretation" in its judgment and relied not only on the wording of the provisions of the Treaty but drew heavily on the spirit and aims of the Community.[98] To make a decision, the Court, therefore, considered that it was necessary to examine "the spirit, the general scheme and the wording" of the Treaty, which could be found in preamble of the Treaty and the institutional structure of the Community.[99]

This reference by the Dutch court, however, received opposition from three Member States: Belgium, Germany and the Netherlands. In briefs submitted to the Court, the three Member States argued that the case referred by the Dutch court was an enforcement case, which could be brought to the Court only by the Commission (as provided for in 169 of the EEC Treaty, renumbered as article 226 EC and article 258 TFEU) or by Member States governments (as provided for in article 170 of the EEC Treaty, renumbered as article 227 EC and article 259 TFEU). Therefore, they considered that the reference initiated by the Dutch court to the ECJ was inadmissible.[100] Furthermore, they argued that the wording of article 12, the provision at the core of the issue, made it clear that the drafters of the Treaty did not intend to create a legal norm of a general nature and general application, in other terms a rule with domestic effect, but rather placed an obligation solely on the Member States.[101]

In response, the Court made a bold statement, declaring that "the objective of the EEC Treaty, which [was] to establish a common market, the functioning of which [was] of direct concern to interested parties in the Community, impl[ied] that the Treaty was more than an agreement which merely create[d] mutual obligations between the Contracting States". The Court went further and reached the conclusion that "the Community constituted a new legal order of international law, for the benefit of which the States ha[d] limited their sovereign rights, albeit within limited fields, and the subject of which comprise[d] not only Member States but also their nationals".[102]

As the EEC Treaty had not dealt with this issue, the ECJ was asked to provide its guidance and established the direct effect principle which the Court subsequently applied, in a series of cases throughout the 1960s and 1970s, not only to Treaty provisions but also to secondary legislation emanating from it.[103] Although this could be implied by the wording of article 189, which conferred general application to Regulations passed by the Council, Directives did not have direct effect and were only binding upon Member States. The Court settled this issue in case 148/78 *Ratti*, in which the Court established the direct effect of Directives, which could be enforced by national courts, and therefore used by individuals, as long as the obligations that they prescribed were unconditional (if their effectiveness was not dependent on the adoption of positive legal measures at national level) and sufficiently precise.[104]

Through this doctrine, which was a cornerstone in the building of EC law, the Court, therefore, established Community law as a source of law to be applied by national courts to individuals as well as national authorities.[105] The Community legal order was therefore distinguished from the other regimes governed by ordinary international law and was used as a first step towards the constitutionalisation of the founding Treaties.[106] Through crucial judgments—*Van Gend en Loos, Reyners, Defrenne v Sabena, Van Duyn* and *Ratti*[107]—the Court also established its monopoly in Treaty interpretation as the direct effect was established centrally by the Court rather than by the various national courts which would be influenced by their own legal traditions and concepts.[108] By establishing the doctrine of direct effect and allowing the application of Community law in Member States, the then ECJ also managed to create rights for individuals, which they could claim in their own national courts.[109]

Through direct effect, the Court laid the first foundation for the effective application and implementation of Community law by imposing it on national legal systems and making it available to individuals in the participating countries.[110] Consequently, and through the preliminary reference procedure, actions brought by individuals allowed the integration process to become a reality.[111] The development of this doctrine was crucial and later on appeared to be very useful in the preservation of the momentum in European integration when the process seemed to have slowed down and while political institutions failed to achieve the legislative harmonisation provided for by the Treaty.[112] This is an important aspect of legal integration, which is going to be analysed in the remaining chapters of this study, considering its application and the effect that it could have within the context of the AEC.

IV.2.2.2. UNIFORM APPLICATION THROUGH THE DOCTRINE OF SUPREMACY

Despite the fact that it was instrumental in the application of the Treaty and its subsequent legal instruments in the Member States, direct effect was not sufficient to ensure the effective application of Community law, as the implementation of supranational norms was left to the discretion of Member State authorities who were still reluctant to give up part of their sovereignty. As through their behaviour, the Member States did not seem to be willing to abide by all the rules provided for in the Treaty,[113] the ECJ needed to come up with a strategy to induce them to apply Community law, ensuring that this was achieved uniformly across countries. The opportunity to achieve this endeavour was given to the Court in the form of a reference for preliminary ruling in Case 6/64 *Costa v ENEL*, through which the Court established the principle of supremacy of Community law.

The facts in this case and involved an Italian national, Flaminio Costa, who challenged the validity of an Act passed by the Italian government, arguing that it conflicted with the EEC Treaty.[114] In its judgment on the case, the Italian Constitutional Court considered that the Italian Constitution, in its article 11, had provided for limitations of sovereignty in favour of international organisations such as the European Economic Community, but argued that the provision did not affect the domestic status of European Treaties or the rules produced by the Community's institutions.[115]

The Constitutional Court, therefore, held that the rules about the efficacy of international obligations had to be applied according to the Italian dualist approach. Under this approach, the EEC Treaty, which had been incorporated and transformed into national law in 1957, could not prevail over an Act of the Italian Parliament which was passed in 1962. The Italian government, therefore, submitted a brief to the then ECJ, arguing that the reference made by a national court to the Court was "absolutely inadmissible", as under Italian law, the lower court had no power whatsoever to set aside an Act of Parliament on the grounds that it was a breach of Community law. The questions about the interpretation of Community law submitted by the national court were therefore pointless, as that court was not allowed to make a decision in breach of Italian law.[116]

All these elements, in addition to the open challenge that the Italian government made to its jurisdiction, encouraged the Court to step up and establish its authority through its doctrine of supremacy of Community law.[117]

The Court started by accepting the Italian government's claim according to which article 177 did not give jurisdiction to the Court to apply the Treaty to a specific case or to decide upon the validity of a provision of national law in relation to the Treaty, as it was restricted to the interpretation of the provisions of the Treaty. However, the Court clarified that it "ha[d] the power to extract from a question imperfectly formulated by the national courts those questions which alone pertain to the interpretation of the Treaty". This was justified by the fact that by contrast with ordinary international treaties, the EEC Treaty had created its own "legal system separate from that of the Member States, but nevertheless intimately and even organically tied to it in such a way that the mutual and constant respect for the respective jurisdictions of the Community and the national bodies [was] one of the fundamental conditions of a proper functioning of the system instituted by the Treaty and, consequently, of the realisation of the aims of the Community".[118]

As a result, the Court held that any provisions and measures adopted at the Community level not only had direct effect in the Member States' legal systems but also rendered automatically inapplicable any conflicting national law provisions. Community law was, therefore, an integral part of national law and took precedence over national law. Moreover, given the special character of Community law, the entry into force of such measures also precluded the adoption of any new national measures which would be conflicting with Community law. This reasoning, which established the supremacy of Community law over national law, was justified by the viability of the Common Market and the integration project as a whole.[119]

The vision that the Court was trying to convey through its decision was that its reasoning was derived from the spirit of the Treaty, which was an agreement to which the Member States had committed themselves, therefore making it impossible for them to accord precedence over conflicting national law. Through the Treaty, Member States are believed to have created a "legal system accepted by them on the basis of reciprocity".[120] In other terms, the obligations under the Treaty—which requires that each Member State promotes the Common Market in its policy-making and the measures that it adopts—prevents those Member States from giving precedence to any national decision or legislation that could hinder the establishment of the Common Market.[121]

Furthermore, in case 106/77 *Simmenthal*,[122] the supremacy of Community law was further established when the Court held that national courts were required to give immediate effect to Community law and to dis-apply conflicting national law if necessary, even when they did not have that authority under national law.[123] In its judgment, the Court recalled the fact that "directly applicable Community provisions produce[d] direct effect and as such confer[red] upon individuals rights which national courts [had to] protect". It further considered that recognising any conflicting national legislation and allowing its application to the detriment of Community law would "imperil the very foundations of the Community".[124] In addition, the effectiveness of Community law would be affected if national courts were prevented from applying Community law "in accordance with the decision or the case law of the Court".[125]

In this latter judgment, the Court made another move in ensuring the effective application of Community law by giving national courts the duty to abide by the principle of supremacy by setting aside any conflicting national norm when applying Community law.[126] The doctrine of supremacy, therefore, played a critical role in forcing Community law into the Member States' legal systems and ensuring its uniform application throughout the jurisdiction of the Community.[127]

Given the way in which it happened and the development of the application of Community law since the principle of direct effect, it is important to note the essential role played by national courts in the creation of the principle of supremacy. By choosing to apply Community law and to refer to directions given by the Court through the preliminary reference procedure, sometimes in an open challenge to other national authorities, national courts constituted themselves as a new type of agents of the Community, with a mission to lay the foundations on which a European legal system could be built.[128] This unexpected active role adopted by national courts and their collaboration with the Court contributed to the effective application of Community law and its imposition to national authorities, sometimes against their will.[129] As a result, national judges were granted powers that they would not have otherwise under national law, and the Court managed to extend its authority to domestic procedural rules, the sum of which supported the favourable reception of Community law in the participating countries.[130]

Through these different cases and the principles which derived from them, the Court managed to give to Community law the status of the highest source of law within the Community and provided the Treaty with the characteristics of a constitution.[131] By ensuring the effective application of the Treaty and other instruments emanating from it, the Court and national courts also managed to activate the integration process by compelling the Member States to achieve the goals that they had provided for in the founding Treaties.[132] Without these fundamental principles, the founding Treaties "would have remained a set of abstract and distant rules, for the most part unknown".[133] Moreover, these two principles granted the Court its constitutional authority and established its monitoring power both at Community and national levels.[134]

The third key contribution that the ECJ made to support the establishment of the European legal order was the doctrine of mutual recognition, which gave a new perspective to the concept of legislative harmonisation. This doctrine will be the focus of the following section.

IV.2.2.3. FURTHER INTEGRATION THROUGH MUTUAL RECOGNITION

From the outset of the European integration project there had been an assumption that for its proper functioning, the Common Market required the elaboration of common rules.[135] Given the disparity of national rules which were applied in the Member States, the harmonisation of these national rules and the generation of common rules governing different fields were seen as the necessary means to advance market integration and achieve the goals set out in the founding Treaties.[136] Having all the Member States giving up on their national rules and complying with a single set of harmonised rules which would be applicable throughout the Community was expected to ease market access and promote the free movement of goods and services.[137]

However, given the exhausting procedure which was required to pass these common rules (the Treaty required unanimous voting in the Council), various fields were still not covered by Community legislation and continued to be governed by national rules and standards. This situation created a segmented market across the Community and constituted an obstacle to the free movement of goods and services, as businesses involved in cross-border trade were required to comply with different sets of national rules.[138] This is the context in which Case 120/78 *Cassis de Dijon*[139] was brought to the then ECJ, a situation which prompted the Court to produce the doctrine of mutual recognition to solve this problem.

The facts in *Cassis de Dijon* involved Rewe-Zentral AG (hereinafter Rewe), a company registered in Cologne, which was denied the right to market a consignment of potable spirits imported from France on the grounds that they did not meet the local standards for alcohol content.[140] Rewe brought an action against the decision to the local courts, claiming that the German law on the matter, which fell under Article 30 of the Treaty on quantitative restrictions, violated the free movement of goods provided by the Treaty. Using the preliminary reference procedure, the local courts, in turn, referred the case to the ECJ, requesting its clarifications on the scope of Article 30 and exceptions to the requirement of non-discrimination.[141]

In its defence, the German government argued that Article 30 of the Treaty concerned discrimination measures only, not the disparities in technical standards. Furthermore, the German government argued that accepting the claim submitted by Rewe and granting its request would amount to replacing German law by French law in Germany. Moreover, the German government considered that the existence of national rules which hindered the free movement of goods and services could only be fixed by Community legislation through harmonisation.[142] In its judgment, the Court considered that "according to [its] settled case-law, any measure of such a kind as to hinder, directly or indirectly, actually or potentially, trade between Member States [fell] under the prohibition contained in Article 30 of the EEC Treaty".[143] In view of this, "the fixing at national level of a minimum wine-spirit content for potable spirits as a condition for authorisation to market within the Member State concerned, where its result is that traditional products of other Member States whose wine-spirit content is below the fixed limit cannot into circulation in the Federal Republic of Germany" fell under the "quantitative restrictions on imports and all measures having equivalent effect" provided in Article 30.

Addressing the issue of a lack of legislative harmonisation in a particular field, the Court considered that "in the absence of common rules relating to the production and marketing of alcohol . . . it [was] for the Member States to regulate all matters relating to the production and marketing of alcohol and alcoholic beverages on their own territory".[144] However, in doing so, Member States were only allowed to cause

> disparities between the national laws relating to the marketing of the products in question . . . in so far as those provisions [would be deemed] necessary in order to satisfy mandatory requirements relating in particular to the effectiveness of fiscal supervision, the protection of public health, the fairness of commercial transactions and the defence of the consumer.[145]

Based on those grounds, the Court held that

> there [was] no valid reason why, provided they [were] lawfully produced and marketed in one of the Member States, alcoholic beverages should not be introduced in any other Member State; the sale of such products [ought not to] be subject to a legal prohibition on the marketing of beverages with an alcohol content lower than the limit set by the national rules.[146]

Through its judgment, the Court created the doctrine of mutual recognition, which was grounded in one of the fundamental rules of the Community: to ensure the free movement of goods and to promote the proper functioning of the Common Market in the absence of common rules resulting from legislative harmonisation in a particular area, the Court compelled the Member States to "recognise" (grant access to) products which were lawfully produced and marketed in another Member State.[147] Through this doctrine, the Court entrusted the Member States with the power to regulate the Common Market in the areas which had not yet been covered by Community legislation.

This doctrine represented a new phase in the integration process, as it completely changed the understanding of harmonisation in the Community. A new approach to integration stemmed from the judgment in *Cassis de Dijon*, an approach whereby the free movement of goods and services was allowed "without the need for harmonisation of national legislation at Community level".[148] This promoted a "decentralised model" of governance of the Community in which Member States were expected to actively participate in the building of the Common Market by opening up their respective markets and making sure they promoted mutual recognition in the exercise of their regulatory powers.[149] This new approach, as well as the doctrines of direct effect and supremacy, which reflected the activism of the Court, inspired the Commission in the preparation of its *White Paper on Completing the Internal Market* in 1985 and inspired the adoption of the Single European Act in 1986, which will be analysed in the following section.

V. Completion of the Common Market Through the Single European Act (SEA)

By the time Denmark, Ireland and the United Kingdom joined the Community in 1973, the integration project appeared to have slowed down. Starting in the late 1960s, the European integration experienced a period of perceived stagnation, as no significant progress had been made either in terms of enlargement of the Community or in terms of economic advancement. Moreover, it appeared that the EEC Treaty was not able to solve the issue, as it contained limitations that seemed almost insurmountable, including the need for unanimity in the Community decision-making process and the reluctance of Member States to abide by Community rules which were intended to help them open up their respective markets. This period has been coined by various authors as Eurosclerosis, a synonym of both economic and political stagnation within the EEC.[150]

To address this issue, the Heads of State and Government decided to strengthen the Community and to reinforce the Community's institutions in order to make them more effective and to improve the functioning of the Community.[151] The participants to the Summit, therefore, submitted several recommendations and, among other things, "invited the Council and the Commission to put into effect without delay the practical measures designed to achieve the reinforcement of the institutions and to improve the relations of both the Council and the Commission with the Assembly".[152]

At the Intergovernmental Conference in Milan in June 1985, European Heads of State and Government agreed on the need to improve the functioning of the Community "in order to give concrete form to the objectives it has set itself".[153] As the deadline for the completion of the Common Market had been set to 1992, it was decided that several measures had to be taken, in particular, the strengthening of the Community institution.[154] For this purpose, it was noted that another Conference was to be held later that year, during which the President of the Council was expected to submit proposals with a view to achieving concrete progress on the European Union.[155]

An Intergovernmental Conference (IGC) was subsequently held in Luxembourg on 2 and 3 December 1985. At this Conference, the Commission submitted its *White Paper on Completing the Internal Market* in which it noted that the Community had lost momentum 'partly through the recession, partly through a lack of confidence and vision'.[156] The Commission noted that, although the Heads of States and Governments had pledged themselves to the completion of the Common Market as a high priority at different European Council meetings (Copenhagen 1982, Fontainebleau and Dublin 1984, Brussels 1985), no progress had been made in the European integration process.[157]

Considering that the time for taking effective action towards the establishment of the Common Market had come, the Commission therefore produced the *White Paper* which detailed 279 legislative proposals, including measures to eliminate a series of physical, technical and fiscal non-tariff barriers which meant that until then, the Common Market continued to exist on paper only[158] (a fact which was similar to the current situation of the AEC). These proposals advocated for the establishment of a comprehensive Common Market which was meant to foster renewed economic and political integration.[159]

Of these proposals, which focused on the removal of physical, technical and fiscal barriers, the most significant included the introduction of the doctrine of mutual recognition as an alternative to legislative harmonisation.[160] Here the Commission acknowledged the work of the Court and adopted the principle as an "effective strategy for bringing about a Common Market in a trading sense".[161] Mutual recognition was preferred to legislative harmonisation which was seen as an instrument which was "over-regulatory, taking a long time to implement, inflexible [which] could [potentially] stifle innovation".[162] Mutual recognition was therefore seen as a better instrument for economic integration as it was more effective and more respectful of national sovereignty and diversity.[163] Consequently, the use of legislative harmonisation was to be significantly reduced and "restricted to laying down essential health and safety requirements".[164] According to this new strategy, mutual recognition would be used as a guiding principle, while Community legislative action would only be required to harmonise the "essential requirements" of products.[165]

Moreover, in order to facilitate the adoption of Community legislation, the Council unanimity voting was to be replaced by Qualified Majority Voting (QMV) in relation to certain Treaty articles, including article 100 of the EEC Treaty which provided for the approximation of laws within the Community.[166] QMV was expected to help overcome the difficulties of securing agreement among Council members in the adoption of Community legislation and thereby ensure the advancement of the integration process.[167]

These measures, combined with several others, were deemed necessary to create a new impetus and recreate a momentum in European integration. At the end of the Intergovernmental Conference,[168] in light of the proposals submitted by the Commission, EEC leaders agreed on the need for a fundamental modification of the EEC Treaty coupled with a reform of the Community's institutions, which were designed to improve its efficiency and extend its powers and responsibilities.[169]

As a result of the approach, the Single European Act (SEA) was signed on 17 February 1986. The SEA, the first substantive modification of the EEC Treaty, stemmed from the desire to "mak[e] concrete progress towards European unity" after a brief period of stagnation.[170] Through this new text, European countries[171] were aiming to streamline their efforts towards economic integration and, based on the different Treaties which established the different European Communities, translate their overall efforts into the establishment of a European Union.[172]

For this purpose, several innovations and additional regulatory techniques were introduced by the SEA to improve the Community's coordination mechanism. One of the major innovations of the SEA consisted in the fundamental shift away from exhaustive harmonisation through the recognition and the adoption of the principle of mutual recognition developed by the ECJ.[173] As noted above, through this new approach the exhaustive harmonisation of national laws was relativised as legislated mutual recognition was expected to accelerate the Community's efforts towards the establishment of a Common Market.

Treaty amendments also included the creation of a European Council (different from the Council of the European Union), in SEA article 2. Comprised of Heads of State or Government of the Member States and the President of the Commission, the European Council was expected to meet twice a year to discuss the general vision of the Community. The Council, an intergovernmental institution, was intended to provide some balance to the Community institutional framework, including by ensuring that the Member States retain some type of control on the Community supranational institutions.[174] The SEA also introduced several measures which were aimed at improving the Community's law-making process, including the co-operation procedure, which associated the European Parliament to the Community's legislative process. This measure was supposed to increase popular participation in the Community law-making process.[175]

As a result of the improvement of the Community's coordination mechanism, the period following the adoption of the SEA witnessed a revival in European integration, which was characterised by the key roles played by two Community institutions: the Commission and the Court. To ensure that the internal market was completed by 1992, the legislative activity of the Community was increased, focusing on the removal of physical, technical and fiscal barriers identified in the Commission's *White Paper* 1985.[176] Thanks to the streamlined and simpler procedure established by the SEA, the legislative activity could also now focus on new areas such as employment, social protection and sustainable growth. In addition, through its jurisprudence and the key doctrines that it had developed throughout the years prior to the SEA, the

ECJ also continued to monitor the effective implementation of Community rules, including the new ones adopted after the SEA.[177]

VI. Conclusion

The analysis conducted in this chapter allowed us to study the different ways in which law has been used in the context of the European integration process and more particularly the contribution that it made to the gradual transformation of the EEC into a Common Market. A special emphasis was placed on the various factors that have influenced its particular design and structure as well as the coordination mechanism that the Community adopted to achieve its objectives, highlighting the fact that the process conducted under the EEC was deemed adapted to its Member States' particular circumstances, used by those states as a means to further their economic growth and gain access to a larger market for goods produced by their national industries. In particular, the chapter was used to provide further details on the Vinerian model of regionalism followed by the European Community, concentrating on the additional legal instruments that were adopted to further the European regional process and promote economic growth and regional trade among the participating countries.

Particular attention was also given to the relative stagnation which was experienced by the European integration process in the early 1970s and to the SEA, which was adopted in response to this situation. The mechanism used to overcome this crisis, as well as the institutional and regulatory arrangements adopted through the Founding Treaties have provided a practical example of how law—through both legislative harmonisation and mutual recognition, and the negative integration conducted by the ECJ through the removal of tariff and non-tariff barriers—was determinant in the advancement of the integration project in Europe and the effective establishment of a Common Market within the European Community and then the European Union.

Moreover, the chapter also concentrated on the institutional and regulatory frameworks created by the EEC Treaty and the key role that they played in furthering the European integration process, including through the strengthening of Community institutions and the elaboration of Community rules to promote cross-border trade and abolish both tariff and non-tariff barriers. Given that the majority of African RECs tend to emulate the process conducted under the European Community, this extended analysis of the principles and techniques provided by the Community's legal framework was provided with a view to grasping the particular context that prompted their creation as well as the specific way in which they were intended to be used in order to support the overall European project.

Furthermore, given the key role played by both the Commission and the ECJ in the advancement of the integration process, the analysis in the chapter also highlighted the benefit of establishing supranational institutions with enough power and autonomy to monitor the proper functioning of the

Community. As discussed above, the ECJ, although it had been established in the European Community Founding Treaties as a second-tier institution, has interpreted its own authority broadly and has thereby grown to play a central role in the establishment of a Common Market in Europe.[178] Through its purposive interpretation of the founding Treaties of the EU, the Court established a robust legal framework which is considered as necessary for the proper and effective functioning of the European Community.[179] Using the preliminary reference procedure provided for in the original Treaties, the Court managed to gain access to the Member States' legal systems and, through the doctrines of direct effect and supremacy, ensured an effective application of the Founding Treaties, conferred rights and obligations on individuals in the Member States and established its authority over national courts.[180]

Building upon its authority, the Court produced a rich case-law which helped establish the authority of Community law and was used by the Court to boost legal integration in Europe. Throughout the years the Court, therefore, focused on refining its legal framework through case-law and managed to play a central role in furthering and deepening the European integration process.[181]

It is for that purpose that it established the doctrine of mutual recognition which, by providing a new approach to harmonisation, played a key role in the development of the free movement of goods, services and factors of production.[182] The legal framework established by the Court and the different contributions that it made to help establish a Common Market within the EU were particularly useful during the period leading to the adoption of the SEA, as they were endorsed by the Commission and provided for a renewed impetus towards deeper integration, whereas the political institutions had failed to do so.[183] The regional courts established in the context of the African regional schemes are going to be examined against such backdrop, with a view to considering the specific role that they could play to advance regionalism efforts in Africa.

This chapter was therefore used to demonstrate that over the years both the ECJ and the legal framework that it created, and the Commission through its participation in the adoption of the SEA played a critical role of in the establishment of a Common Market within the European Union.[184] This particular model of regionalism, characterised by a coordination mechanism which is both rules-based and highly institutionalised, therefore seemed to be adequate to support and further develop the process of European integration.

The particular role played by law in the various integration models that were identified in the previous chapters will be used to inform the analysis conducted in the African context. The remaining chapters will therefore refocus on the AEC and, after conducting a political economy of regional integration efforts in Africa in order to identify the particular circumstances in which this process is conducted, will be used to investigate the different ways in which law could be used to help achieve the objectives of the Treaty of Abuja.

Notes

1. Treaty of Abuja, article 4.2(h).
2. This analytical approach in the study of regionalisation processes is presented as the most effective way to grasp the differences among various regional schemes in Van Langhenhove, L. (2013) 'Why We Need to "Unpack" Regions to Compare Them More Effectively' in Fioramonti, L. (ed.) *Regionalism in a Changing World*, London: Routledge.
3. Subsequently European Community (EC) and European Union (EU).
4. These issues were also identified in the context of MERCOSUR.
5. This characteristic was enshrined in the pledge for an "ever closer union" which was included in the EEC Treaty.
6. The Treaty of Rome was signed in 1957 and entered into force on 1 January 1958; hereinafter EEC Treaty.
7. Swann, D. (1996) *European Economic Integration: The Common Market, European Union and Beyond*, Cheltenham; Brookfield: Edward Elgar, p. 9.
8. See Davies, K. (2013), *Understanding European Union Law*, 5th ed., London: Routledge, p. 7. In the African context, sustainable and self-reliant economic growth is considered as the ultimate goal rather than a means to achieve an overall objective.
9. See Hogan, M.J. (1987), *The Marshall Plan: America, Britain and the Reconstruction of Western Europe, 1947–1952 (Studies in Economic History and Policy: USA in the Twentieth Century)*, Cambridge: Cambridge University Press.
10. The Organisation for European Economic Cooperation (OEEC, later superseded by the Organisation for Economic Co-operation and Development—OECD) was established in 1948 to coordinate the recovery programme among European countries. This organisation required a degree of institutionalised coordination and cooperation between the states which were the recipient of the aid programme and provide a good example of early forms of shared decision-making between the European states.
11. This accounts for the factors which influenced the creation of the European Coal and Steel Community in 1951. Further details are provided in Alter, K.J. (2012) 'Understanding the European Court's Political Power' in Zimmerman, H. and Dur, A. (eds) *Key Controversies in European Integration*, Basingstoke: Palgrave Macmillan, p. 81.
12. See Ward, I. (2009), *A Critical Introduction to European Law*, 3rd ed., Cambridge: Cambridge University Press, p. 8. See also Laski, H.J. (1930), *Liberty in the Modern State*, Harmondsworth, Middlesex: Penguin Books.
13. Baldwin, R.E. (2005) 'Sequencing and Depth of Regional Economic Integration: Lessons for the Americas from Europe' 31(1) *World Economy*, p. 5.
14. However, as discussed in the previous chapter, other models, including the intergovernmental arrangement under ASEAN, might provide alternative options likely to be more appropriate to support the AEC countries' economic development while preserving their independence and autonomy.
15. Pollack, M.A. (2002) *The Engines of European Integration: Delegation, Agency and Agenda Setting in the EU*, Oxford: Oxford University Press, p. 3.
16. See Treaty of Paris, article 2. This approach adopted under the ToP corresponds to one of the economic aspects of the regional developmentalism approach which, rather than conducting trade liberalisation across all sectors of the participating countries' economies, focuses on specific sectors that are more likely to promote economic growth. The same approach was attempted in the context of ASEAN through the adoption of several Protocols aimed at conducting a targeted integration in sectors considered as necessary to

improve their international competitiveness. Similarly, the various integration initiatives under the AEC could be used to identify and further develop key economic sectors which could both promote their economic growth and increase their cooperation. The significance of selectivity in RTAs involving developing countries is also highlighted by the authors in Chauffour, J-P. and Maur, J-C. (2011) 'Beyond Market Access' in Chauffour, J-P. and Maur, J-C. (eds) *Preferential Trade Agreement Policies for Development: A Handbook*, Washington DC: The World Bank, p. 34.

17. Hansen, J.D. and Schroder, P.J.H. (2001) 'Economic Integration in Europe: Setting the Stage' in Hansen, J.D. (ed.) *European Integration: An Economic Perspective*, Oxford, Oxford University Press, p. 4.
18. See Heater, D. (1992) *The Idea of European Unity*, Leicester: Leicester University Press, p. 175.
19. See Baldwin (2005), p. 5. On sectoral integration, see Balassa (1962), p. 15.
20. Treaty of Paris, article 4.
21. On European trade liberalisation, see Hoeller, P., Girouard, N. and Colecchia, A. (1998) 'The European Trade Policies and Their Economic Effects' *OECD Economic Department Working Paper No.194*, p. 8. As discussed in the context of NAFTA and MERCOSUR, the market approach could prove adequate for countries which have already developed strong domestic markets with relatively strong industries, whereas it could have adverse effects on developing countries such as the AEC Member States which could be looking to develop infant industries in order to promote their economic growth.
22. See Davies (2013), p. 8. These powers were vested in the institutional framework provided to this effect in articles 3 and 7 of the Treaty of Paris, which included a High Authority, a Common Assembly, a Special Council of Ministers and a Court of Justice.
23. This aspect of the early efforts towards regional integration in the context of Europe will be contrasted with African integration projects in subsequent chapters when considering the different steps necessary for the effective establishment of the AEC.
24. The concept of "supranational rule of law" has been introduced in Alter (2012), p. 81.
25. See Pollack (2002), p. 77.
26. Belgium, France, Germany, Italy, Luxembourg and the Netherlands.
27. See Ward (2009), p. 12.
28. See Davies (2013), p. 10. As provided in the Preamble of the EEC Treaty, the 6 countries were "calling upon the other peoples of Europe who share[d] their ideal to join in their efforts". See also Article 2, which provides that "the [EEC] was created to promote throughout the Community a harmonious development of economic activities" (emphasis added).
29. See Preamble of the EEC Treaty. The move to an "ever closer union" implied, *inter alia*, furthering the integration process between the participating countries and enhancing their ability for collective action. As discussed in previous sections, this strategy, which resulted from the particular circumstances that triggered the inception of the integration process, was intended to promote the participating countries' welfare through common decision-making and the establishment of supranational institutions with increased powers and relative autonomy.
30. Hansen and Schroder (2001), p. 6.
31. These manufactured goods within the EEC included motor vehicles, motorcycles, textiles, transport equipment, etc. These economic sectors are not currently well developed in most AEC countries. For further details on exchanges

in manufactured goods within the EEC see Jovanovic, M.N. (ed.) (2011) *International Handbook on the Economics of Integration, Volume II: Competition, Spatial Location of Economic Activity and Financial Issues*, Cheltenham; Northampton: Edward Elgar, p. xiv. See also Balassa, B. (1984) 'Trade Between Developed and Developing Countries: The Decade Ahead' (3) *OECD Economic Studies*, p. 8.

32. Those four principles are covered in article 3(a) which provides for the "elimination, as between Member States, of customs duties and of quantitative restrictions on the import and export of goods, and of all other measures having equivalent effect; article 3(b) "the establishment of a common customs tariff and of a common commercial policy towards third countries", and article 3(c) which provides for "the abolition, as between Member States, of obstacles to freedom of movement for persons, services and capital".
33. A Common Market is different from a Single Market for commodities, which involved the removal of all restrictions on trade within a specific market, but does not include the free movement of factors of production. See Hansen, J.D. and Nielsen, J.W. (1997) *An Economic Analysis of the European Union*, 2nd ed., London: The McGraw-Hill Companies, p. 5.
34. See Craig, P. (2002) 'The Evolution of the Single Market' in Barnard, C. and Scott, J. (eds) *The Law of the Single European Market: Unpacking the Premises*, Oxford: Hart, p. 2.
35. Article 145 of the EEC Treaty. This provision has not only been renumbered (after The Treaty of Maastricht and the Treaty of Amsterdam, becoming Article 202 EC); it has also been replaced in substance by the Treaty of Lisbon.
36. See Article 137 of the EEC Treaty, renumbered after the Treaty of Amsterdam, becoming article 189 EC and later on replaced in substance by the Treaty of Lisbon.
37. See Article 155 of the EEC Treaty (which became article 211 EC and later on replaced in substance by the Treaty of Lisbon).
38. See Article 164 of the EEC Treaty (which became article 220 EC and later on replaced in substance by the Treaty of Lisbon). As discussed in the context of MERCOSUR and further analysed in the section on negative integration, a central judicial institution is necessary to ensure the uniform application of common policies adopted by the participating countries.
39. See Article 177 of the EEC Treaty (which became article 234 EC and later on article 267 TFEU). This provision introduced the preliminary procedure which will be subject to a detailed analysis below.
40. See Articles 164 and 169 of the EEC Treaty. (Article 169 became article 226 EC and later on article 258 TFEU).
41. In general terms, these roles are played by the European Parliament and the Council (legislative branch), the Commission (executive branch) and the Court of Justice (judicial branch). However, this supranational system of governance was new territory and it was still too early to foresee with precision which definite role would be assigned to each institution.
42. As it will be discussed in subsequent sections, beyond the establishment of regional institutions, the issues faced by the African RECs might require the adoption of the various techniques and methods that were developed over the years by the EEC institutions.
43. Hervey, T. (2009) 'European Treaties' in Cane, P. and Conaghan, J. (eds) *The New Oxford Companion to Law*, Oxford: Oxford University Press, p. 2.
44. Craig (2002), p. 4.
45. EEC Treaty, article 189 (renumbered after the Treaty of Amsterdam and the Treaty of Lisbon, and later on became article 249 EC and article 288 TFEU). See also Craig (2002), p. 4.

46. See Arnull, A. (2009) 'European Community Legal Instruments' in Cane and Conaghan (eds) *The New Oxford Companion to Law*, Oxford: Oxford University Press, p. 1. See also Hervey (2009), p. 2.
47. Regulations are therefore supposed to be more appropriate instruments as they are considered as part of the participating countries' legal systems and are therefore not subject to further implementation in countries following a dualist approach towards international law (this issue was discussed in the case of Brazil in the context of MERCOSUR).
48. Regulations adopted on 29 June 1968, in accordance with articles 28 and 11 of the EEC Treaty.
49. Adopted on 15 October 1968.
50. EEC Treaty, article 189, above n10.
51. Ibid., article 13(2).
52. See EEC Treaty, article 100 (renumbered after the Treaty of Amsterdam and the Treaty of Lisbon, and later on became article 94 EC and article 115 TFEU).
53. Directives are considered as flexible instruments designed to create some degree of similarity between the participating countries' legal systems in order to facilitate the achievement of their common goals. This approach seems more appropriate than the unification strategy adopted under the Organisation for Harmonisation of Business Law in Africa (OHADA), as with Directives the countries retain the power to choose the means that they consider as the most adequate to achieve the common goals.
54. See EEC Treaty, article 100.
55. EEC Treaty, article 3(d), (e), (f), (g) and (h).
56. Smith, M.P. (2003) 'From Competition to Competitiveness: A New EU Industrial Policy?' Paper presented at the Eighth Biennal International Conference of the European Studies Association, Nashville, TN, 27–29 March, p. 1.
57. See EEC Treaty, article 80.2. The regional policy is now covered by articles 130a and 130b of the Treaty on European Union (Treaty of Maastricht) which amended the Treaty of Rome and was signed on 7 February 1992. These policies are delivered to the concerned countries through the European Development Fund, the European Cohesion Fund and the European Social Fund. The regional policy was adopted to address the regional disparity, a key issue identified in the context of MERCOSUR, and is aimed at promoting a harmonious economic development within the Community including by providing financial aid to specific sectors or countries. Similar policies are analysed in the context of the East African Community, to promote targeted industries and sectors likely to promote economic growth in the region. For further details on the EU regional policy, see Nicolaides, P. (2011) 'EU Policies and Policy-Making' in Jovanovic, M.N. (ed.) *International Handbook on the Economics of Integration, Volume I: General Issues and Regional Groups*, Cheltenham; Northampton: Edward Elgar, p. 316.
58. The distinction between positive and negative integration that is analysed in this section was initially discussed in Tinbergen, J. (1954) *International Economic Integration*, Amsterdam: Elsevier, p. 79. The author defined negative integration as the "removal of trade barriers and the principle of non discrimination, and positive integration as the creation of new institutions and their instruments or the modification of existing instruments". On positive integration, the author provided a further explanation, arguing that "positive integration should consist of the creation of all institutions required by the welfare optimum which have to be handled in a centralised way".

59. See Pelkmans, J. (1997) *European Integration, Methods and Economic Analysis*, London: Longman, p. 8. Article 100 of the EEC Treaty provided for the approximation of laws within the Community.
60. Weatherill, S. (2004) 'Why Harmonise?' in Tridimas, T. and Nebbia, P. (eds) *European Union Law for the Twenty-First Century*, Oxford: Hart, p. 20.
61. This aspect of Community legislation is discussed by the ECJ in Case 26/62 Van Gend en Loos, p. 12 and Publico Ministero v Ratti, Case 148/78 [1979] ECR 1629. See also Hervey (2009), p. 1.
62. The Court was renamed Court of Justice of the European Union with the Lisbon Treaty. For a discussion on the renaming and transformation of the Court, see Birkinshaw, P. (2012) 'National Courts and European Union Courts' in Hayward, J. and Wurzel, R. (eds) *European Disunion: Between Sovereignty and Solidarity*, Basingstoke: Palgrave Macmillan, p. 129.
63. See Dehousse, R. (1998), *The European Court of Justice, The Politics of Judicial Integration*, Basingstoke: Palgrave Macmillan, p. 1.
64. See Davies (2013), p. 69.
65. This analysis of the evolution of the work of the Court is conducted to investigate the key role that regional courts could play to support regional integration efforts in the context of the AEC.
66. Article 31 of the Treaty of Paris provides that the Court was created to "ensure that in the interpretation and application of th[e] Treaty, and of rules laid down for the implementation thereof, the law [was] observed. For further details, see also Pollack (2003), p. 160 and Dehousse (1998), p. 5.
67. Judicial review of the acts of other institutions was provided at article 173 of the EEC Treaty while article 165 covered its role in dispute settlement. Carubba, C.J. and Murrah, L. (2005) 'Legal Integration and Use of the Preliminary Ruling Process in the European Union' 59(2) *International Organization*, p. 400.
68. See Weiler, J.H.H. (1988) 'The White Paper and the Application of Community Law' in Bieber, R. et al. (eds) *1992: One European Market?* Baden-Baden (Germany): Nomos. This attitude can be observed for instance through the various measures and reactions adopted by participating countries in the context of the East African Community in response to the proactive role that the regional court attempted to play to support the application of regional rules.
69. Coutts, S.D. (2011) 'The Lisbon Treaty and the Area of Freedom, Security and Justice as an Area of Legal Integration' 7 *Croatian Yearbook of European Law and Policy*, pp. 87, 89.
70. See Alter (2012), p. 82.
71. As discussed above, the work of the Court constituted one of the major ways in which law was used to support the establishment of a Common Market within the European Union, a role that could potentially be replicated by African regional courts to support the establishment of the AEC.
72. See Dehousse (1998), p. 41.
73. See Alter (2012), p. 82.
74. This aspect of the contribution of the Court will be discussed in the section on the SEA.
75. This vision considered a strong legal order as the bedrock of the European Community.
76. See Dehousse (1998), p. 71. See also Keohane, R.O. and Hoffmann, S. (1991) 'Institutional Change in Europe in the 1980s' in Keohane, R.O. and Hoffmann, S. (eds) *The New European Community, Decision-Making and Institutional Change*, Boulder, CO; Oxford: Westview Press, p. 278. This

aspect of the work of the Court proves particularly important as if provides for an effective tool to ensure the effective application of regional rules. Moreover, as highlighted in the context of MERCOSUR and subsequently the EAC, this arrangement might also prove significant to secure a uniform and harmonious implementation of the common policies adopted by countries in the context of a Customs Union as well coordinating the participating countries' macroeconomic policies.

77. See article 177 of the EEC Treaty. The first version of this provision appeared in Article 41 of the ECSC Treaty, which provided that "when the validity of acts of the High Authority or the Council is contested in litigation before a national tribunal, such issue shall be certified to the Court, which shall have exclusive jurisdiction to rule thereon".
78. Broberg, M. and Fenger, N. (2010), *Preliminary References to the European Court of Justice*, Oxford: Oxford University Press, p. 2.
79. The same arrangement has been provided in the context of the East Africa Community and OHADA. However, the OHADA Court has been used mainly as a Supreme Court, reviewing cases already judged by national courts on matters concerning OHADA law. As it will be discussed in the chapter dedicated to OHADA, this structure may not prove very effective, as it runs the risk of affecting rather than promoting collaboration between national courts and the Regional Court, thereby missing the opportunity to improve the national courts' involvement in the integration process and increase the direct interaction between regional and national legal orders.
80. See Shapiro, M. (1999) 'The European Court of Justice' in Craig, P. and Búrca, G. (eds) *The Evolution of EU Law*, Oxford: Oxford University Press, p. 322. See also Davies (2013), p. 89.
81. See Dehousse (1998) p. 47. This issue was identified in the context of MERCOSUR.
82. See Broberg and Fenger (2010), p. 3.
83. Miller, L. (2011) *The Emergence of EU Contract Law, Exploring Europeanization*, Oxford; New York: Oxford University Press, p. 158. See also Alter, K. (2009) 'The European Court's Political Power' Northwestern University School of Law, Faculty Paper 175, p. 95.
84. Alter (2009), p. 95.
85. See Dickson, J. and Eleftheriadis, P. (eds) (2012) *Philosophical Foundations of European Union Law*, Oxford: Oxford University Press, p. 2.
86. This procedure was provided in article 173 of the EEC Treaty.
87. See Dehousse (1998), p. 21. See also Lenz, C.O. (1994) 'The Role and Mechanism of the Preliminary Ruling Procedure' 18(2) *Fordham International Law Journal*, p. 389.
88. Maduro, M.P. (1998), *We the Court: The European Court of Justice and the European Economic Constitution: A Critical Reading of Article 30 of the EC Treaty*, Oxford: Hart, p. 9. See also Mattli, W. and Slaughter, A-M. (1998) 'Revisiting the European Court of Justice' 52(1) *International Organization*, p. 180.
89. Stone Sweet, A. (2010) 'The European Court of Justice and the Judicialisation of EU Governance' *Living Reviews in EU Governance*, p. 36.
90. Dehousse, R. and Weiler, J.H.H. (1990) 'The Legal Dimension' in Wallace, W. (ed.), *The Dynamics of European Integration*, London: Pinter for the Royal Institute of International Affairs, p. 247.
91. De la Mare, T. and Donnelly, C. (1999) 'Preliminary Rulings and EU Legal Integration: Evolution and Stasis' in Craig, P. and Búrca, G. (eds) *The Evolution of EU Law*, Oxford: Oxford University Press, p. 347.

92. See Case 26/62 Van Gend en Loos v Nederlandse Administratie der Belastingen (1963) ECR 1. See also Birkinshaw (2012), p. 116.
93. Broberg and Fenger (2010), p. 3.
94. Davies (2013), p. 70.
95. De Witte, B. (1999) 'Direct Effect, Primacy, and the Nature of the Legal Order' in Craig, P. and Búrca, G. (eds) *The Evolution of EU Law*, Oxford: Oxford University Press, p. 323.
96. Case 26/62 Van Gend en Loos v Nederlandse Administratie der Belastingen (1963) ECR 1.
97. Article 12 of the EEC Treaty provided that "Member States [should] refrain from introducing between themselves any new customs duties on imports or exports or any charges having equivalent effect, and from increasing those which they already appl[ied] in their trade with each other".
98. See Davies (2013), p. 73. The author used the wording "purposive method of interpretation" to explain the fact that the Court used this judgment as an opportunity to advance Community law and establish its authority over national provisions in order to create a European legal order.
99. See Dehousse (1998), p. 38.
100. Pollack (2002), p. 163.
101. See Dehousse (1998), p. 38. This attitude of the three Member States is an evidence of their initial reluctance to accept the general application of regional rules in their national legal systems as well as the proactive role of the Court.
102. Van Gend en Loos (1963), p. 12. See also Cahill, M. (2012) 'European Integration and European Constitutionalism: Consonances and Dissonances' in Augenstein, D. (ed.), *'Integration Through Law' Revisited: The Making of the European Polity, Farnham, Surrey*, England: Burlington, VT: Ashgate. The Court, therefore, established that Community law provided both Member States and individuals with rights and obligations which were enforceable in their national courts. This principle contrasted with normal practice in international law where international treaties were only binding upon their contracting parties (States), their effect in national legal orders being determined by constitutional law rules of these contracting parties. This particular point is argued in De Witte (1999), p. 324. See also De Waele, H. (2010) 'The Role of the European Court of Justice in the Integration Process: A Contemporary and Normative Assessment' 6(1) *Hanse Law Review*, p. 4.
103. See Davies (2013), p. 70. See also Dehousse (1998), p. 37.
104. In its judgment, the Court considered that "[a] Member State which has not adopted the implementing measures required by the directive in the prescribed periods may not rely, as against individuals, on its own failure to perform the obligations which the directive entails. It follows that a national court requested by a person who has complied with [a] directive not to apply a national provision incompatible with the directive must uphold that request if the obligation in question is unconditional and sufficiently precise". Case 148/78 Ratti, p. 1642.
105. See De Witte (1999), p. 339. See also Svensson, S. (2008) 'The Role of the European Court of Justice in the integration of the European Community' Thesis, Lund University Department of Political Science, Lund, Sweden, p. 17.
106. Mac Amhlaigh, C.S. (2011) 'Concepts of Integration Through Law (and the Price of Constitutional Pluralism)' in Augenstein, D. (ed.) *Integration Through Law Revisited: The Making of European Polity*, Farnham, Surrey, England: Burlington, VT: Ashgate, p. 69.

107. Case 2/74 Reyners [1974] ECR 631; Case 43/75 Defrenne v Sabena [1976] ECR 455; Case 41/74 Van Duyn [1974] ECR 1337 and Case 148/78 Ratti [1979] ECR 1629.
108. See Joerges, C. (1996) 'Taking the Law Seriously: On Political Science and the Role of Law in the Process of European Integration' 2(2) *European Law Journal*, p. 110. This was important in order to ensure the uniform application of common policies adopted by the participating countries.
109. Birkinshaw, P. (2003) *European Public Law*, London: Butterworths, p. 12.
110. De Witte (1999), p. 327. See also Birkinshaw (2003), p. 46. By granting direct effect to Community law, the Court addressed the issue of the effective application of regional rules, which constitutes a major issue in the context of the African RECs.
111. Barnard, C. (2013) *The Substantive Law of the EU: The Four Freedoms*, fourth edition, Oxford: Oxford University Press, p. 16. See also Mattli and Slaughter (1998), p. 186 and Tamm, D. (2012) 'The History of the Court of Justice of the European Union Since its Origin' in Rosas, A. and Levits, E. and Bot, Y. (eds) *The Court of Justice and the Construction of Europe: Analyses and Perspectives on Sixty Years of Case-law—La Cour de Justice et la Construction de l'Europe: Analyses et Perspectives de Soixante Ans de Jurisprudence*, Dordrecht Springer, p. 27.
112. Dehousse (1998), p. 39.
113. This was evidenced, for example, in the facts of Van Gend en Loos, where the Netherlands did not hesitate to impose customs duties which did not go in line with the objectives of the EEC Treaty.
114. Case 6/64 Flaminio Costa v ENEL (1964) ECR 585, p. 593.
115. Costa v ENEL (1964), p. 593.
116. Case 6/64 Costa v ENEL, p. 593. See also Stein, E. (1981) 'Lawyers, Judges, and the Making of a Transnational Constitution' 75(1) *The American Journal of International Law* 1, p. 11.
117. De Witte (1999), p. 328.
118. Case 6/64 Costa v ENEL, p. 593.
119. Costa, Case 6/64, p. 594. See also Dehousse (1998), p. 43 and Cahill (2012), p. 2.
120. Costa v ENEL (1964), p. 594.
121. Ibid. See also Cahill (2012), p. 2. These facts are similar to those in the 2007 case Anyang' Nyongo and others in which the East African Court of Justice decided on the breach of Community law by domestic rules in Kenya and opted for the supremacy of regional rules over national rules.
122. Case 106/77 Administrazione delle Finanze dello Stato v Simmenthal.
123. See Davies (2013), p. 71.
124. The Court expressed the same opinion in Internationale Handelsgesellschaft, Case 11–70, p. 1134. Here, the Court considered that "the law stemming from the Treaty, an independent source of law, cannot because of its very nature be overridden by rules of national law, however, framed, without being deprived of its character as Community law and without the legal basis of the Community itself being called into question".
125. Simmenthal (1976), p. 644.
126. See De Witte (1999), p. 341.
127. See Eleftheriadis, P. (1998) 'Begging the Constitutional Question' 36 *Journal of Common Market Studies* 255, p. 257.
128. This demonstrates the important role played by national courts in the coordination of the Common Market by contributing to the effective application and enforcement of regional rules. This approach could prove effective in

the context of the African RECs where states are still reluctant to accept the supremacy of regional rules over domestic law.

129. See Dehousse (1998), pp. 41–43.
130. Ibid, p. 45. See also Stone Sweet, A. (1999) 'The European Court of Justice' in Craig, P. and Búrca, G. (eds) *The Evolution of EU Law*, Oxford: Oxford University Press, p. 133.
131. Starr-Deelen, D. and Deelen, B. (eds) (1996) 'The European Court of Justice as a Federator' 26(4) *Publius*, p. 84.
132. Svensson (2008), pp. 1–20.
133. See Dehousse (1998), p. 46.
134. Cahill (2012), p. 15.
135. Weatherill (2004), p. 11
136. Maduro (1998), p. 110.
137. Armstrong, K. (2002) 'Mutual Recognition' in Barnard, C. and Scott, J. (eds) *The Law of The Single European Market*, Oxford: Hart, p. 229. This is an assumption shared by the drafters of the OHADA Treaty who consider the unification of business laws in Africa was a means to promote intra-regional trade across Africa.
138. Barnard (2013), p. 11.
139. Case 120/78 Rewe-Zentral AG v Bundesmonopolverwaltung für Branntwein [1979] ECR 649.
140. Case 120/78 Cassis de Dijon, p. 651.
141. See Maduro (1998), p. 105.
142. Ibid.
143. Case 120/78 Cassis de Dijon, p. 652.
144. Ibid, p. 662.
145. Ibid.
146. Ibid, p. 664.
147. Armstrong (2002), p. 226.
148. Action Plan for the Single Market, SEC (97), 1 Final.
149. See Maduro (1998), p. 107.
150. Ward (2009), p. 20.
151. See the Statement from the Paris Summit, Bulletin of European Communities, October 1972, No.10, p. 26.
152. Ibid.
153. Bulletin of the European Parliament, Special Edition 8 July 1985, p. 5.
154. These measures included improvement of the Council's decision-making, the enlargement of the European Parliament's role, the Commission's administrative powers and the strengthening of political co-operation in the general context of the transition to the European Union
155. Bulletin of the European Parliament, Special Edition 8 July 1985, p. 6.
156. COM (85) 310, 14 June 1985, para 5.
157. COM (85) 310, 14 June 1985, para 5.
158. See Craig (2002), p. 12.
159. Ward (2009), p. 25.
160. COM (85) 310, 14 June 1985, para 63. A more detailed description of mutual recognition is provided later in the chapter.
161. European Commission, Completing the Internal Market, COM (85) 310 final, para 63.
162. European Commission, Completing the Internal Market, COM (85) 310 final, para 64.
163. See Nicholaidis, K. (2007) 'Mutual Recognition "on trial" the Long Road to Services Liberalisation, 14(5) *Journal of European Public Policy*,

pp. 717–734. See also Schmitt, S.K. (2007) 'Mutual Recognition As a New Mode of Governance' 14(5) *Journal of European Public Policy*, p. 672.

164. European Commission, Completing the Internal Market, COM (85) 310 final, para 65.
165. European Commission, Completing the Internal Market, COM (85) 310 final, paras 65 and 66. See also Armstrong (2002), p. 227.
166. Ibid, p. 17.
167. Ibid, p. 22.
168. The 1985 Luxembourg Conference, which gathered the participating countries' Heads of State and Government.
169. Luxembourg European Council, Bulletin of the European Communities, No. 11/1985, p. 7.
170. See Article 1 of the SEA.
171. Which now included Greece (1981) and Portugal and Spain (1986).
172. See Preamble of the SEA.
173. Mutual recognition was introduced through article 100b of the SEA, which provided that "the Council, acting in accordance with the provisions of Article 100a [on harmonisation], may decide that the provisions in force in a Member State must be recognised as being equivalent to those applied by another Member State".
174. A similar arrangement is likely to be considered as appropriate in the African context, given the participating countries' concerns regarding their sovereignty.
175. See Craig (2002), p. 13. The co-operation process was provided in Articles 6, 7, 49, 54(2), 56(2), 57, 100a, 100b, 118a, 130 (e), 130q(2) in which the phrase "after consulting the Assembly" was replaced by "in co-operation with the European Parliament".
176. Craig (2002), p. 20.
177. The subsequent amendments to the EEC Treaty were used to sustain the momentum created by the SEA and to deepen European integration even more by reinforcing the established legal order
178. Garret, G., Kelemen, D.R. and Schulz, H. (1998) 'The European Court of Justice, National Governments, and Legal Integration in the European Union' 52(1) *International Organization* 149, p. 151.
179. Maduro (1998), p. 8.
180. Birkinshaw (2012), p. 115.
181. Svensson (2008), p. 1. See also Schmidt, S. and Kelemen, R.D. (eds) (2013) *The Power of the European Court of Justice*, London: Routledge, p. 1.
182. Gormley, L. (1985) *Prohibiting Restrictions on Trade Within the EEC*, Amsterdam; New York: North-Holland; New York, NY: Elsevier Science, p. 249.
183. Starr-Deelen and Deelen (1996), p. 88. See also Radkin, J. (2012) 'The European Court of Justice: A Strange Institution' in Zimmerman, H. and Dur, A. (eds) *Key Controversies in European Integration*, Basingstoke: Palgrave Macmillan, p. 91.
184. Kelemen, R.D. (2012) 'The Political Foundations of Judicial Independence in the European Union' 19(1) *Journal of European Policy* p. 43.

6 Regional Developmentalism Through Law Within SADC, ECOWAS and EAC

I. Introduction

This chapter provides a critical analysis of the application of the conceptual framework developed in the previous chapters in the context of the African Regional Economic Communities (RECs) recognised by the African Union as the pillar upon which the African Economic Community (AEC) is to be built. In particular, this chapter is used to further the general argumentation developed in the previous chapters by highlighting the various issues that arise in most African regional schemes following the Vinerian model and by considering the particular way in which law could address those issues and support the successful establishment of an AEC that corresponds to the needs of the African economies.

Similar to previous chapters, the concept of *regional developmentalism through law* constitutes both the conceptual framework and the main methodology used throughout this chapter.[1] This analysis is conducted in light of the various aspects of law that were examined in the previous chapters, with a view to identifying the particular way in which these can be applied as normative tools to support regional schemes across the continent as well as help address the various issues arising in the context of the African RECs. A particular emphasis is placed on the economic and the political aspects of the legal frameworks provided within the RECs, including the regulatory and institutional frameworks adopted to implement the regional objectives. This holistic method is adopted to ensure that beyond legal integration—which includes mainly harmonisation of national policies and mechanisms for the effective implementation of regional law, often identified as the major legal issues in the context of regionalisation in Africa—the analysis conducted in this chapter also assesses the relevance of the legal principles and techniques adopted by the RECs to achieve regional development.

This analysis concentrates on three particular RECs, namely the Southern African Development Community (SADC), the Economic Community of West African States (ECOWAS) and the East African Community (EAC), as these provide different points allowing us to cover various aspects of regionalism in Africa which are relevant to the overall argumentation developed throughout the monograph. In particular, while the process conducted in SADC's early years provides us with an example a primarily state-led (interventionist) regionalism in which the main focus is on *economic cooperation* and regional capacity-building, ECOWAS presents the example of a regional scheme following the classical (Vinerian) model of regionalism which prioritises *economic integration* and the gradual elimination of barriers to cross-border trade as main objectives to be achieved. The EAC, which appears to be the most advanced regional scheme to date in terms of progress made towards the achievement of its objectives, offers the example of a comprehensive approach to regionalism in which participating countries engage in both market-led economic integration and state-led capacity-building.[2]

These RECs are examined in light of their objectives as well as the different coordination mechanisms that they have adopted to achieve those objectives. As will be demonstrated in this chapter, despite the fact that the three RECs are all considered as pillars of the AEC and therefore are expected to follow the Vinerian (linear) model of regionalism aimed at the establishment of a continental Common Market,[3] they nevertheless provide for different paths to achieve this objective which involve different sets of issues. This constitutes a particular feature of regionalism efforts in the African context, given that regional schemes are examined both in light of their respective objectives as well as by taking into consideration their progress towards the achievement of the objectives of the African Economic Community. By examining these RECs, this chapter is therefore also aimed at assessing the processes conducted under the AEC, which has been assigned with the role of coordinating the RECs' activities as well as influencing their approach towards regionalism.[4]

Given the crucial role that they are supposed to play in determining the success of regionalism efforts,[5] the analysis conducted in this chapter focuses on the regulatory frameworks provided by the three RECs, especially on the legal rules and techniques particularly designed to promote sustained economic growth and development within their respective regions.[6] A particular emphasis will also be placed on two key issues, including the institutional framework created to manage the RECs as well as the specific mechanism put in place or developed to ensure the achievement of their goals. Focusing more particularly on the implementation and the enforcement of community rules, which are considered to be the major issues faced by regional schemes in Africa, this analysis will also be devoted to the judicial institutions established within the RECs and will consider the role played by these institutions to ensure the effective implementation of community rules and thereby advance the regional processes.

For this purpose, the different aspects of legal integration discussed in the context of the European Court of Justice (ECJ) will be highlighted, namely positive integration through harmonisation of national laws within those communities, as well as negative integration through the decisions of their regional courts, with a particular emphasis placed on the theories of direct effect and supremacy of community rules, as well as preliminary reference mechanism and the participation of national courts and private stakeholders in the regional processes. In addition, the chapter will also be used to consider the application of the various legal arrangements provided under NAFTA, MERCOSUR and ASEAN, emphasising their ability to promote regional development in the context of the African RECs.

It will be contended in this chapter, and in the broader monograph, that regional processes which are meant to progress towards a deeper level of integration (in this case, a Common Market) need to meet two key requirements to be successful: key supranational institutions need to be established in order to coordinate the activities of the RECs and support the achievement of their specific goals,[7] and both popular participation and commitment at the national level are necessary to advance the regional agenda and to determine the scope and content of the regional schemes.[8]

As mentioned above, the following sections will be used to examine these various issues in the context of SADC, ECOWAS and EAC.

II. State-Led Development Coordination and Capacity-Building Through SADCC/SADC

The SADC constitutes an interesting case study among the African RECs, given the singular model of regionalism that was adopted by the region in its early years. This model, which was based on heavy state interventionism through a production coordination approach, provides a practical example of an alternative to the classical market-led economic integration followed by schemes like ECOWAS and a case of the application of the ideological component of regional developmentalism. This section, therefore, provides a critical analysis of regional efforts within SADC, focusing particularly on its initial formation under the Southern African Development Coordination Conference (SADCC) and drawing upon the political and economic underpinnings for the establishment of the regional scheme. This section is also used to highlight the lack of an appropriate regulatory and institutional framework under SADCC and reinforces the importance of the political component of the concept of regional developmentalism through law.

II.1. Project Coordination Approach Under SADCC

SADCC was established in 1980 by nine Southern African countries with the aim of promoting collective self-reliance and the harmonisation of the economic development of the region, with a view of subsequently improving the living conditions of Southern African populations.[9] In particular, SADCC was created with the primary goal of reducing the participating countries' external economic dependence (dependence on South Africa in particular) and to create closer ties and interdependence among them.[10] A planned approach to regionalism was adopted to achieve this goal, focusing on regional cooperation and the coordination of the participating countries' efforts to support their national development priorities as well as to promote a harmonised regional development.[11]

Production coordination was given a central role in the development strategy adopted by SADCC, which focused on the formulation and the management of various projects aimed at enhancing the participating countries' capacity in key sectors and industries, as well as building the infrastructures to support it.[12] This particular strategy—production coordination through projects—was adopted with a view to accommodating the participating countries' sovereignty and autonomy, as it allowed them to make clear and limited commitments and was believed to promote a balanced development among the participating countries in which each state would both contribute to and benefit from the regional scheme equitably.[13] Through these various measures, SADCC was therefore supposed to provide a flexible and realistic approach to regionalism which was intended to promote regional development while being also adapted to the needs and particular circumstances of the participating countries.

II.1.1. The Role of Trade and Economic Integration

Both regional and international trade were included under the SADCC approach to regionalism but were however expected to play a secondary role as means to achieve the region's main objectives.[14] Full trade liberalisation and economic integration were particularly avoided, as there was a general assumption that they would only benefit the most advanced participating countries, therefore promoting an unequal regional development.[15]

Moreover, pure trade liberalisation was deemed to be more suited for countries with larger markets and production capacity.[16] The Vinerian (linear) model of regional integration—which includes the establishment of Free Trade Areas, Customs Unions and Common Markets—was considered as particularly unsuited for the region, as it would potentially deprive the participating countries of important customs revenue, including import and export taxes.[17] These measures were deemed to cost the participating countries important losses without providing them with readily available alternatives.[18] There was, therefore, a general assumption that several preconditions needed to be met before engaging in full-fledged regional economic integration, including production enhancement, infrastructure-building and gradual integration in key sectors of mutual interest.[19] These measures were intended to be particularly designed to rely on collective action and regional resources in order to address the participating countries' national needs and support their national development strategies.[20]

Various programmes and projects were initiated to this effect, and their management was entrusted to different participating countries through an institutional framework specifically designed to achieve this goal.

II.1.2. Decentralised Institutional Framework

In contrast with other regional schemes, including ECOWAS or the European Union, for example, SADCC adopted a significantly decentralised institutional framework, which reflected the participating countries' preference for a highly intergovernmental approach to regional governance.[21] This particular approach was adopted in order to provide the organisation with a non-confrontational, consensus-based governance structure, characterised by a strong central political organ and weak administrative institutions with no executive power.[22]

The SADCC Memorandum of Understanding, therefore, provided for a Summit of Heads of State and Government—the highest institution, responsible for the management and the coordination of the organisation; a Council of Ministers—composed of representatives from national government and responsible for overseeing the implementation of the various projects; and a Secretariat—in charge with the coordination of the execution of the tasks of the organisation as well as ensuring the liaison between the organisation's institutions.[23] Sectoral Commissions and a Standing Committee of Officials were also provided to support the Summit in the achievement of its objectives.[24]

The specific institutional framework adopted under SADCC was deemed to be particularly suited for its project coordination approach, given the fact that individual countries were expected to be responsible for particular programmes in sectors or areas falling within the remit of the regional scheme. Angola, for example, was responsible for energy conservation and development, while Mozambique was entrusted with transport and communication and Zimbabwe with food security and agricultural research.[25] This approach was particularly suitable for the region's development, as it was expected to promote production integration among the participating countries and to facilitate the creation of production linkages between various sectors and industrial activities across the region. Both integration and linkages were intended to support the creation of regional value chains, which would subsequently promote industrial development and product diversification in less developed countries and areas.[26]

However, despite the adoption of these various measures aimed at building the participating countries' production capacity, external dependence remained high due to the lack of industrial development and export diversification.[27] This external dependence was further exacerbated by the fact that the region relied on external financial and technical assistance to implement its various projects and programmes, hence hampering the efforts towards collective self-reliance and policy autonomy. Moreover, the institutional framework provided under SADCC was both controlled by and heavily dependent on each participating countries' government and indirectly on national elites, which often considered regional initiatives as a means to increase their international credibility and cling to an apparent state sovereignty rather than a tool to advance national interests.[28] Consequently, despite the multiple instruments formally adopted by the participating countries' governments, the regulatory and institutional frameworks provided by the SADC MOU did not impose any actual obligations on the participating countries and therefore failed to establish an appropriate coordination mechanism to ensure the effective implementation of regional policies.[29]

It is against such a backdrop that SADC was established in 1992, with the aim of addressing this particular problem and furthering regional efforts towards deeper integration and capacity-building.

II.2. The Move to Regional Economic Integration Under SADC

The Treaty establishing the Southern African Development Community (hereinafter SADC Treaty) was adopted on 17 August 1992 and marked the switch from economic cooperation and the project coordination approach under SADCC to a stronger emphasis on trade and market-led economic integration.[30] This transformation reflected the switch to the neoliberal paradigm in the continent's development discourse which had occurred in the 1980s. The region's new strategy was further developed in the SADC Protocol on Trade (hereinafter SADC Trade Protocol, adopted in 1996)—through which trade was given a prominent role and which provided for the liberalisation of intra-regional trade by means of fair, equitable and beneficial arrangement;[31] and the Regional Indicative Strategic Development Plan (hereinafter RISDP, adopted in 2003)—which was aimed at deepening regional economic integration through the establishment of a Customs Union, a Common Market and a Monetary Union.[32] Regional integration, therefore, became the organisation's main objective, as it was believed to promote regional development through boosting of economic growth and, indirectly, the enhancement of the living standards of the population in the region.[33]

The adoption of the classical model of regional integration through the SADC Treaty and other secondary instruments reflected the abandonment of a state-led and coordination-based regional scheme and the adoption of a neoliberal approach to regionalism in which regional development was superseded by economic integration and trade liberalisation as the main objectives. In addition, under this approach, the establishment of a regional market through the gradual elimination of tariff and non-tariff barriers to trade was believed to be the most appropriate method to promote economic growth, which is believed to be a prerequisite for the achievement of regional development.[34] This assumption reflects the adoption by SADC of a "global" approach to development, which is expected to be achieved through the implementation of an *ideal* model of regionalism—i.e. economic integration—without taking account the region's particular circumstances.[35]

The transformation of the organisation significantly impacted its overall strategy, which is now aimed at promoting a market-led process and at establishing a favourable environment within which private enterprise can operate smoothly and prosper. This includes the Community's approach towards industrialisation, infrastructure-building and investment.

The SADC industrial strategy places a strong emphasis on regional integration and prescribes the establishment by SADC Member States of a macroeconomic environment "to enhance growth and support regional integration industrialisation and competitiveness".[36] In addition, the SADC Spatial Development Initiatives (SDIs)—which are considered as the remnant of the project coordination approach followed under the SADCC, focusing particularly on infrastructure-building—are designed to facilitate private investment and to be adjustable to private immediate demands, with a view to promoting international economic integration rather than focusing primarily on key sectors and areas which are more likely to promote sustainable economic growth and economic transformation in the region.[37] Moreover, the SADC Protocol on Finance and Investment, which was adopted on 18 August 2006, provides various rules and measures that also place a strong emphasis on regional integration and are aimed both at promoting the harmonisation of national investment policies and at establishing a closer cooperation among participating countries.[38]

These various instruments, which constitute the regulatory framework upon which the overall SADC strategy is based, demonstrate the overemphasis placed on regional economic integration, which has become the ultimate objective of the regional efforts rather than the means used by the participating countries to achieve regional development. In contrast, under an approach based on regional developmentalism through law, regional efforts would focus on the adoption of regional rules targeting the enhancement regional production, including through the inclusion of specific measures in the Investment Protocol which would be aimed at promoting particular sectors and areas in the region, as well as the adoption of both partial and gradual integration in sectors of common interest.[39]

As highlighted in the context of ASEAN, the regulation of both regional trade and investment through legal instrument similar to the ASEAN Trade in Good Agreement (ATIGA) and the ASEAN Comprehensive Investment Agreement (ACIA), as well as the concentration of regional integration efforts in key sectors considered as a priority in the regional development strategy, could prove particularly important in order to support the progression of the regional process conducted under SADC. In addition to these legal instruments, special measures similar to the Regional Policy in the context of the European Economic Community need to be adopted to monitor punctual interventionist actions taken by the region in order to promote a harmonious regional development and address the redistribution issues likely to arise among the participating countries.

However, this approach proves rather impractical in the context of SADC, given the fact that the Community operates under GATT article XXIV which provides for restrictive measures aimed at substantial trade liberalisation among the participating countries.[40] As highlighted in chapter three, operating under the World Trade Organization (WTO) Enabling Clause could prove more beneficial to a regional scheme such as SADC, given that it will provide it with the flexibility that is necessary to take a more interventionist approach in the promotion of regional development and adopt special measures which would be considered as non WTO-compliant under GATT 94 article XXIV.

II.2.1. SADC's Improved Institutional Framework

The SADC Treaty was also elaborated with a view to improving both the regulatory and institutional frameworks of the organisation, including through the adoption of a binding Treaty and the improvement of its institutional framework.[41] The new SADC institutional framework is therefore composed of institutions with similar responsibilities to those of the institutions under SADCC, namely the Summit of Heads of State and Government, the Council of Ministers, the Sectoral and Custer Ministerial Committee, the Standing Committee of Officials and the Secretariat[42] as well as new institutions, including the Organ on Politics, Defence and Security Co-operation, the SADC National Committees and the SADC Tribunal.[43]

The modification of the SADCC original organs and the creation of new institutions are intended to improve the functioning of the Community by ensuring the effective implementation of regional policies and other legal instruments. Similar to the EC Commission in the context of the European Economic Community, the role of the SADC Secretariat has been reinforced under the SADC Treaty, as it now constitutes the executive organ of the Community which is responsible, *inter alia*, of strategic planning and the management of SADC's programmes, the implementation of the decisions of the Summit and the coordination and harmonisation of the policies and strategies of the Member States.[44] SADC National Committees were established with the aim of gathering key stakeholders in each participating country and providing input at the national level in the formulation of regional instruments, including policies and programmes of action.[45] As discussed in the context of the European Economic Community, the establishment of an institution with such autonomy and increased powers dedicated to the monitoring of regional programmes is expected to ensure the smooth operation and progression of regional processes.

A Tribunal was also established with the specific responsibility of ensuring the application and correct interpretation of SADC law (Treaty and secondary instruments).[46] However, the vast majority of cases brought to the Tribunal were based on issues that are not directly relevant to regional integration, including the enforcement of both human and employment rights.[47] This situation, which characterises the majority of African RECs, is possibly due to the low level of intra-regional trade in Africa.[48] As highlighted in the context of regional processes conducted under NAFTA, MERCOSUR, ASEAN and OHADA, as legal certainty and predictability constitute one of the key issues arising in the context of the African regional schemes, the establishment of a SADC regional arbitration institution could prove more beneficial than a formal judicial institution such as a tribunal, given that it would provide businesses operating in the region with a regional judicial system that is both consensual and suitable to their needs.

However, one particular case concerning the enforcement of Human Rights requires a particular attention, given the unique circumstances surrounding the case and the various measures that were adopted subsequently, which significantly impacted both the institutional framework and the implementation of SADC law within the participating countries.

II.2.2. Mike Campbell (Pvt) Ltd and Others v. Republic of Zimbabwe[49]

This case involved a group of applicants who filed an application at the SADC Tribunal disputing the acquisition by the Republic of Zimbabwe of their agricultural land as well as their removal from their same land. The applicants argued that the respondent (Zimbabwe) was in breach of its obligations under the SADC Treaty by enacting and implementing amendment No. 17, 2005 of the Zimbabwean Constitution which provided for the organisation of a major land reform programme in the country. In particular, the facts were presented as a case of gross violations of Human Rights by the Zimbabwean government, especially by its denying the applicants access to national courts to challenge the legality of the compulsory acquisition of their land and its refusal to provide them with subsequent compensation. In addition, the Zimbabwean government was also accused of racial discrimination, since they were the only community which had seen their land being confiscated by the same government.[50]

Basing its decision on article 15(1) of the SADC Tribunal Protocol, which provided for its jurisdiction over disputes concerning human rights, democracy and the rule of law, the Tribunal decided that the Respondent's action was in breach of its obligations under Articles 4(c) and 6(2) of the SADC Treaty[51] and required the Respondent to take all necessary measures to protect the possession, occupation and ownership of the lands of the Applicants as well as to compensate those who had already been evicted.

The Tribunal subsequently referred the case to the SADC Summit for non-compliance by the Respondent, the Republic of Zimbabwe, despite several injunctions to abide by the Tribunal's decision.[52] In response, and in contradiction with the request contained in the referral, Summit took several measures which significantly alter the institutional framework of the Community, including the *de facto* suspension of the SADC Tribunal in 2010 and the decision in 2012 to establish a new Tribunal with a mandate limited to the interpretation of SADC law only in cases involving disputes between Member States.[53] Through these decisions, the Summit significantly reduced popular participation in the regional process and deprived the Tribunal of the ability to support the achievement of regional objectives by ensuring the effective implementation of SADC law.[54]

As a result, SADC's institutional framework was seriously altered, thereby hampering the Community's efforts towards both regional integration and regional developmentalism. As highlighted in the discussion on neofunctionalism in Chapter 2 as well as in the context of the European Economic Community, to ensure the smooth evolution of a regional process, a sound regional regulatory framework should not be exclusive and, beyond state actors, it needs to include key stakeholders who could either benefit from or be affected by the regional process. By preventing private parties from bringing cases to a regional judicial or quasi-judicial institution, therefore, runs the risk of seriously affecting the regional process, given the crucial role that they are expected to play in the promotion of regional trade.

Following on from this analysis on SADC, the next section concentrates on ECOWAS, which provides another example of an African REC following the Vinerian model of regionalism with has made relative progress towards deeper integration, including through the strengthening of its legal framework.

III. The Classical Model of Regional Integration Under ECOWAS

This section is dedicated to the study of the process conducted under ECOWAS which, from its inception, was aimed at achieving economic integration and in which participating countries are expected to engage in a market-led development process.[55] In particular, ECOWAS provides an evolving approach to regional economic integration in which both regulatory and institutional frameworks have been improved in order to advance the integration process. This section is therefore used to identify more issues likely to arise in regional schemes aimed at achieving economic integration in the African context, including the adoption of an adequate coordination mechanism to support the effective implementation of regional policies and the relevance of trade liberalisation in the African context.

III.1. Initial Efforts Through the 1975 ECOWAS Treaty

ECOWAS was initially established in 1975 by the Treaty of Lagos which signature had been influenced by various factors including the Pan-African wave which was blowing on the continent at the time, pressure from the private sector and encouragements of the United Nations Commission for Africa (UNECA).[56] The majority of ECOWAS Member States, having accessed their independence and acquired their political autonomy in the previous decade, were confronted with various political and economic issues that the creation of a regional organisation was expected to address more effectively.[57]

The Community was established with the ultimate goal of fostering economic and social development in its member states,[58] a goal which was to be achieved through an "effective cooperation largely through a determined and concerted policy of self-reliance".[59] As highlighted in the previous chapter, this approach was adopted in order to accommodate the participating countries' concerns over their newly acquired sovereignty and independence.[60] This cooperation between Member States was designed to be centred on the removal of tariff and non-tariff barriers to trade and to the free movement of persons, services and capital. This strategy, which was geared towards trade liberalisation and the gradual establishment of a Customs Union among the ECOWAS Member States, was expected to help attract more foreign direct investment and thereby promote economic and social development.[61]

Under the Treaty, the integration efforts were expected to focus mainly on key areas, including industry, telecommunications, energy, agriculture, natural resources, commerce, monetary and financial issues and social and cultural matters.[62] This functional approach to regional integration was expected to promote and develop local businesses and increase intra-regional trade, allowing the Member States to increase their self-reliance and alter a pattern of strong external dependence which characterised the political economies of most countries in the region. This situation, seen as a consequence of colonisation, was believed to have shaped the trade system of most countries in the region in such a way as to serve the needs of the former colonial powers in raw materials.[63]

III.1.1. Intergovernmental Institutional Framework

ECOWAS was therefore established in order to address this multi-faceted issue of promoting economic development through a strategy which involved the strengthening of co-operation among Member States, the attraction of more foreign investment and the increase of intra-regional trade and self-reliance. To achieve this goal, the participating countries recognised early the need for a strong institutional framework to successfully achieve co-operation among them and therefore provided in chapter II of the 1975 Treaty for what was seen as adequate institutional machinery established for this purpose.[64] Five main institutions were established to manage and further develop the co-operation among the ECOWAS Member States: an Authority of Heads of State and Government, which was responsible for the general direction and the development of the Community; a Council of Ministers, composed of two representatives of each participating country and established to ensure the efficient and harmonious functioning of the Community; an Executive Secretariat, established to support the other institutions and to be responsible for the day-to-day administration of the activities of the Community; and technical and specialised commissions designed to assist the Secretariat in the elaboration of reports and recommendations with respect to issues relating to their specific areas.[65]

An ECOWAS Tribunal was also established and was responsible for the implementation and enforcement of the Treaty by ensuring the observance of law and justice in the interpretation of the provisions of the Treaty. Moreover, the Tribunal was responsible for settling any disputes arising among Member States and which could not be settled amicably by direct agreement.[66] However, regarding disputes among participating countries, precedence was given to an amicable and consensual approach, thereby relegating the use of the tribunal as a second option and ensuring that the participating countries retained control over the implementation of the Treaty provisions which were not likely to be enforced against their own will.

Therefore, although they might have appeared relatively and nominally similar to the institutions of the European Union (in which case the Authority would be the counterpart of the European Council while the Council of Ministers would be the equivalent of the Council of the European Union), these institutions were completely different as they reflected the strong and rather absolute intergovernmental character of the Community at the time. All the institutions, including the Council of Ministers, were tightly controlled by the Member States, which retained their hold on them through the Authority.[67] The management and further development of the Community were therefore left to the goodwill of the Member States whose sovereignty was left untouched and who had the freedom to decide the pace and rate at which economic integration in the region would evolve.[68]

III.1.2. Non-Binding Regulatory Framework

The provisions of the Treaty constituted the fundamental text and primary source of law for the Community. These provisions were meant to be implemented through secondary legislation to be produced by the Authority and the Council. The Treaty, therefore, provided for decisions and directions to be elaborated by the Authority and the Council in order to achieve the goals of the Treaty.[69] Several decisions were therefore made by both the Authority and the Council relating to key areas such as the consolidation of import duties and non-tariff barriers, trade liberalisation in industrial products or trade liberalisation of unprocessed products.[70] On the removal of barriers to trade in particular, through a series of meetings in 1978 and 1980 the Authority adopted a Trade Liberalisation Scheme (TLS) which was aimed at the "total removal of tariffs on all unprocessed goods and handicrafts as well as the progressive elimination of tariffs on all industrial products from 1981 to 1989 [. . .]".[71] However, these decisions and directions constituted very limited and rather ineffective instruments for the implementation of the Treaty, as they were only binding on the institutions of the ECOWAS institutions and not on the Member States.[72]

Protocols and conventions were intended to be the main means through which the ECOWAS Member States decided to implement the provisions of the Treaty. Protocols were used particularly to provide some clarifications on the provisions of the Treaty and to further develop some key areas of regional integration.[73] In this vein, some important Protocols were passed during the initial years of the Community, including protocols on key issues such as the assessment of loss of revenue by Member States, the funding of the Community, the re-exportation within the Community of goods imported from third countries or the definition of the concept of products originating from Member States.[74] Rather than using the mechanism provided for at article 4 of the Treaty and put to use the institutions established to manage the Community, Member States chose to negotiate and ratify various Protocols to ensure the implementation of the Treaty.[75]

One of the main pieces of legislation adopted by the ECOWAS Member States was the Protocol relating to the Free Movement of Persons, Residence and Establishment on 29 May 1979.[76] This Protocol, and its subsequent Supplementary Protocols,[77]provides (in three phases) the citizens of the ECOWAS Member States with the right to enter, reside and establish economic activities within the territory of the Community. These instruments were intended to provide for a mechanism to achieve one of the main goals of the Treaty which is the "complete freedom of movement" within the Community'.[78]

The harmonisation of the policies of the different Member States was recognised as a mechanism necessary for the effective functioning of the Community.[79] Harmonisation (or approximation of laws) was preferred to unification as exercised by OHADA, given the diversity of legal systems present within the Community and the difficulty that such an exercise would generate.[80] The Treaty had provided for harmonisation of policies in key areas, including harmonisation of industrial incentives, industrial development plans and economic policies.[81] Other areas which were expected to be covered by the harmonisation process included the free movements of goods, services, persons and capital, aimed at creating a legal environment broadly the same in all Member States in order to facilitate the implementation of the Treaty provisions.[82]

III.1.3. Shortcomings of the 1975 ECOWAS Treaty

Although through the 1975 Treaty they had recognised and emphasised the various benefits and potential profits that they could gain from an increased cooperation among them and from economic integration in the region, the participating countries nevertheless did not provide the Community with the legal framework necessary to achieve a successful integration. The Treaty provided the Community with an institutional framework which, although it seemed sophisticated enough on paper, lacked the autonomy necessary to effectively play its role. The institutions were tightly controlled by the Member States governments which determined the pace of economic integration in the region.[83] This was also evidenced in the regulatory framework established by the Treaty, a framework which was equipped with legal instruments that either lacked any binding effect on the Member States (decisions and directions) or were subject to ratification by the Member States before they could produce any effects (Protocols).

The combination of these various factors (both the weak institutional framework and the lack of binding effect) hampered the effective implementation of the Community's regulatory framework in the participating countries and Treaty provisions in all Member States.[84] In addition, despite the fact that the Treaty provided for the establishment of an ECOWAS Tribunal in order to ensure the observance of the law in the interpretation of Treaty provisions, it provided neither for the mechanism through which the tribunal was supposed to operate nor the relationship that the tribunal was expected to maintain with the participating countries' national courts.

The intergovernmental arrangement which operated under the 1975 Treaty failed to work because it required the presence of a country economically and politically strong to provide the impetus for regional integration. This is a role which could have been played by Nigeria, which was economically strong in the early years of the Community but which unfortunately lost its hegemony after the 1970s energy crisis.[85] As a consequence of the lack of strong leadership in the region, Member States failed to agree on a mechanism which would have permitted further economic integration in the region. Whereas Nigeria encouraged the building and strengthening of local industries within the Community, the Francophone countries, which had maintained strong ties with France, were more interested in granting access to the regional market to foreign investors.[86] These tensions among Member States eventually managed to paralyse the functioning of the Community and affect the progress of the integration process in the region.

III.2. Improvement of the Legal Framework Through the 1993 ECOWAS Treaty

To salvage the integration process in the region and to ensure the success of ECOWAS in achieving its objectives, a Committee of Eminent Persons (CEP) was established in order to review the 1975 ECOWAS Treaty and identify its shortcomings as well as areas which still needed to be improved.[87] The CEP reviewed the Treaty in depth and highlighted some key issues which constituted the main obstacles to the good functioning of the Community. The CEP noted the lack of a strong legal framework necessary to both give effect to the provisions of the Treaty and carry out the objectives of the Community.[88] More particularly, the CEP highlighted the lack of binding force of ECOWAS decisions on the Member States; the cumbersome policy-making process, which required unanimity for the adoption of the ECOWAS Protocols, and the random implementation of the same Protocols, which was left to the discretion of the Member States through a ratification procedure,[89] and the lack of participation of national interest groups in the decision-making process of the Community.

The CEP submitted several recommendations for the improvement of the Treaty, including the need for the Community to switch from a voluntary cooperation system to a supranational and more coercive one. It argued that the Member States needed to give up part of their sovereignty in favour of supranational institutions whose operations and efforts would be aimed solely at the advancement of economic integration in the region.[90]

In response to the recommendations of the CEP, the ECOWAS Member States decided to revise the Lagos Treaty and adopted a new Treaty in Cotonou, Benin on 24 July 1993. Through the 1993 Treaty, the Member States recommitted themselves to economic integration by proceeding to the relevant amendments of the 1975 Treaty and by setting clear timetables for the establishment of the next stages of the integration process.[91] The 1993 Treaty was aimed at addressing the shortcomings identified with the 1975 Treaty and at improving the legal framework of the Community. Various measures were therefore adopted to improve both the regulatory and the institutional structures of the Community. These will be detailed in the following sections.

III.2.1. Binding Effect of Community Law

With a view to ensuring the effective implementation of Community law, the new Treaty extended the binding effect of the Authority's decisions of the Authority and the Council's regulations to the Member States.[92] However, to be binding on the Member States, the regulations adopted by the Council required the approval of the Authority. In addition to the new binding force granted to the Decisions and Regulations, the Treaty improved the Community law-making process by providing for the adoption of the decisions and regulations by consensus or by two-thirds majority.[93] This procedure was expected to facilitate the adoption of new Community measures and therefore.

Despite this significant progress, the Treaty did not, however, address the issue of the effect of the Decisions and Regulations in the Member States' legal systems and the relation between Community law and national law.[94]

III.2.2. Improvement of the Institutional Framework

In parallel to the strengthening of the Community's regulatory framework, the 1993 Treaty provided for the establishment of new institutions which were supposed to reflect the Member States' efforts to give a more supranational character to the organisation and an increasing popular participation in the Community decision-making. Although the Authority and the Council remained generally unchanged, the Secretariat was strengthened and the Community Parliament, the Economic and Social Council and the Court of Justice were introduced.[95] Under the 1993 Treaty, the Secretariat has been given more autonomy and independence from the Member States, in order to ensure its effective functioning.[96]

A Community Parliament, which composed of 120 members of whom at least five from each Member State, was introduced in order to represent the "Peoples of the Community" in the decision-making structure of the Community.[97] The Parliament is supposed to discuss issues "concerning the Community, in particular issues relating to Human Rights and Fundamental Freedom and make recommendations to the Institutions of the Community".[98] The Parliament "may also be consulted for its opinion on matters concerning the Community".[99]

The Treaty also provides for an Economic and Social Council, which is expected to play an advisory role to the Community policy-making institutions (Authority and Council).[100] It is composed of "representatives of the various categories of economic and social activity", which include members from the Member States' interest groups, including the private sector and civil society. The inclusion of these groups in the ECOWAS policy-making process was expected to increase popular participation in the Community with a view to using their input both to shape and to extend the scope of the integration process.[101]

III.2.3. Establishment of an ECOWAS Court of Justice

A Community Court of Justice (hereinafter ECCJ) was established by article 15 of the 1993 Treaty as the judicial institution of ECOWAS.[102] Similar to the ECOWAS Tribunal, the ECCJ was established to "ensure the observance of law and of the principles of equity in the interpretation and application of the provisions of the Treaty".[103] However, the competence of the Court is extended compared to that of the Tribunal, as the ECCJ is now the primary institution for the settlement of disputes arising between one or more Member States and the institutions of the Community on the interpretation and the application of the provisions of the Treaty.[104] In addition, under this new regime, a Member State could also initiate proceedings on behalf of its nationals against another Member State or an institution of the Community relating to the interpretation and the application of the Treaty.[105] The ECCJ also plays the role of an advisory body, and its opinion may be requested by the other institutions of the Community or the Member States.[106]

The establishment of the Court with an extended competence compared to its predecessor (the Tribunal) may be explained by the need for the uniform application of Community law, with the Court expected to play the role of guardian of the spirit of the ECOWAS Treaties.[107] Especially through its dispute resolution mechanism, the ECCJ is expected to play a significant role in the integration process of the region by compelling both Member States and Community institutions to apply the Treaty in a uniform manner.[108]

However, although the establishment of the ECCJ constituted a significant progress in the integration process, the jurisdiction of the Court remains very limited. The jurisdiction of the Court may be further hampered by the non-compliance of Member States with the Court's decision, a situation that would not be surprising on the part of the Member States given their tendency not to respect their commitments.[109] Moreover, the Protocol which established the Court provides standing only for the Member States and the institutions of the Community. Both natural and legal persons can only access the Court through their respective states, with no remedy in a case where the same state has decided to reject their request or in a situation where they would like to initiate proceedings against their own State. This issue was addressed by the Court through case law in the *Afolabi* case, which prompted a significant change in the Community's legal environment.

III.2.3.1. AFOLABI OLADJIDE V NIGERIA[110]

The jurisdiction of the Court took a major turning point in 2004, in a case involving a Nigerian national and his country. The case involved Mr Afolabi Oladjide, a businessman based in Nigeria who entered into an agreement with another party to purchase goods from Benin. However, the transaction could not be completed when Nigeria unilaterally decided to close its border with Benin. Afolabi, therefore, filed a suit with the ECCJ against Nigeria, alleging that by closing its border, the country had violated Community law on the right to free movement of persons and goods.[111] Proceeding to a very strict interpretation of the 1991 Protocol by which it was established, the Court decided that Afolabi did not have standing with it and therefore rejected his application. Through this decision, the ECCJ missed the opportunity to establish increase its powers and advance the Community's integration process.[112]

The ruling in the Afolabi case provoked a variety of reactions from the civil society in the region which exerted a lot of pressure on the Community, an action which resulted in the adoption by the Authority of the 2005 Supplementary Protocol expanding the Court's competence to include matters related to human rights and the Court's jurisdiction to also include standing for private litigants.[113] This Protocol constituted a major turning point in the legal environment of the Community, as it provided Member States' nationals with the opportunity to both monitor and ensure the application of Community law by the Member States.[114]

However, this measure did not manage to produce the effects that one could have expected, as the majority of cases brought by private litigants to the ECCJ from that period have mostly been related to the breach of the applicants' human rights and not to matters directly related to the advancement of the integration process in the region.[115] This trend can be observed in recent cases decided by the ECCJ, including, *inter alia*, *Konso Kokou Parounam v République du Togo* (Case ECW/CCJ/JUD/02/16),[116] *Société Anonyme Maseda v République du Mali* (Case ECW/CCJ/JUD/02/17)[117] and *Wing Commander Danladi Angulu Kwasu v Republic of Nigeria* (Case ECW/CCJ/JUD/04/17).[118] However, despite the fact that it has not decided many cases directly related to economic integration matters in the region, the ECCJ has nevertheless played a key role in the advancement of both political and economic fundamental rights of ECOWAS citizens, an issue that proves very important in the pursuit of socio-economic development in West Africa.

III.2.4. The Adoption of a New Legal Regime

The year 2006 marked the last step in the improvement of the legal framework of the Community, with the transformation of the Executive Secretariat into the ECOWAS Commission.[119] The new ECOWAS Commission was further restructured to play a more effective role in the integration process, including by providing it with a president, a vice-president and different commissioners in charge of several departments working on specific areas to be developed through regional co-operation.[120] Alongside the transformation of the Commission, the Community proceeded to the reorganisation of its legal regime. To reflect its stronger supranational character, the Community regulatory framework underwent several transformations, including the creation of Supplementary Acts to be adopted by the Authority to revise the Treaty; the establishment of the direct effect of the Council's Regulations, which are now enforceable in the Member States; and the adoption by the Council of Directives, which are binding on all Member States who have discretion in deciding their own methods for achieving the objectives of a specific Directive.[121] A Common External Tariff (CET) was also adopted by the Authority of Heads of State and Government, to ensure the transformation of the Community into a Customs Union.

However, despite this modification of the ECOWAS legal regime, which constitutes a significant improvement of the original legal framework established by the 1975 ECOWAS Treaty, it must be pointed out that two key elements have been left undeveloped, namely the Member States' compliance with Community law and with the ECCJ's decisions and the relationship between the ECCJ and the Member States' national courts. The two concepts are strongly connected because, as was highlighted in the case of the European Court of Justice, national courts could participate in the integration process and thereby provide Member States nationals with a better and more accessible opportunity to benefit from Community law. Moreover, by working closely with the Member States' national courts, the ECCJ could potentially further expand its jurisdiction to the Member States' legal systems and benefit from the involvement of national judges which could prove useful in ensuring the application of Community law at the national level at the expense of national law.[122] Not having to decide on the substance of particular cases, the ECCJ would, therefore, have the opportunity to further specialise in its role of ensuring uniformity in the interpretation and the application of Community law.

III.3. Impact of ECOWAS and the Adoption of Regional Development Policies

As has been highlighted through the analysis of the creation and gradual evolution of the ECOWAS legal framework, in its early years, the Community was provided with a regulatory framework which was mostly ineffective because it lacked the proper legal force to produce any effects and an institutional framework which lacked any decision-making power because it was tightly controlled by the Member States. Through subsequent revisions of the Treaty and adoption of several key instruments, the legal framework of the Community was significantly improved to become more effective. However, this analysis of the ECOWAS legal framework also indicates that legal integration in the context of ECOWAS has mostly happened through legislative measures or the adoption of various legal instruments at the regional level.

However, despite the gradual improvement of both its regulatory and institutional frameworks, little progress has been made by ECOWAS to achieve its objective of achieving deeper economic integration and thereby promoting regional development. In particular, while the Community has successfully established a Free Trade Area in 2000, a majority of ECOWAS Member States still have not managed to remove both tariff and non-tariff barriers to intra-regional trade in order to implement a fully functioning Customs Union.[123] In addition, the region continues to be overly dependent on primary-commodity exports, a situation which contributes to maintaining the region's economic subordination and dependence on external markets, thereby hampering their efforts towards economic transformation, production diversification and sustainable economic development.[124]

To address these particular issues, the Community has adopted key regional instruments, including a regional Agricultural Policy (ECOWAP—ECOWAS Agricultural Policy) in 2005 and an Industrial Policy (WACIP- West African Common Industrial Policy) in 2010. ECOWAP, which is intended to apply the Comprehensive Africa Agricultural Programme developed through NEPAD,[125] provides a Regional Agricultural Investment Plan (RAIP), which is aimed at giving general principles to be applied in each Member State through various National Agricultural Investment Plans (NAIPs).[126] WACIP, on the other hand, is aimed at accelerating the industrialisation of the region through the endogenous transformation of locally produced raw materials and the development of regional infrastructure.[127] These regional instruments, however, are impeded by multiple limitations which prevent their effective implementation. While efforts to materialise the Member States' planned interventions under ECOWAP have been relatively slow or have been undermined by multiple financial constraints, WACIP has not provided for an adequate mechanism for the application of its policies at the national level.[128] Moreover, WACIP does not provide for appropriate incentives aimed at reversing the current production structure, which is mainly based on primary commodities.[129] As highlighted with the case of the ASEAN Comprehensive

Investment Agreement and the Framework Agreement for the Integration in Priority Sectors, an appropriate WACIP needs to identify the key industrial sectors and areas which have potential to promote economic growth in the ECOWAS region and ensure that both foreign and regional investment are directed towards these sectors and areas.

As has been noted through this analysis, the process conducted under ECOWAS has allowed us to further emphasise the unsuitability of a model of regionalism based solely on market-led economic integration in the African context. In particular, despite the fact that it has established fairly developed regulatory and institutional frameworks aimed at promoting deeper integration and regional development ECOWAS's progress has been relatively slow, this section was used to reject the claim that legal frameworks provided under regional schemes should be designed primarily to promote freer trade and deeper economic integration. This analysis was therefore used to highlight the need for a model of regionalism that is more appropriate to address the recurring issue of industrialisation and economic transformation shared by the majority of African countries. Following on from this observation, the following section is dedicated to the East African Community (EAC) which has provided for a comprehensive approach to regionalism, which has managed to advance both economic integration and capacity-building in East Africa.

IV. Comprehensive Regionalism Under the EAC

The EAC constitutes an interesting case study among the African RECs, given the relative fast pace in which it has progressed and managed to achieve most of its goals.[130] More importantly, the EAC provides a practical example of a model of regionalism based on regional developmentalism, given the greater emphasis placed on regional development and state interventionism aimed at creating comparative advantage and supporting regional capacity-building. Moreover, and similar to the process conducted under ASEAN, EAC has adopted a dirigiste approach to regionalism in which regional markets and economic integration efforts are considered as a component of the participating countries' overall development strategy and are used to serve the particular needs of the region.

For this purpose, this section highlights the different attempts towards regionalism undertaken by the East African countries which initially followed a model similar to the one under ECOWAS before switching to a model based on regional developmentalism.

The inception of the first EAC dates back to the end of the nineteenth century and the beginning of the twentieth century, with the introduction of various regional major projects including the construction of a Kenya—Uganda railway in 1897, the establishment of a Customs Collection Centre in 1900 and a Postal Union in 1905.[131] The original efforts towards regional economic integration in the region were initiated with the creation of a Customs Union between Kenya and Uganda in 1917; the then Tanganyika joining them in

1927.[132] This Customs Union constituted a fairly advanced form of regional economic integration and included measures for the adoption of a common external tariff, the promotion of free trade among the Member States of the Customs Union, the free movement of labour and capital as well as the establishment of a common institution for the collection of import duties.[133] As noted in previous chapters, these measures were aimed at advancing colonial mercantilist interests in the region through the efficient production of resources to be exported to markets located in European metropoles.[134]

These initial initiatives towards economic integration in the region eventually led to the signing of the Treaty for East African Co-operation in Kampala, Uganda on 6 June 1967, Treaty which established the first EAC.[135]

IV.1. Initial Efforts Based on Regional Economic Integration

The establishment of the first EAC was based not only on the early economic integration efforts in the region but also on a common history which was characterised by underdevelopment in the region and a long period of colonial exploitation.[136] The Community was therefore established to address these issues, with the ultimate goal of "strengthen[ing] and regulat[ing] the industrial, commercial and other relations of the Partner States to the end that there [should] be accelerated, harmonious and balanced development and sustained expansion of economic activities the benefits whereof [should] be equitably shared".[137] For this purpose, and similar to ECOWAS, which was established eight years later, the strategy chosen was trade-liberalisation and the strengthening of economic integration in the region, which included the gradual establishment of a Common Market and ultimately an Economic Union among the Partner States.[138]

To help the Partners States coordinate their co-operation, the Treaty provided for the establishment of an institutional framework which, although it was most similar to the original institutional under ECOWAS, provided for additional institutions with different roles.[139] In addition to the East African Authority (the equivalent of the original ECOWAS Authority),[140] the three East African Ministers (equivalent to the original ECOWAS Council) appointed to assist the Authority[141] and the Central Secretariat (similar to the ECOWAS Secretariat),[142] several councils were also established to work on and develop specific areas of economic integration.[143] The Treaty also provided for the establishment of an East African Legislative Assembly, composed of the East African Ministers as well as other members appointed by the Authority and responsible for the elaboration of the Acts of the Community.[144]

Alongside these institutions three judicial and quasi-judicial institutions were also established to be in charge of the enforcement of the law within the Community. A Common Market Council (CMC) was to be created to "ensure the functioning and development of [a] Common Market in accordance with the Treaty and to [keep a review of its operations] and to settle problems arising from the implementation of the Treaty concerning the Common Market

[. . .]".[145] The CMC could also receive and consider any references related to a breach of any obligations under the Treaty. To this effect, the CMC had the power to issue binding Directives to any Partner States which would fail to fulfil its obligations under the Treaty. Two other judicial institutions, the Common Market Tribunal—which had the responsibility to ensure the observance of the law in the interpretation and application of the Treaty;[146] and the Court of Appeals for East Africa (CAEA)—which had jurisdiction to "hear and determine such appeals from the courts of each Partner State [. . .]",[147] were also established to promote judicial integration within the Community.

Despite its apparently well-designed organisation, which constituted a significant improvement compared to the institutional frameworks provided under SADC and ECOWAS, the institutional arrangement provided by the 1967 EAC Treaty was not effective, as most institutions, apart from the Authority, did not have the adequate authority to effectively coordinate the Community.[148]

The Treaty provided for the implementation of its provisions through Community Acts in the form of Bills passed by the Assembly.[149] These Acts should have the approval of the Authority before producing any effect. However, no provision determined the binding force of the Community Acts. Next to Community Acts, the Authority could also issue directions to the Councils or to the East African Ministers. These directions were only binding on the Community institutions.[150]

IV.1.1. Collapse of the Community

The establishment of the EAC brought with it a set of issues specific to regional integration, including the equitable sharing of benefits among the Partner States, regional governance and competition, strong divergences of opinion among the Partner States' leaders and the lack of popular participation.[151] The situation was further exacerbated by the limitations of the Community's institutional framework and the lack of an adequate approach to regionalism would be adapted to the particular needs of the region, and managed to cause the collapse of the first EAC.

However, with a view to identifying the shortcomings of the original Community, a negotiation process was launched by the three participating countries in order to revive cooperation between them.[152] Several initiatives were conducted for this purpose and eventually led to the adoption of the Treaty establishing a new EAC in 1999 in Arusha, Tanzania.

IV.2. The Move to Regional Developmentalism Through Law Under the 1999 EAC Treaty

The new EAC Treaty, whose essence is based on fundamental principles that all participating countries are supposed to follow, provides the new Community with a new approach to regionalism which is intended to promote a comprehensive regional development.[153] The objective of the new Treaty, therefore, places a greater emphasis on the development of policies and programmes aimed at deepening cooperation among the Partner States[154] in political, economic, social, cultural and other matters for their mutual benefit.[155] To achieve this objective, the Treaty has provided for the establishment Partner States of a Customs Union, a Common Market, a Monetary Union and, ultimately, a Political Federation, a strategy which is intended to help the Partner States promote regional development and expand their economic activities.[156] For this purpose, the Treaty provides for the adoption of various measures and the coordination of their policies "to the extent necessary to achieve the objectives of the Community".[157]

In addition, the Treaty also provides a set of operational principles, which are aimed at addressing the issues which hampered the smooth functioning of the previous Community.[158]

Moreover, several provisions were introduced in the Treaty to address the major issues which caused the collapse of EAC 1, including article 3 (b), which addresses the balanced, harmonious and equitable development of all Partner States, and article 8, which provides for more reliance on the Community institution in order to achieve the objectives of the Treaty. The Treaty also brings changes to both the Community institutional and regulatory frameworks which will be analysed in the following sections.

IV.2.1. Improved Regulatory Framework

Departing from the previous regime under the first EAC, which had only provided for the Bills of the EALA and the directions of the Authority's as the Community law, the new Treaty provides for a sophisticated and well-designed regulatory framework aimed at facilitating the governance of the Community. For this purpose, the Treaty provides for the Bills passed by the East African Legislative Assembly (EALA) and the Regulations, Directives, Decisions and Recommendations issued by the Council.[159] The Regulations, Directives and Decisions enacted by the Council are binding on the Partner States and Community institutions other than the Summit, the EALA and the EACJ.[160] The Treaty merely provides for the binding force of the Regulations, Directives and Decisions, but it is silent on the effect of the same instruments in the Partner States' legal systems.

This also applies to the Bills enacted by the EALA of which the Treaty only provides that they require the Summit's assent to be valid but does not specifically provide for their binding effect or their effect in national legal systems.[161] Alongside to the Acts of the Community, the Summit has also adopted various Protocols to establish the EAC Customs Union, Common Market and Monetary Union.[162] In contrast with ECOWAS, in the context of the EAC, Protocols have been used only to allow the integration process to proceed to its next level instead of implementing various Treaty provisions.

IV.2.1.1. HARMONISATION OF NATIONAL ECONOMIC POLICIES

The EAC Treaty also provides for the harmonisation of the policies and strategies relating to the development of the Community.[163] Harmonisation is considered here as the approximation of Partner States' national law to create an enabling environment for economic integration and the progress of the Community. The harmonisation process is conducted by the Secretariat, assisted in this matter by the Co-ordination Committee.[164] To this effect, the Secretariat commissioned a study in 2010 in order to identify commercial laws in the Partner States which needed to be harmonised. Various areas were identified as priorities in the context of the EAC, including banking laws, laws governing transactions, finance and fiscal legislation, investment laws, laws relating to trade, etc.[165] This strategy is more appropriate and less onerous for the Partner States, contrary to the process carried out by OHADA, which is based on the unification of business laws in all its Member States. In addition to the work of the Secretariat, a Sectoral Council on Legal and Judicial affairs was also set up to ensure that the Community Acts adopted by the EALA are conformed to the Treaty and that national laws are harmonised in accordance with the Treaty.[166] This arrangement, however, creates confusion, as it is not clear whether the Secretariat or the Council are in charge of harmonisation within the Community.

Further harmonisation efforts were required from the Partner States with the adoption of the Protocol on the Establishment of the EAC Common Market.[167] The Protocol provides for harmonisation in various domains, including laws and legal systems in general, tax policies, social policies, academic and professional qualifications and labour policies.[168] The approximation of laws and policies in these areas are expected to guarantee the free movement of goods, persons, labour, services and the right of establishment and residence.[169] Mutual recognition is another means for harmonisation provided for in the Common Market Protocol, however, limited to academic and professional qualifications.[170] Similar to the situation in the European Economic Community, through mutual recognition Partner States give free access to their territory to goods or persons who meet a certain standard.[171]

IV.2.2. Regional Development Policies

To address the particular economic issues faced by countries in the region, the Treaty has also provided for specific instruments which are aimed at promoting the region's industrial development by creating linkages among industries "through diversification, specialisation and complementarity . . . [and] the development of small-and-medium scale industries".[172] Through these measures, which represent the interventionist aspect of the process conducted under EAC, states are expected to create a dynamic comparative advantage through economic transformation and product diversification. It is in this context that the Partner States adopted a Model Investment Code in 2006 and as well as the EAC Industrialisation Policy 2012–2032.

Similar to the ASEAN Comprehensive Investment Agreement, the EAC Investment Code provides for measures intended to regulate and direct foreign direct investment in the region, including through the establishment of national investment promotion agencies, and the creation of special economic zones targeting specific areas and industries.[173] In addition, the Investment Code provides for investment disputes to be resolved in accordance with national laws and procedures or international arbitration if provided accordingly.[174]

The Industrialisation Policy, on the other hand, provides for various legal rules particularly aimed at promoting the development of regional value chains, strengthening national and regional industrial capabilities, enhancing the region's competitiveness and developing supporting infrastructure along selected economic corridors.[175] The EAC Secretariat is responsible for coordinating the implementation of the Industrialisation Policy, in collaboration with the Partner States (through assigned ministers) and the Private Sector.[176] Several programmes and projects have been initiated in this context, including several transportation corridors linking various cities in the region,[177] and the identification of strategic sectors in which the region has a potential comparative advantage, including agro-processing, iron-ore and other mineral processing, and fertilisers and agrochemicals.[178] Through the Investment Code and the Industrialisation Policy, the EAC Treaty has therefore provided the Partner States with key legal instruments allowing them to use the regional process both to promote economic integration while also enhancing their production capacity.

To implement these various policies and measures, the Treaty has provided for an improved institutional framework, which is composed of both intergovernmental and supranational organs.

IV.2.3. Establishment of a Hybrid Institutional Framework

The Treaty provides a new configuration of the Community institutions, with more autonomy and decision-making power being granted to most institutions (especially the Council, the Secretariat and the Court), which is a significant progress compared to the previous EAC where most institutions only served to assist the Authority in its task. The powers of several institutions, including the Council of Ministers and the Secretariat, are increased with a view to ensuring that the good functioning of the Community is not disrupted by tensions which might arise among the Partner States and which could potentially cause the stagnation of the regional process. A similar institutional arrangement was provided in the context of the European Community where key Community supranational institutions, including the Commission and the Court of Justice, have played a crucial role to support the effective establishment of a Common Market in Europe.

The East African Authority has been renamed the Summit and remains responsible for 'giv[ing] general directions and impetus as to the development and achievement of the objectives of the Community'.[179] The East African Ministers are replaced by the Council of Ministers (the Council), composed of the ministers in charge of regional cooperation of each Partner State.[180] The Council is the policy organ of the Community and ensures the good functioning and development of the Community in accordance with the Treaty.[181]

The East African Legislative assembly remains the legislative organ of the Community[182] and, to reflect the people-centred character of the new Treaty, shall liaise with the national assemblies in the Partner States on matters related to the Community, to create more awareness of Community matters at a national level.[183] The Secretariat, consisting of the Secretary-General and Deputy Secretaries, is reinforced and becomes the executive organ of the Community. It intervenes in the policy-making process and is responsible for initiating, receiving and submitting recommendations to the Council and forwarding Bills to the EALA.[184]

Other institutions are also established to support the work of the main institutions. The Co-ordination Committee, which consists of the Permanent Secretaries responsible for regional co-operation in each Partner State, is responsible *inter alia* for submitting from time to time reports and recommendations to the Council concerning the achievement of the objectives of the Treaty.[185] The Sectoral Committees, which work under the control of the Council, assist the Council in the elaboration of implementation programmes with respect to their respective sectors.[186]

Next to these institutions which have been established to work towards the implementation of the Treaty by issuing legal instruments aimed at creating an "enabling environment" for the integration process in the region, a judicial institution, the East African Court of Justice (EAJC), was also created to ensure the uniform application and interpretation as well as compliance with these legal instruments.[187]

IV.2.4. The East African Court of Justice

The EACJ constitutes one of the key drivers of the regional process under EAC, given the active role that it has played since its establishment as the judicial organ of the Community.[188] Through legal activism and key decisions, the Court has been particularly active with a view to supporting the achievement of the objectives of the Community.

The Court consists, after amendment in 2006, of a First Instance Division and an Appellate Division.[189] It is responsible for ensuring the adherence to law in the interpretation and the application of and compliance with the Treaty.[190] The Court is guided in this role by the fundamental principles and the operational principles provided in the Treaty.[191] It is also responsible for the adjudication process in case of a breach of Community law by a Partner State or a Community institution. This procedure is initiated by the Partner

States;[192] it can also be initiated by the Secretariat, after consultations with the concerned Partner State and the Council.[193]

Similar to the ECJ under the European Community, the Court is also competent for adjudicating cases concerning the legality of Community law or any action of a Partner State or a Community institution on the ground that it is an infringement of the provisions of the Treaty as well as disputes between the Community and its employees.[194]

IV.2.4.1. NATIONAL COURTS' INVOLVEMENT AND PRELIMINARY REFERENCE PROCEDURE

To ensure the application of Community law at the national level, article 33 of the Treaty has provided for the jurisdiction of the Partner States' national courts over Community matters. Moreover, article 34 of the Treaty has provided for a preliminary reference procedure similar to that of the ECJ, which is supposed to help the EACJ in its task to ensure the uniform application of Community law in all Partner States.[195]

These provisions prove to be very important, as they provide national courts with jurisdiction over Community matters and also establish a direct link between national courts and the EACJ. Under this procedure, the EACJ is expected to provide national courts with guidance on the interpretation of Community law, whereas national courts retain the authority to decide on the substance of the concerned cases.[196] This special feature, which differs from the top-down approach followed by the OHADA process, is supposed to improve the EACJ's visibility in the Partner States' legal systems, and in turn to support the harmonisation process by enabling national judges in the various Partner States to apply Community law uniformly.[197]

IV.2.4.2. LEGAL INTEGRATION THROUGH CASE LAW

This section is dedicated to the legal integration process conducted under the EACJ and focuses more particularly on key cases that have been used to address several issues arising in the context of regionalism as well as to advance the efforts towards regionalism. A particular emphasis is placed on the approach adopted by the EACJ towards the various challenges both to the integration process and to its own jurisdiction, as well as the contribution made by entities from the regional and national civil societies.

IV.2.4.2.1. Anyang' Nyongo and Others v Attorney General of the Republic of Kenya and Others This first case tackles the issue of the application of Community law in national legal systems. It was based on a suit filed by Prof Anyang' Nyong'o who was contesting the election of nine Kenyan parliamentarians to the EALA on the grounds that the Kenyan rules used to elect them were in breach of the EAC Treaty.[198]In response the opposition and pressure exercised by Kenya, which considered that the Court did not have jurisdiction to adjudicate on the validity of Kenyan national law, the Court rendered what can be seen as a milestone decision in the region and considered that the Kenyan rules were in breach of article 50 of the Treaty. For this purpose, the Court used a rationale which was particularly aimed at advancing the EAC regional process:

> When the Partner States entered into the treaty, they embarked on the proverbial journal of thousands of miles which of necessity starts with one step. To reach the desired destination they have to ensure that every subsequent step is directed towards that destination and not backwards or away from that destination. There are bound to be hurdles on the way. One such hurdle is balancing individual state sovereignty with integration. While the Treaty upholds the principle of sovereign equality, it must be acknowledged that by the very nature of the objectives they set out to achieve, each Partner State is expected to cede some amount of sovereignty to the Community and its organs in limited areas to enable them to play their role.[199]

The Court's decision resulted in a negative reaction by the Partner States who, in retaliation, decided to amend the Treaty with a view to create an Appellate Division within the Court, as well as extending the grounds for the removal of the judges of the EACJ, two decisions which were intended to limit the independence and autonomy of the Judiciary in the region.[200] However, despite this reaction by the Partner States' Heads of States and Government, the Court stood its ground and considered in subsequent judgments that the Treaty amendments conducted by the Partner States in response to their initial decision ran the risk of undermining the "overall supremacy of the Court over the interpretation and application of the [EAC] Treaty".[201] This case proves to be significant in the context of legal integration in the region, as it reflected the desire for the EACJ to use the purposive approach when deciding on Community matters and to work towards the establishment of a specific legal order for the region.[202]

IV.2.4.2.2. East African Law Society and Others v Attorney General of Kenya and Others[203] Moreover, in the aftermath of the Anyang case and the different Treaty amendments that resulted from it, a reference was made by the East African Law Society and other national civil society groups before the Court to challenge the amendments of the Treaty. Here again, the Court adopted the same purposive approach to the case and considered in its judgment that part of the Treaty amendments which resulted from the Anyang' case constituted an infringement of article 38 (2) of the EAC Treaty, which could potentially affect the judicial integrity and the judicial independence of the Court.[204] Basing part of their reasoning on article 31 of the Vienna Convention, the Court's judges considered that they '[had] to interpret the terms of the Treaty not only in accordance with their ordinary meaning but also in their context and in light of their objectives and purpose'.[205]

This case proves particularly important, as it serves to confirm the tendency of the Court to direct its decisions towards the advancement of the EAC regional process. This highlights the crucial role played by an autonomous regional court in ensuring the application and effective implementation of regional law by both participating countries and other Community institutions. In addition, this also highlights the key contribution made by national law societies to promote the work of the Court. This case, therefore, constitutes a practical example of national and regional civil societies' intervention to ensure the proper application and enforcement of the Treaty as well as to promote the integration process.[206]

IV.2.4.2.3. James Katabazi v Secretary General of the EAC[207] Similar to Afolabi case before the ECOWAS Court, this case involved the violation of human rights and proves to be important as it provides an example of the Court's approach towards human rights issues. The file involved James Katabazi, a Ugandan national who filed a suit to the EACJ against the Ugandan government and the EAC, arguing that by holding him and his inmates into custody despite a decision by the Ugandan High Court to grant them bail was a violation of the rule of law and therefore of the EAC Treaty. In its decision the Court considered its role provided in article 23 of the EAC Treaty "the Court shall be a judicial body which shall ensure the adherence to law in the interpretation and application and compliance with this Treaty" and, considering law broadly as to include the rule of law, granted the applicant's request on the grounds that the rule of law was listed as one of the EAC's fundamental principles.[208]

This decision by the Court to adjudicate on a case involving the violation of human rights and not directly related to regional integration could have suggested that, like the ECOWAS Court, the EACJ ran the risk to be distracted from its primary mission of supporting the integration process and to turn itself into a human rights court instead. However, given the fact that the Court decided more economic cases in subsequent years, this attitude could rather be understood to reflect the Court's desire to advance the overall regional process by adapting its action to the particular needs of the region which, in this case, included the promotion of human and people's rights.[209] This attitude of the Court reflects the holistic approach to regional development adopted through the EAC Treaty which, beyond trade liberalisation and economic integration, also includes political and social issues. This trend can also be verified in a more recent case, *Ololosokwan Village and 3 others v The Attorney General of the United Republic of Tanzania*,[210] in which the Court reasserted the right for

> any person who is resident in a Partner State [to refer] for determination by the Court, the legality of any Act, regulation, Directive, decision

or action of a Partner State or an institution of the Community on the ground that such Act, regulation, directive, decision or action is unlawful or is an infringement of the provisions of the Treaty.[211]

IV.2.4.2.4. British American Tobacco Uganda Limited v Government of Uganda[212] On 25 January 2018, an interim injunction was granted by the EACJ First Division, preventing the Government of Uganda (and the Uganda Revenue Authority) from collecting excise duty on British American Tobacco Uganda Limited (BAT Uganda Limited) due to the fact that it could turn out to constitute a discriminatory act.

In 2014, Uganda adopted the Excise Duty Act No.11 of 2014 which was aimed at introducing an excise duty on cigarettes applicable uniformly to all such goods in all EAC Member States. In 2017, the Act was amended to make a distinction between locally manufactured goods and imported goods, thereby introducing a discrimination between goods considered as *locally* manufactured and goods from the other Member States. BAT Uganda Limited, therefore, filed a case to the EACJ, challenging the legality of the 2017 amendment, arguing that it violates provisions of the EAC Treaty as well as those of the Customs Union and the Common Market Protocols.[213]

The Court, therefore, granted the interim injunction with a view to, pending the determination of the reference by BAT Uganda Limited, preventing the Uganda Revenue Authority from levying an excise duty that could turn out to be exorbitant and in breach of Community law. This case showcases the concern for the Court to play an active role in ensuring the scrupulous application of Community law and, thereby, the achievement of the EAC objectives.

V. Conclusion

The analysis conducted in this chapter has proved important as it served to identify certain patterns that characterise most regional integration processes in Africa. In particular, it allowed us to highlight the need for African RECs to adopt a legal framework that is particularly adapted to their specific needs and particular circumstances and the critical need for the adoption of suitable legal instruments that can serve both as a foundation upon which regional schemes can be built, but also as tools that can provide the impetus necessary to achieve regional objectives and promote regional development.

This study of the evolution and transformation of SADC, ECOWAS and the EAC helped to identify the key issues arising in the context of regionalism in Africa and to highlight the particular role that law could play to address them. These issues can be classified into two main categories, including the adoption of appropriate regional development strategies and the effective coordination of the regional process and of the participating countries' collective actions through both regulatory and institutional frameworks.

On the one hand, concerning the regulatory framework, the analysis placed a strong emphasis on the need for the establishment of an efficient and well-organised regulatory framework to ensure the effective implementation of Treaty provisions. In particular, the chapter was used to emphasise the importance of the binding effect of regional regulatory frameworks, which is likely to guarantee the implementation of regional policies. The case of SADC and ECOWAS's early years were therefore used to highlight the disadvantages and the detrimental effect that an inadequate regulatory framework can have on the progression of regional processes.

On the other hand, regarding the institutional framework, it was pointed out that the mere existence of a highly intergovernmental structure ran the risk of being ineffective in the absence of a country economically and politically strong enough to provide the impetus necessary to further integration efforts in the region. This issue was evidenced in the context of the three RECs which all experienced significant difficulties in their early years in the coordination of their collective actions and the implementation of regional policies. The chapter argued that the adoption of a set of supranational institutions, including the ECOWAS Commission and the EAC Secretariat which had increased autonomy and decision-making powers, allowed the two Communities to operate more efficiently and to monitor the advancement of their respective regional processes.

The chapter also highlighted the crucial role played by regional judicial institutions to ensure the effective implementation of regional policies and their uniform application in all participating countries. While the SADC Tribunal did not provide for a well-functioning regional jurisdiction, given its suspension in 2010, the study of the work of both ECOWAS and EAC Courts allowed us to note their respective evolutions, with the ECOWAS Court turning into a human rights court and the EAC Court adopting a purposive approach to the cases brought before it. This was demonstrated the ability of the EAC Court of Justice to play a key role in the EAC integration process and to serve as a driving force of its regional process. This analysis also highlighted the potential key role played by both national courts and private litigants in pushing the integration processes forward by taking advantage of the judicial framework provided for by the Treaties. Here the analysis focused more closely on national and regional civil societies and the key role that they could play in securing Treaty amendments (ECOWAS) or opposing any actions by the Member States which could endanger the implementation of the Treaties (EAC).

In addition, and equally important, the study of the process conducted under the EAC highlighted the fact that beyond adequate regulatory and institutional frameworks, there is also a need for the African RECs to adopt an appropriate development strategy based on key legal instruments such as regional industrial and investment policies directed towards regional capacity-building and the enhancement of the participating countries' production diversification. These key instruments were presented as specially designed to address the structural problems faced by a majority of African economies and to enhance production capacity through cooperation in key activities and sectors and regional capacity-building.

Lastly, even though it was not included in the analysis conducted in the chapter, the rules-based coordination mechanism provided under the North American Trade Agreement could prove particularly suitable for the new Tripartite Free Trade Area which has just been launched between the EAC, SADC and the Common Market for Eastern and Southern Africa (COMESA),[214] given the fact that the new Free Trade Area to be established will be aimed, in its initial stage, at providing market access to all parties involved in the trade of goods and services in the region.

Notes

1. The different components of Integration through law are used as theoretical framework to develop the concept of regional developmentalism through law which considers the various aspects of the role that law could play to promote development in the context of the African RECs.
2. See UNECA (2012) *Assessing Regional Integration in Africa V: Towards an African Continental Free Trade Area*, Addis Ababa: UNECA, p. 17.
3. As discussed in Chapter 2, this approach, which was developed mainly by Jacob Viner and Bela Balassa, provides for increasingly advanced levels to be achieved for countries to achieve regional economic integration, including a Free Trade Area, a Customs Union, a Common Market and an Economic Union.
4. See article 3(b) of the Protocol on Relations Between the African Economic Community and the Regional Economic Communities which requires the RECs' processes to be in line with the objectives of the AEC, including the removal of barriers to trade and the establishment of a continental Common Market.
5. See Franck, T.M. (1964) *East African Unity Through Law*, New Haven; London: Yale University Press, p. 2.
6. Kaahwa, A. (2008) *Reforming Justice in East Africa: A Comparative Review of Legal Sector Processes*, Kampala: Fountain Publishers, p. 17.
7. UNECA (2013) *Assessing Regional Integration in Africa VI: Harmonizing Policies to Transform the Trading Environment*, Addis Ababa: UNECA, p. 12.
8. Ibid, p. 10.
9. Matambalya, F.A.S.T. (1995) *The Impact of Regionalisation Schemes on the Export and Economic Performance of Developing Countries: A Case Study of the Southern African Development Community (SADC)*, Frankfurt: Brandes & Apsel, p. 43. SADCC was established through a Memorandum of Understanding for Economic Development signed in Lusaka, Zambia on 01 April 1980 by nine Southern African states which included Angola, Botswana, Lesotho, Malawi, Mozambique, Swaziland, Tanzania, Zambia and Zimbabwe. Current membership also includes Namibia (which joined in 1990), South Africa (1994), Mauritius (1995) and the Seychelles and the Democratic Republic of Congo (1997).
10. See Afadameh-Adeyemi, A. and Kalula, E. (2011) 'SADC at 30: Re-examining the Legal and Institutional Anatomy of the Southern African Development Community' in *Monitoring Regional Integration in Southern Africa Yearbook* 2010, Stellenbosch: Trade Law Centre for Southern Africa, the Konrad-Adenauer-Stiftung, pp. 5–22.

11. See generally See Mtengeti-Migiro, R. (1992) *Institutional Arrangements for Economic Integration in Eastern and Southern Africa: A Study of SADCC and the PTA With Experiences From the EEC*, Konstanz: Hartung-Gore. See also Mvungi (1994) *Constitutional Questions in the Regional Integration Process: The Case of the Southern African Development Community With References to the European Community*, Freidrich Naumann Foundation Southern Africa Regional Office, p. 79.
12. Weggoro, N.C. (1995) *Effects of Regional Economic Integration in Southern Africa and the Role of the Republic of South Africa: A Study of Project Coordination Approach in Industry and Trade in SADCC/SADC*, Berlin: Köster, p. 78. See also Ofstad, A. et al. (1986) *SADCC Intra-Regional Trade Study*, Gaborone: SADCC.
13. See Hanlon, J. (1984) SADCC: Progress, Projects and Prospects. The Trade and Investment Future of the Southern African Development Co-ordination Conference, EUI—The Economist Intelligence Unit, Special Report No.182.
14. See Matambalya (1995), p. 39.
15. See SADCC Industry and Trade Coordination Division (1986) 'SADCC Industry and Trade Development Activities (prepared for Regional Investment Promotion Meeting for SADCC Countries, Harare 3–7 November 1986), Dar-Es-Salaam'. Similar concerns were expressed in the case of Mexico within the North American Free Trade Agreement.
16. See Ortergaard, T. (1989) *SADCC, Beyond Transportation: The Challenge of Industrial Co-operation*, Uppsala: CDR Publications No.8.
17. See generally Herbst, J. (1990) "War and the State in Africa", 14 *International Security*, pp. 126–127. See also Tsie, B. (1996) "States and Markets in the Southern African Development Community (SADC): Beyond the Neo-Liberal Paradigm", 22 *Journal of Southern African Studies.*
18. Ibid. See also Langhammer, R.J. (1993) "The Developing Countries and Regionalism", 31 *Journal of Common Market Studies*, p. 218 and Sidaway, J. and Gibb, R. (1998) 'SADC, COMESA, SACU: Contradictory Formats for Regional Integration in Southern Africa' in Simon, D. (ed.) *Reconfiguring the Region: South Africa in Southern Africa*, London: James Currey, p. 179. The authors emphasise the importance of customs revenue for the participating countries' national elites who use them to entertain their respective patron-client networks. This argument refers to a similar argument developed in chapter two of this monograph which highlighted the critical role played by the African national elites in shaping various regional schemes which are often used to increase their credibility at the international level.
19. See Weggoro (1995), pp. 2 and 69.
20. See Mtengeti-Migiro (1992).
21. As will be noted in a subsequent section, decentralisation and intergovernmentalism were greater under SADCC that they were in the context of ECOWAS.
22. See, generally, Witulski, U. (1990) Macroeconomic Linkages Among Southern African Countries, Munich; London: Weltforum-Verl.
23. SADCC Memorandum of Understanding (hereinafter SADCC MOU), articles I and VI.
24. SADCC MOU, article I.
25. See Weggoro (1995), p. 68.
26. Ibid, p. xvi. The method was similar to the method adopted in the context of ASEAN, which was aimed at establishing a regional production base in the region and regulating regional value chains among participating countries.
27. Exports continued to be concentrated in low-priced primary commodities while imports constituted mainly in high-priced manufactured goods. In

addition, while the imports level from South Africa decreased, it remained fairly high compared to intra-regional trade.

28. See Sidaway, J. and Gibb, R. (1998) 'SADC, COMESA, SACU: Contradictory Formats for Regional Integration in Southern Africa' in Simon, D. (ed.) *Reconfiguring the Region: South Africa in Southern Africa*, London: James Currey, p. 179. As noted in the context of ASEAN, the advancement of national interests and the use of the state to promote countries' economic development were key factors in the economic success of most ASEAN Member States.
29. See Matambalya (1995), p. 36.
30. This switch was evidenced in article 5(2) of the SADC Treaty which provided for "[the development] of policies aimed at the progressive elimination of obstacles to the free movement of capital and labour, goods and services, and of the people of the region generally, among the Member States".
31. See article 2 of the SADC Trade Protocol.
32. See SADC RISDP, p. 7. See also Kalaba, M., Willcox, O., Fundira, T., Williams, B. and Alves, P. (2006) *Deepening Integration in SADC: South Africa—SADC's Economic Engine*, Gaborone: Friedrich Ebert Foundation, p. 21.
33. See, generally, Gaolathe, B. (2002) 'Reducing Poverty in the SADC Region through Collective Action—the Role of Governments' Paper presented at the 2002 SADC Consultative Conference, Gaborone, cited in Kalaba et al. (2006). See also Chingono, M. and Nakana, S. (2009) 'The Challenge of Regional Integration in Southern Africa' 3 *African Journal of Political Science and International Relations* 396, p. 397.
34. See Gaolathe (2002).
35. This assumption can be found in SADC RISDP, p. 64 which reads, "Global trends and developments indicate that those nations or groups of countries that are successfully implementing trade and economic liberalization policies are experiencing high economic growth and an improvement in the quality of life of their peoples. Given the changing global environment, the creation of large markets has become synonymous with increased foreign investment and economic growth as investors search for economies of scale and efficiency gains in the production process".
36. This industrial policy is provided in the SADC Industrialisation Strategy and Roadmap 2015–2063, which was approved by the SADC Summit on 29 April 2015.
37. See Jourdan, P. (1998) 'Spatial Development Initiatives (SDIs)—the Official View" 15(5) *Development Southern Africa*, p. 20 and Soderbaum, F. (2004) 'Modes of Regional Governance in Africa: Neoliberalism, Sovereignty Boosting, and Shadow Networks' 10(4) *Global Governance* 419, p. 424.
38. See SADC Trade and Investment Protocol, articles 1 and 2.
39. This is the case under the Framework on the ASEAN Investment Area and the ASEAN Comprehensive Investment Agreement, which provided for specific sectors in which investment could be directed, as well as the EAC Model Investment Code, which has provided for the establishment of Special Economic Zones aimed at encouraging investment in specific areas.
40. As noted in the World Trade Organization Regional Agreements Gateway, the SADC Free Trade Area was notified to the World Trade Organization in 2004 under GATT Article XXIV. See www.wto.org/english/tratop_e/region_e/region_e.htm [30 September 2015]
41. These measures were aimed at improving the implementation of the various policies and legal instruments adopted by the participating countries, an evolution compared to the SADCC MOU, which did not constitute a binding instrument.

42. These institutions are provided in article 9 of the consolidated version of the SADC Treaty.
43. Ibid.
44. SADC Treaty, article 14.
45. SADC Treaty, article 16A.
46. SADC Treaty, article 16. Similar to the ECOWAS Court of Justice, the SADC Tribunal was expected to support the advancement of the integration process by emulating the ECJ and thereby ensuring the effective application of Community law. This mechanism was expected to address the issue of lack of implementation of regional policies, which constituted one of the major obstacles faced by SADCC.
47. See, for example, cases on employment rights: Kanyama v. SADC Secretariat (SADC (t) 05/2009), (2010) SADCT 1 (29 Jan.2010); Mondlane v. SADC Secretariat (SADC (T) 07/2009) (2010) SADCT 3 (5 Feb. 2010); cases on Human Rights: Mike Campbell (Pvt) Ltd and Others v. Republic of Zimbabwe (2/2007) [2008] SADCT 2 (28 Nov.2008); Tembani v. Republic of Zimbabwe (SADC (T) 07/2008) [2009] SADCT 3 (14 Aug. 2009). Cases cited in Osiemo, O. (2014) 'Lost in Translation: The Role of African Regional Courts in Regional Integration in Africa' 1 *Legal Issues of Economic Integration* 87, p. 100.
48. This observation was made in Osiemo (2014), p. 100.
49. Mike Campbell (Pvt) Ltd and Others v. Republic of Zimbabwe (2/2007) [2008] SADCT 2 (28 Nov.2008)
50. These facts are provided in the judgment rendered by the Tribunal.
51. These articles provide that "SADC and its Member States shall act in accordance with [various] principles, including human rights, democracy and the rule of law" and that "SADC and its Member States shall not discriminate against any person on grounds of gender, religion, political views, race, ethnic origin, culture, ill health, disability, or such other grounds as may be determined by the Summit".
52. This referral was based on article 32(5) of the SADC Tribunal Protocol, which provides that "if the Tribunal establishes the existence of [the failure by a Member State to comply with its decision], it shall report its findings to the Summit for the latter to take appropriate action".
53. See Du Plessis, M. and Malebakeng, F. (2010) 'Enforcing the SADC Tribunal's Decisions in South Africa: Immunity: South African Judicial Decisions' 35 *South African Yearbook of International Law*, pp. 265–269 and Hemel, D. and Schalkwyk, A. (2010) 'Tyranny on Trial: Regional Courts Crack Down on Mugabe's Land 'Reform' *The Yale Journal of International Law*, pp. 517–523. See also Osiemo (2014), p. 110.
54. As analysed in the context of the European Community, both popular participation and community law enforcement are considered as key components of the mechanism through which law can be used to advance regional processes.
55. Several other RECs have also chosen to follow the same model of regionalism and are therefore faced with similar issues to those that are identified in the context of ECOWAS. These RECs includes the Arab Maghreb Union (UMA), the Community of Sahel-Saharan States (CEN-SAD), the Intergovernmental Authority on Development (IGAD), the Economic Community of Central African States (ECCAS) and the Common Market for Eastern and Southern Africa (COMESA).
56. See Jebuni, C.D., Ogunkola, E.O. and Soludo, C.C. (1999) 'A Case-Study of the Economic Community of West African States (ECOWAS)' in Oyejide, A., Elbadawi, I. and Yeo, S. (eds) *Regional Integration and Trade Liberalization in*

Subsaharan Africa, Vol. 3: Regional Case-Studies, Basingstoke: Palgrave Macmillan, p. 24. Original members included Benin, Burkina Faso, Cote d'Ivoire, Gambia, Ghana, Guinea, Guinea-Bissau, Liberia, Mali, Mauritania, Niger, Nigeria, Senegal, Sierra Leone and Togo. Cape Verde joined the Community in 1977, while Mauritania withdrew its membership in December 2000.

57. As discussed in previous chapters, upon their independence, the majority of African countries inherited truncated economies and weak political structures which significantly limited their ability to address the multiple economic challenges that they faced. It is against such a backdrop that regionalism was proposed as a strategy and expected to support these countries' national efforts. Further details on this particular issue are provided in See Jones, C.A. (1983) *The North-South Dialogue: A Brief History*, London: Frances Pinter, pp. 1–15 and Holland, R.F. (1985) *European Decolonization 1918–1981: An Introductory Survey*, Basingstoke; London: Palgrave Macmillan, p. 112.
58. See preamble of the 1975 ECOWAS Treaty, which provides that the Treaty was signed to express the desire to "accelerate, foster and encourage the economic and social development of their states in order to improve the living standards of their people".
59. Ibid. This particular provision mirrored the approach adopted in article II (1) (b) of the Charter of the Organisation of African Unity.
60. See Mahiou, A. (1993) La Communauté Economique Africaine, 39(1) *Annuaire français de Droit International*, p. 799.
61. On the common assumption that trade liberalisation and common markets can be used to attract foreign investment and foster development, see Alter, K.J., Helfer, L.R. and McAllister, J.R. (2013) 'A New International Human Rights Court for West Africa: The ECOWAS Community Court of Justice' 107 *American Journal of International Law* 737, p. 741.
62. These areas are listed under the "aims of the Community" provided in article 2 of the 1975 ECOWAS Treaty.
63. On the external dependence of the majority of countries, especially on France and the United Kingdom, see Mytelka, L. (1977) 'The Lome Convention and a New International Division of Labour' *Journal of European Integration*, I, p. 72 and Asante, S.K.B. (1984) 'ECOWAS, the EEC and the Lome Convention' in Mazzeo, D. (ed.) *African Regional Organizations*, Cambridge: Cambridge University Press, p. 187. See also Burfisher, M.E. and Missiaen, M.B. (1990) 'Intraregional Trade in West Africa' in Okolo, J.E. and Wright, S. (eds) *West African Regional Cooperation and Development*, Boulder; Oxford: Westview Press. Here the authors point out that the key trading partners for West African countries are located outside the region.
64. See Asante (1984), p. 172.
65. See 1975 ECOWAS Treaty, articles 5 to 9. A similar intergovernmental institutional framework has been provided by the other RECs. However, among these RECs, only COMESA has managed to establish several institutions that are functional, while a majority of other RECs have provided for regional institutions that are barely operational. In addition, while COMESA and UMA are the only RECs that have provided for the establishment of regional courts, the COMESA Court of Justice is the only one to be fully operational to date.
66. Id, article 11.
67. In the context of the EEC, Community institutions were equipped with greater power. While the Council was responsible for the coordination of the Member States' economic policies and was entrusted with legislative powers (EEC Treaty, article 145), the Commission was responsible for the effective implementation of Community policies (EEC Treaty article 137) and the

ECJ's role included the interpretation of Community law, review of the legality of the actions of the Member States and the other institutions as well as jurisdiction over cases brought by the Commission against any Member States which would fail to fulfil their obligations (EEC Treaty, articles 164 & 169).

68. As discussed in the context of MERCOSUR and the European Union, while this approach could prove adequate in the initial phase of the integration process, a more robust institutional framework in which increased powers are given to Community institutions is more likely to ensure the smooth progression of the regional process and an efficient coordination of collective action, thereby avoiding any stagnation in case of a lack of political will by the Member States.
69. The 1975 ECOWAS Treaty, article 5 (3) provided for the decisions and directions of the Authority whereas article 6 (3) provided for the ones by the Council.
70. Decision a./dec.8/5/79 of the authority of heads of state and government of ECOWAS relating to the consolidation of import duties and non-tariff barriers adopted in May 1979; Decision a/dec.18/5/80 of the authority of heads of state and government of ECOWAS relating to trade liberalisation in industrial products adopted in May 1980; and Decision c/dec.8/11/79 of the council of ministers on the trade liberalisation of unprocessed products.
71. Omogorobe, Y. (1992) 'The Legal Framework for Economic Integration in the ECOWAS Region: An analysis of the Trade Liberalisation Scheme' in Spring Communications (ed.) The Trade Liberalisation Scheme of the Economic Community of West African States (ECOWAS): Papers Presented at the 2nd National Seminar on TLS, p. 22.
72. 1975 ECOWAS Treaty, articles 5 (3) and 6 (3). Of all the other RECs (except for EAC, which will be analysed in the following section), only COMESA has provided that the Directives and Decisions of the COMESA Council of Ministers have binding effect on the Member States and all subordinate organs of the Community (see article 9 (3) of the COMESA Treaty). As discussed in the context of the European Community, the doctrine of direct effect, through which Community law became binding on the Member States, was necessary to ensure the effective implementation of Community law across the Community. However, this was unlikely to be the case under the 1975 ECOWAS Treaty, given that the Member States were not bound to apply Community law and the limited powers which were assigned to the ECOWAS Tribunal to ensure the application of the same Community law.
73. See Jebuni et al. (1999), p. 32.
74. The Protocol on Assessment of Loss of Revenue by Member States was adopted to implement the provisions of paragraph 2 of article 25 of the Treaty; the Protocol relating to the Fund for Co-operation, Compensation and Development of ECOWAS was adopted in accordance with articles 50 and 51 paragraph 3 of the Treaty; the Protocol relating to the Re-Exportation within ECOWAS of Goods imported from Third Countries was adopted to implemented article 22 of the Treaty; the Protocol relating to the Definition of the Concept of Products originating from ECOWAS Member States was adopted to implement paragraph 2 of article 15 of the Treaty. All three Protocols were signed on 5 November 1976.
75. This opinion is shared by Jebuni et al. (1999), p. 32 where authors highlight the fact that by 1989, 30 different Protocols had been negotiated by the ECOWAS Member States.
76. Protocol A/P.1/5/79 Relating to the Free Movement of Persons, Residence and Establishment.

77. Supplementary Protocol A/SP.1/7/85 on the Code of Conduct for the Implementation of the Protocol on Free Movement of Persons, the Right of Residence and Establishment; Supplementary Protocol A/SP/.1/86 on the Second Phase (Right of Residence) of the Protocol on Free Movement of Persons, the Right of Residence and Establishment; Supplementary Protocol A/SP/.2/5/90 on the Implementation of the Third Phase (Right of Establishment) of the Protocol on Free Movement of Persons, Right of Residence and Establishment.
78. See Adepoju, A., Boulton, A. and Levin, M. (2007) 'Promoting Integration Through Mobility: Free Movement and the ECOWAS Protocol' UNHCR Research Paper No.150, p. 1. These phases include Phase I, right of entry and abolition of visas; Phase II, right of residence; and Phase III, right of establishment.
79. 1975 ECOWAS Treaty, article 2 (g) provides for "the harmonisation of the economic and industrial policies of the Member States and the elimination of disparities in the level of development of the Member States".
80. Most of the ECOWAS Member States' legal systems are derived from the Common law and the Civil law families, systems which they received through colonisation by France, Portugal, Spain and the United Kingdom. On the diversity of legal systems in the region, see Ndulo, M. (1992) 'The Promotion of Intra-African Trade and The Harmonisation of Laws in the African Economic Community: Prospects and Problems' Conference of the African Economic Community Treaty, 27–30 January, Abuja, Nigeria, p. 4 and Ovrawah, O.A. (1994) 'Harmonisation of Laws within the Economic Community of West African States (ECOWAS)' 6 *Afr.J.Int'l & Comp. L.* 76, p. 82.
81. 1975 ECOWAS Treaty, article 30.
82. Ovrawah (1994), p. 83–84.
83. Alter et al. (2013), p. 741.
84. See Asante (1984), p. 179. This is likely to be the case for UMA, CEN-SAD, IGAD and ECCAS which, as of 2013, are yet to establish fully functioning Free Trade Areas.
85. Gambari, I.A. (1991) *Political and Comparative Dimensions of Regional Integration: The Case of ECOWAS*, New Jersey; London: Humanities Press, p. 18. See also Kufuor, K.O. (2006) *The Institutional Transformation of the Economic Community of West African States*, Aldershot: Ashgate, p. 22.
86. See Alter et al. (2013), p. 743.
87. The CEP was established by the Authority's Decision A/DEC 10/5/90 of 30 May 1990.
88. See Mutharika, B. (1972) Toward Multinational Economic Cooperation in Africa, New York; London: Praeger, p. 15. See also Asante (1984), p. 179. The author considers this aspect of most RECs in Africa as a political reality which needs to be taken into consideration when addressing development challenges at the regional level.
89. See Asante, S.K. (1986) *The Political Economy of Regionalism in Africa: A Decade of the Economic Community of West African States (ECOWAS)*, New York: Praeger, p. 70; See also Ladan, M.T. (2009) *Introduction to ECOWAS Community Law and Practice: Integration, Migration, Human Rights, Access to Justice, Peace and Security, Zaria, Kaduna*, Nigeria: Ahmadu Bello University Press, p. 7 and Kufuor (2006), p. 87. Kufuor particularly notes that "between 1978 and 1989, the Authority of the Community has adopted and signed a total of 21 protocols. [Up to 2006], only 1 [Protocol had] been ratified by all the sixteen [ECOWAS] Member States [and] only ten [had] been ratified by more than half of the ECOWAS membership".

90. See Kufuor (2006), pp. 29–32.
91. Article 3 (2) provides for clear stages supposed to lead the Community towards the establishment of a Common Market. Moreover, articles 35 and 54 provide for fixed deadlines for the establishment of a Customs Union (within ten years from 1 January 1990) and a Monetary Union five years after the customs union.
92. 1993 ECOWAS Treaty, articles 9 (4) and 12 (3). The instruments adopted by the Council were renamed "regulations" in order to distinguish them from the "decisions" made by the Authority.
93. Ibid. articles 9(2) and 12 (2).
94. In other terms, the 1993 Treaty did not provide for the direct effect and supremacy of Community law, as it is the case in the European Union.
95. 1993 ECOWAS Treaty, article 6.
96. This can be evidenced at article 20 (2) of the 1993 Treaty which provides that "Every Member State undertakes to respect the international character of the office of the Executive Secretary, the Deputy Executive Secretaries, and other staff of the Community and undertakes not to seek to influence them in the performance of their duties".
97. The Community Parliament was introduced in article 13 of the 1993 Treaty, but it was not until the adoption of various Protocols and Decisions (Protocol A/P/2/94 relating to the Community Parliament, Supplementary Protocol A/SP/.3/06/06 amending the previous Protocol, Decision A/DEC.6/01/06 relating to the Modalities for the Effective Implementation of Article 6 of Protocol A/P/2/94) that it was eventually established in 2006.
98. Protocol A/P/2/94 relating to the Community Parliament, article 6.
99. Protocol A/P/2/94 relating to the Community Parliament, article 6 (2). Whereas this article provides that the Parliament may be consulted in general on matters concerning the Community, its paragraph 2 provides that the Parliament shall be consulted on specific matters, including, *inter alia*, Treaty review, Community citizenship and public health policy for the Community.
100. 1993 ECOWAS Treaty, article 14.
101. See Lodge, J. and Herman, V. (1980) 'The Economic and Social Committee in EEC Decision-Making' 34(2) *International Organization*, p. 265. The authors develop in details the role of interest groups in the integration process.
102. The CCJ was initially established through Protocol A/P.I/7/91 in 1991 to replace the ECOWAS Tribunal and extend its jurisdiction.
103. Protocol A/P.I/7/91 relating to the Community Court of Justice (hereinafter CCJ Protocol), article 9 (1).
104. Ibid, article 9 (2).
105. This procedure, provided in article 9 (3) of the CCJ Protocol, is, however, subject to the failure of attempts to settle the dispute amicably.
106. CCJ Protocol, article 10.
107. See Ovrawah (1994), p. 86.
108. Kufuor, K.O. (1996) 'Securing Compliance with the Judgments of the ECOWAS Court of Justice' 8 *Afr. J. Int'l & Comp. L.* 1, p. 1.
109. See Kufuor (1996), p. 7. See also Kelly, J.P. (1987) 'The International Court of Justice: Crisis and Reformation' 12 (2) *The Yale Journal of International Law*, pp. 342–374 where the author develops the concept of non-compliance by countries with the decisions of international courts in general.
110. Case ECW/CCJ/JUD/01/04.
111. This includes the provisions of the 1993 Treaty at articles 3 (2) (d) (iii) which pertain to the obligation by the Community to remove any obstacles

to the free movement persons, goods, services and capital, which Afolabi labelled as human rights provided for at 4 (g) of the Treaty.

112. See Alter et al. (2013), p. 738. The authors consider the impact that the Court could have had if it had decided to grant access to private litigants. As examined in the context of the European Community, the ECJ used the Van Gend en Loos case to establish the binding effect of Community law and establish itself as protector of the Treaty. The Court's decision in Van Fend en Loos constituted one of the major milestones which allowed the Court to play a key role in the advancement of the European integration process.
113. See article 3 of Supplementary Protocol A/SP.1/01/05.
114. As discussed in the context of the European Community, for example, the doctrine of direct effect created by the ECJ opened the supervision of the application of Community law to individuals in addition to the Commission and the Member States, thereby establishing a system of "dual diligence" within the Community. The concept of dual diligence is discussed in Weatherill, S. (2007) *Cases and Materials on EU Law*, Oxford: Oxford University Press, p. 96
115. See Alter et al. (2013), p. 738. See also Oppong (2011), p. 126. Here the author deplores the fact that the majority of cases recently handled by the ECCJ are cases related to the violation of human rights and not concerning economic integration issues. A similar situation can be observed in the context of the COMESA Court of Justice where a majority of cases are based on employment disputes. See, for example, Kabeta Muleya (Dr) v. The common market for Eastern and Southern Africa and Erastus Mwencha [2003] COMESACJ 1 (4 Apr. 2003); Bilika Harry Simamba v. Common Market for Eastern and Southern Africa (2002) COMESACJ 5 (25 Oct. 2002); Eastern and Southern African Trade and Development Bank (PTA BANK) and Dr. Michael Gondwe v. Martin Ogang [2001] COMESACJ 2 (26 Apr. 2002). Cases cited in Osiemo (2014), p. 100.
116. This 2016 case concerns the violation of the appellant's human rights through arbitrary detention perpetrated by state military. Here the Court stressed the fact that, while it did not have the mandate to refer to Member States' national laws, it nevertheless had jurisdiction under international legal instruments pertaining to Human Rights.
117. In this 2017 case, the Court ordered damages to be paid to the appellant by the state of Mali for the violation of its contractual obligations. This case is of particular interest, as it showcases the ability of the Court to use its Human Rights mandate to contribute to the establishment of a sound investment environment by enforcing the rights of a private actor against a Member State.
118. In this case, which was decided in October 2017, the Court addressed the fundamental right to life and ordered the state of Nigeria (respondent) to pay damages to the appellant (Winger Danladi Angulu Kwasu) for the unlawful and arbitrary killing of his son by the National Defence Army (the deceased, an NDA cadet, was pushed into water during an exercise when he did not know how to swim).
119. See generally Kufuor (2006) and Gathii, J.T. (2011) *African Regional Trade Agreements as Legal Regimes*, Cambridge: Cambridge University Press, p. 155.
120. These departments include Administration and Finance; Agriculture, Environment and Water Resources; Human Development and Gender; Infrastructure; Macroeconomic Policy; Political Affairs, Peace and Security; Trade, Customs, Industry and Free Movement.

121. The new nomenclature of the Acts of the Community is provided at ECOWAS Commission at a glance—www.comm.ecowas.int.
122. See Akinrinsola, I. (2004) 'Legal and Institutional Requirements for West African Economic Integration' 10 *Law & Bus. Rev. Am.* 493, p. 512. The author argues that compliance with Community law at a national level is necessary for the success of economic integration in the region. See also Oppong (2011), p. 126.
123. See ECOWAS Vision 2020 Document (adopted by the Summit of Heads of States and Government on 15 June 2007), p. 2. See also UNECA (2013).
124. See ECOWAS Vision 2020 Document, p. 3.
125. The CAADP was established by NEPAD in 2003 to promote agricultural development across the continent.
126. ECOWAS Agricultural Policy, p. 6.
127. West African Common Industrial Policy, p. 2.
128. See Open Society Initiative for West Africa (OSIWA) 'Review of ECOWAS Policies in the Agricultural and Industrial Sectors' A Study by Dalberg and OSIWA.

     Available online at www.osiwa.org/publication/view/review-of-ecowas-policies-in-the-agricultural-and-industrial-sectors
129. Ibid.
130. See Odhiambo, W. (2005) 'The East African Customs Union and its Implications' in Ajulu, R. (ed.) *The Making of a Region—The Revival of the East African Community*, Midrand, South Africa: Institute for Global Dialogue, pp. 63–75. See also van der Mei, A.P. (2009) 'Regional Integration: The Contribution of the Court of Justice of the East African Community' *ZaöRV* 69, p. 404. The authors highlight the fact that the EAC has managed to establish its Customs Union and Common Market in the in the lapse of just ten years.
131. These projects are mentioned in the Preamble of the EAC Treaty 1999.
132. See Kasekende, L.A., Ng'eno, N. and Lipumba, N. (1999) 'Regional Integration and Economic Liberalization in Eastern and Southern Africa' in Oyejide, A., Elbadawi, I. and Yeo, S. (eds) *Regional Integration and Trade Liberalization in Sub-Saharan Africa*, Vol. 3: Regional Case-Studies, p. 154. The two countries were later on joined by the then Tanganyika.
133. Oloka-Onyango, J. (2005) 'Who Owns the East African Community?' Makerere University Human Rights and Peace Centre Occasional Paper Series No.1, p. 2. See also Tulya-Muhika, S. (2000) 'Revival of the East African Co-operation and its Institutional Framework' in Perspectives on Regional Integration and Cooperation in East Africa: Proceedings of 1st Ministerial Seminar on East African Cooperation Arusha, 25–26 March 1999, EAC Secretariat.
134. See Jones (1983), pp. 1–15. See also Trebilcock, M.J. and Prado, M.M. (2014) *Advanced Introduction to Law and Development*, Cheltenham: Edward Elgar, p. 187.
135. See Oloka-Onyango (2005), p. 2.
136. See Franck (1964), p. 95.
137. This aim is provided in article 2 of EAC Treaty 1967.
138. Article 2 (2) of the EAC Treaty 1967 provided, *inter alia*, for the abolition of restrictions on trade among the Partner States, the adoption of a Common External Tariff or the inauguration of a common agricultural policy.
139. These institutions were provided for at article 3 of the EAC Treaty 1967 and included an East African Authority, an East African Legislative Assembly, the East African Ministers, the Common Market Tribunal and several Councils.

140. EAC Treaty 1967, articles 46 to 48.
141. Ibid., articles 49 to 51.
142. Ibid., article 3 (3).
143. Article 53 of the EAC Treaty provided for the establishment of a Common Market Council, a Communications Council, an Economic Consultative and Planning Council, a Finance Council and a Research and Social Council.
144. EAC Treaty 1967, articles 56 to 60.
145. Ibid., article 30.
146. Ibid., article 32 to 36.
147. EAC Treaty 1967, article 80.
148. See Mazzeo, D. (1984) 'The Experience of the East African Community: Implications for the Theory and Practice of Regional Cooperation in Africa' in Mazzeo, D. (ed.) *African Regional Organizations*, Cambridge: Cambridge University Press, p. 154. Under the provisions of the EAC Treaty 1967, the other institutions were created either to assist or support the Authority in its tasks.
149. EAC Treaty 1967, article 59
150. Ibid., article 48 (3).
151. Mugyenyi, O. and Zeija, F. (2006) 'The East African Customs Union Protocol: An Audit of the Stakeholders' participation in the Negotiation Process' ACODE Policy Research Series No.14, p. 4. See also Mazzeo (1984), p. 151.
152. Hazlewood, A. (1979) 'The End of the East African Community: What are the Lessons for Regional Integration Schemes?' *Journal of Common Market Studies*, pp. 40–58.
153. These fundamental principles, which are inspired by the past experience of cooperation in the region, are provided in article 6 of the 1999 EAC Treaty. These principles include, *inter alia*, equitable distribution of benefits; good governance including the adherence to the principles of democracy, the rule of law, accountability, transparency, social justice, equal opportunities, gender equality as well as the recognition, promotion and protection of human and peoples' rights in accordance with the provisions of the African Charter on Human and People's Rights and peaceful settlement of disputes.
154. The terms "participating countries" and "Partner States" are used interchangeably in this section.
155. EAC Treaty, article 5 (1).
156. EAC Treaty, article 5 (2). See also article 8 (b), which provides that "the Partner States shall plan and direct their policies and resources with a view to creating conditions favourable for the development and achievement of the objectives of the Community". This constitutes a distinctive feature of the EAC, which places a stronger emphasis on regional development and economic cooperation and provides for a significantly deeper level of integration in the form of a Political Federation.
157. EAC Treaty, article 8 (a).
158. These operational principles are provided in article 7 of the EAC Treaty and include a people-centred and market-driven cooperation.
159. EAC Treaty articles 14 (d) and 59.
160. Ibid., article 16.
161. Ibid., article 63.
162. See, for example, Protocol on the Establishment of an East African Customs Union, adopted on 2 May 2004; Protocol on the Establishment of the East African Community Common Market, adopted on 20 November 2009 and the Protocol on the Establishment of an East African Monetary Union, adopted on 30 November 2013.

163. EAC Treaty, articles 71 1 (e) and 126 (2) (b). Article 126 of the EAC Treaty provides for the harmonisation of the Partner States' laws and goes as far as requiring the elaboration of a common syllabus for the training of lawyers within the Community.
164. Ibid.
165. Kitonsa, E. (2012) 'The Status of the EAC Legal Harmonisation Process in Uganda' Paper presented at the Conference on Creating a Predictable and Facilitative Legal Environment For Business in The East African Community, 6–7 August 2012, Arusha, Tanzania, pp. 5–6. Other priorities identified by the Secretariat included intellectual property laws; public-private partnership law; laws on recognition of judgments; business registration law; and the law related to enforcement measures and procedures for debt recovery.
166. See Kitonsa (2012), p. 3.
167. The Common Market Protocol was adopted to implement articles 76 and 104 of the Treaty.
168. See EAC Treaty, articles 11, 12, 32, 39 and 47.
169. Ibid, article 2 (4).
170. Ibid., article 11.
171. This concept was introduced in case 120/78 Cassis de Dijon.
172. EAC Treaty, article 80 (a) & (b).
173. See East African Investment Code, 2006. These particular measures are intended to provide incentives for the private sector to invest in areas and sectors considered as more likely to promote economic development across the region.
174. Ibid.
175. See EAC Industrialisation 2012–2032.
176. Ibid, p. 30.
177. These corridors include the Northern Corridor from the port of Mombasa in Kenya, linking Kenya, Uganda, Rwanda, Burundi and Eastern DRC; and the Southern Corridor from the port of Dar es Salaam and going through Tanzania, Zambia, Rwanda, Burundi and Eastern DRC. More details on the corridors are provided on the EAC website at www.eac.int/infrastructure/index.php?Itemid=129
178. See East African Industrialisation Strategy 2012–2032.
179. EAC Treaty, article 11.
180. Ibid., article 13.
181. Ibid., article 14 (1) and (2).
182. On the reinforcement of the EALA see Wanyande, P. (2005) 'The Role of the East African Assembly' in Ajulu, R. (ed.) *The Making of a Region—The Revival of the East African Community,* Midrand, South Africa: Institute for Global Dialogue, pp. 63–75. See also Oloo, A.G.R (2005) 'The EALA and the national Assemblies of Partner States: Conflict or Harmony? in Ajulu, R. (ed.) *The Making of a Region—The Revival of the East African Community*, Midrand, South Africa: Institute for Global Dialogue, pp. 76–94.
183. Ibid., article 49 (2). This new feature is further developed in article 65. See also Oloka-Onyango (2005), p. 2, where the author considers that these provisions reflect the desire by signatories of the Treaty to enable the general public to take the leading role in the Community.
184. EAC Treaty articles 66 to 71.
185. Id., article 18.
186. Id., Article 21 (a).
187. Nsekela, J.H.R. (2009) 'The Role of the East African Court of Justice in the Integration Process' Paper presented during the 3rd East African

Community Media Summit, Imperial Royale Hotel, Kampala, Uganda, 21–22 August 2009, p. 5.
188. The Court is established by article 9 of the EAC Treaty.
189. EAC Treaty, article 23 (2).
190. Under article 23, the Court has two functions: ensuring the adherence to law and ensuring compliance with the Treaty.
191. See Nsekela (2009), p. 6.
192. EAC Treaty, article 28.
193. Ibid., article 29.
194. Ibid. articles 30 and 31.
195. See Oppong (2011), p. 48.
196. See the guidelines on the preliminary reference procedure, which are provided on the EACJ website at Guidelines on a reference from national courts for a preliminary ruling information note —www.eacj.org
197. Nsekela (2009), pp. 10–12.
198. Ruling of 27 November 2006, Ref.Nr.1 of 2006.
199. Ruling of 27 November 2006, Reference No.1 of 2006, in Prof. Peter Anyang' Nyong'o et al. vs the Attorney General of the Republic of Kenya et al.
200. Van Der Mei, A.P. (2009) 'The East African Community: The Bumpy Road to Supranationalism. Some Reflections on the Judgments of the Court of Justice of the East African Community in Anyang' Nyong'o and others and East African Law Society and others' *Maastricht Faculty of Law Working Paper 2009–2007*, p. 5. See also Nsekela (2009), p. 8 and Osiemo, O. (2014) 'Lost in Translation: The Role of African Regional Courts in Regional Integration in Africa' 1 *Legal Issues of Economic Integration* 87, p. 103.
201. This opinion was expressed by the Court in the subsequent Anyang cases which resulted from the appeals filed by Kenya before the Appellate Division.
202. See Van Der Mei (2009), p. 9. The two subsequent judgments can be found in Prof. P. Anyang' Nyong'o et al vs Attorney General of the Republic of Kenya et al and East African Law Society et al vs the Attorney General of Kenya et al.
203. This case (No.3 of 2007) was referred to the Court by the East African Law Society, the Law Society of Kenya, the Tanganyika Law Society, the Ugandan Law Society and the Zanzibar Law Society.
204. See Case No. 3/07 of 2007 EALS and others v AG and others.
205. Ibid., p. 24.
206. This case, as well as other cases, including Case No. 09 of 2007, were used as reference by the Court in other subsequent cases.
207. Case Ref. No. 1 of 2007, 20 November 2007, EACJ First Instance Division.
208. EAC Treaty, article 6 lists the rule of law and the recognition, promotion and protection of human and people's rights among the fundamental principles of the Community. Furthermore, article 7 (2) provides "The Partner States undertake to abide by the principles of good governance, including adherence to the principles of democracy, the rule of law, social justice and the maintenance of universally accepted standards of human rights".
209. See Kent, J.L. (1991) 'Effectiveness of the European Court of Justice and its role in the Process of Integration' Paper presented at the Second International Conference on 'The Challenges of a New European Architecture: Implications for the European Community's Internal and External Agendas' George Mason University, Fairfax, VA, 22–24 May, p. 2. Here the author considers this notion in view of the ECJ.
210. Application No.15 of 2017. Arising from Reference No.10 of 2017.
211. See Article 30 of the EAC Treaty.

212. See www.eacj.org, (accessed on 27/01/2018).
213. More particularly, BAT Uganda Limited argues that the Act infringes articles 6 (d), (e), which provide for equal treatment as a fundamental principle of the Community; articles 7 (1) (c), which are aimed at the establishment of export-oriented economies in all Member States; and articles 75(1), (4), (6) of the Treaty, which prevents the Member States from enacting new legislation that would create any discrimination between goods produced by the Member States; articles 15 (1) and (2) of the EAC Customs Union Protocol, which prevent the Member States from enacting any legislation that would discriminate between domestic goods and those produced in other Member States; as well as articles 4,5,6 and 32 of the Common Market Protocol, which provide for measures to ensure the effective establishment of a Common Market among the Member States.
214. See Communiqué of the Third COMESA-EAC-SADC Tripartite Summit, 10 June 2015, Sharm El Sheikh, Arab Republic of Egypt.

7 The Issue of Harmonisation Within the AU/AEC

I. Introduction

Taking into consideration the analysis provided in the previous chapter, which identified various constraints and challenges in the context of African regional integration efforts, this chapter will examine the issue of legal harmonisation as a key instrument to foster the effective establishment of the African Economic Community (AEC).[1]

As highlighted in previous chapters, regionalism constitutes one of the key instruments used by African states in their search for an appropriate strategy to promote sustainable economic growth and development across the continent. This has led to the proliferation of several regional schemes in Africa intended to help the African states achieve their objectives. Based on a functionalist approach towards regionalism, legal integration—through the harmonisation of the Regional Economic Community (REC) Member States' policies, the adoption of common rules and the establishment of regional judicial institutions—is considered as one of the major avenues which can be used to achieve economic integration. Based on the experience in the context of European integration, there is a broad consensus that through the adoption of common rules and their enforcement by regional courts, harmonisation can be used to guide the actions of different stakeholders involved in regional schemes and should, therefore, be given a more prominent role in regional projects.[2]

The rationale for harmonisation undertakings resides in the fact economic integration addresses the issue of fragmented markets all over the continent and results in economic convergence among states taking part into a regional process; economic convergence, in turn, calls for harmonisation of economic rules, to ensure the smooth and effective establishment of internal markets with the same standards and the same basic rules.[3] Harmonisation is believed to help promote legal certainty and economic efficiency within a specific region, as the rules governing key sectors of the economy become similar and increase the region's attractiveness for foreign direct investment.[4]

However, even though harmonisation is recognised as a key instrument to foster economic integration, this continues to be a hotly debated topic, especially on the particular harmonisation approach that should be adopted by the RECs that make up the AEC, to ensure that they achieve their goals of promoting regional development. In particular, there is a debate among advocates of the minimalist approach (minimal harmonisation), in which a regional bloc adopts a series of minimum standards through Community legislation, but participating countries retain the right to provide for higher standards, whereas advocates of the maximalist approach (maximal harmonisation) argue for the adoption of common rules enacted at the Community level, directly applicable in all participating countries which are, in turn, precluded from producing any new legislation in the same area of law.[5] Moreover, the question also arises in terms of the harmonisation techniques to be used in order to achieve this objective, whether the use of Protocols ratified by all Member States or the development of special rules and policies by Community institutions is the most appropriate method to harmonise the laws of the participating countries.

II. Harmonisation Within the AU/AEC Framework

As analysed in the context of the European Community, the level of harmonisation as well as the approach and techniques used depend on the particular stage of economic integration pursued by the participating countries. The approximation of the national economic rules becomes necessary only when the participating countries decide to establish Customs Unions and Common Markets, insofar as the existence of various rules constitute an impediment to the free movement of goods, services and people.[6]

As highlighted in the discussion on the adoption of the principle of *mutual recognition* by the European Court of Justice, the mere existence of different legal systems (the concept of legal pluralism) within the same region does not in itself constitute an impediment of cross-border trade and economic integration, and approximation/harmonisation measures should be aimed at accommodating those legal systems, hence creating some sort of similarity among them, rather than eliminating all the differences and replacing them with a set of new rules.[7] This approach, therefore, allows the Member States to develop rules and policies that are adapted to their own national circumstances and priorities, while regional rules are specifically developed and designed to facilitate regional projects and cross-border business transactions.[8]

This is the approach that has been adopted by the East African Community (EAC), which has entrusted its Secretariat with the responsibility to coordinate and harmonise the policies and strategies relating to the development of the Community through a Co-ordination Committee.[9] Through this Co-ordination Committee, the Secretariat works with relevant stakeholders in the EAC Member States to identify national laws which do not comply with EAC Community Law and provides them with the relevant assistance needed in order to make the necessary amendments to their national legislation. This particular approach is believed to be relatively efficient, as it allows a central institution, the Secretariat, both to encourage and to follow up the harmonisation process undertaken by the Member States within a specific timeframe, rather than leaving it to the Member States to take action at their own pace.[10] This harmonisation process is limited and targets key sectors and specific laws which are important to achieve the objective of establishing a Common Market among the Member States.

III. Harmonisation/Unification Through the Organisation for Harmonisation of Business Law in Africa (OHADA)

With its seventeen current Member States, the Organisation for Harmonisation of Business Law in Africa (OHADA—French acronym for Organisation pour l'Harmonisation en Afrique du Droit des Affaires) represents the largest harmonisation project at the continental level that one must analyse in order to consider its relevance to the overall AEC process and its ability to advance both economic integration and regional development in Africa. OHADA provides for a different approach to harmonisation, which is based on a rules-based model of regionalism aimed at promoting regional development and economic integration. While it is not listed as one of the African RECs upon which the AEC is expected to be built, OHADA presents a unique case of the use of law to promote regional development in Africa with a view to supporting the establishment of the AEC.[11]

This section is concerned more particularly with the overemphasis placed on the necessity of a strong and extensive legal framework to facilitate regional trade and thereby stimulate economic growth.

OHADA was established with the objective of harmonising business law in order to facilitate business transactions within its Member States, given the general assumption that cross-border trade is significantly limited in an environment where countries subscribe to different sets of rules and legal systems.[12] The establishment of a legal and regulatory framework allowing private transnational exchanges to securely take place is therefore considered as essential in the OHADA context, providing its Member States with the ability to promote the development of their local private sector and to attract increased foreign investment.[13]

Moreover, given the OHADA founding members' underlying aspiration to establish a secure and reliable legal framework by adopting common rules intended to be simple and *modern*,[14] this section engages with both modernisation and neoliberal theories which, as noted in Chapter 2, have influenced both the meaning of and the process towards development in Africa. The section focuses more particularly on the general assumption that the adoption of *ideal* types of market-friendly economic rules, which are deemed to increase legal predictability and legal certainty across the OHADA region, is expected to be one of the most appropriate approaches to regionalism, specifically designed to be adapted to each country's needs and particular circumstances.[15] This critical analysis of the process carried out by OHADA proves particularly important, given the particular interest that it generates in the context of regionalism efforts in Africa.[16]

In light of the concept of regional developmentalism through law developed throughout this monograph, it will be argued in this section that although it provides for various mechanisms which could be used to support regional development, including the promotion of regional arbitration and the adoption of several rules likely to improve the business environment in its Member States, the particular approach followed by OHADA, which is primarily based on a unification and judicial integration, runs the risk of undermining rather than promoting the efforts towards the establishment of an AEC. As highlighted in the case of NAFTA which, similar to OHADA, has provided for an extensive rules-based coordination mechanism, such an approach does not offer to its Member States enough flexibility to allow them to provide the necessary impetus for economic transformation and industrialisation. The limitations of the OHADA model are further emphasised by the lack of a clear political goal beyond harmonisation in the context of OHADA, stressing the need for legal integration to be tailored for specific regional processes and particular needs rather than being considered as an objective *per se*.

For this purpose, this section's analysis is organised into three parts dedicated to the key aspects of OHADA that are relevant to the overall argument developed throughout the monograph.

The first part provides a brief overview of the organisation's historical background which is intended to provide the particular context within which the organisation was created as well as the rationale for its particular approach to regionalism. This part is particularly aimed at providing further details on the various economic challenges faced by a majority of African countries. The following part focuses on the particular mechanisms and legal techniques adopted by OHADA in order to achieve its objectives. A particular emphasis will be placed on the institutional framework of the organisation, its law-making process, the adoption of OHADA Uniform Acts and the specific way in which these are expected to support legal integration in the context of OHADA. The last part is dedicated to the OHADA Common Court of Justice and Arbitration (CCJA) and focuses on both its judicial and arbitral functions. This section focuses more particularly on the evaluation of the judicial framework and the enforcement procedure established by the CCJA.

These various aspects are analysed with a view to assessing the relevance of the process carried out by OHADA to the objective of the Treaty of Abuja and its ability to support the effective establishment of the AEC.

III.1. Overview of OHADA's Historical Context

From the outset of regional integration initiatives in Africa, promoting the economic development and sustainable growth of the various states involved in regional groupings have often constituted one of the main objectives.[17] Regionalism (especially regional integration) occupies a prominent place in most African states' development strategy, as it is supposed to provide them with the opportunity to better exploit their wealth and to attract more foreign and local investments. This explains why a thriving environment designed to both attract and increase foreign direct investment constitutes a key objective which is supposed to sustain the economic growth of African countries.

This is the idea which motivated a few West African states which, facing a decrease in investments during the 1990s, decided to combine their efforts with a view to addressing the problem caused by foreign investors' reluctance to come to the region due to apparent disparity and anachronism of business law. A "High-Level Mission" (hereinafter "the Mission") was established with the goal of identifying the different issues faced by the concerned countries and find the most appropriate solutions to address them.[18] The findings of the Mission showed that the non-attractive environment for investment was due to a lack of adequate regulatory and judicial frameworks in a majority of countries. To address this problem, the Mission suggested the creation of a new business law, intended to be "modern" and "harmonised", interpreted by "lawyers well trained in business law", and the application of which would be secured by a "unique supranational court".[19]

This process resulted in the signing on 17 October 1993 of the Treaty on the Harmonisation of Business Law in Africa (hereinafter OHADA Treaty), in Port-Louis, Mauritius.[20] This Treaty, which established OHADA, was aimed at harmonising the business laws of its Member States by elaborating common rules deemed to be *simple*, *modern* and adapted to each country's situation, and particularly designed to enhance the Member States' international competitiveness.[21] Because the common rules are designed to be simplified and harmonised, both substantively and in their application in local courts, there is a likelihood that the process conducted by OHADA will stimulate economic growth by encouraging foreign businesses to invest in the Member States.

The establishment of the OHADA was seen as significant and critical as it emerged following a long period when the legislative activity within French-speaking African states had led to disparities that were considered as prejudicial to the establishment and growth of businesses. While a few countries had undertaken the modernisation of their laws from the 1980s onwards, a majority of them to use the Code Napoléon, dating from 1807, alongside laws dating back to 1887 and 1926 (as it was the case in D.R. Congo before its accession to OHADA).[22] This situation was seen as counterproductive within the context of economies with the ambition to achieve regional integration. In addition to those disparities, there was also the uncertainty as to the exact meaning of the body of law from one country to another, and even within individual countries.[23] As this surfaced, it was considered as a necessity to establish a regional institution to issue the new body of law, a court to apply it, a regional school for the training and further specialisation of judges at a high level and a streamlined administrative body to coordinate the operations of the various institutions.

The OHADA process is therefore seen as an important tool designed to achieve several objectives. On the one hand, this process is designed to promote and enhance domestic and regional trade across the OHADA region, and to provide increased legal certainty by inciting greater legal predictability and security, thereby guaranteeing high returns for foreign investments.[24] On the other hand, by adopting common rules and legal principles that are supposed to be modern and based on international standards, OHADA is conducting a legal reform process which is considered as essential in order to facilitate both regional and international economic integration in its Member States.[25] Ultimately, OHADA is expected to promote legal integration within its Member States, with a view to generating sustainable economic growth and advance economic integration.[26]

III.2. OHADA's Harmonisation Approach

As discussed above, harmonisation can be defined as the coordination of different legal systems in order to reduce their differences and reach common goals.[27] With harmonisation, nations are supposed to agree on a set of objectives and targets and let each nation amend their internal legal regimes to fulfil the chosen objectives, giving their laws some sort of similarity. Here the focus is therefore placed on making the laws of different countries *similar*,[28] on the "removal of discord, the reconciliation of contradictory elements, between the rules and effects of two legal systems which continue in force as self-sufficient bodies of law".[29] There is a general assumption that increased economic growth and enhanced trade are the main objectives pursued by harmonisation processes across the world, given that it is believed to reduce transaction costs and to remove obstacles to trade.[30] However, as discussed in the context of European Economic Community, legislative harmonisation is more likely to have such an impact when used adequately and in the appropriate context (rather than a stand-alone process), including as a tool to support a wider objective such as the establishment of a Common Market.

There is a general understanding that differences in national legal traditions and laws are one of the major challenges faced by regional integration initiatives.[31] These disparities are believed to tamper the free circulation of goods and are deemed to create obstacles to the development of a common market to the same extent as the maintenance of tariff borders or different national policies in the various economic fields.[32] The harmonisation of trade laws, therefore, seems critical for regional integration, as without harmonisation, a meaningful economic integration might not be achieved. A strong legal framework is deemed necessary to foster and support economic integration,[33] as well as to support various activities and processes, including the free flow of investments, cross-border trade and economic growth.

However, the fact that OHADA has opted for the adoption of common rules (the Uniform Acts) which are meant to be the same in every Member State suggests that unification rather than harmonisation is the approach upon which the OHADA process is based and the mechanism that has been chosen to achieve its objectives.[34] Unification (also called "maximal harmonisation") is a process in which nations agree to replace national rules and adopt a unified set of rules chosen at the interstate level.[35] It is a process which is aimed at reducing the discrepancies between the national legal systems by inducing them to adopt common principles of law. The method used in unification is to produce a uniform law on the basis of work by experts in comparative law and to incorporate the law in a multi-partite treaty which constrains the signatories, as a matter of international law, to adopt and apply the uniform law as their municipal law.[36] Through the unification of laws, the OHADA Member States have decided to share a set of rules, the defining element here being the voluntary sharing of laws.[37]

Furthermore, OHADA was also created to address legal risk, which is believed to be caused by the concept of unpredictable rules applying to a business relationship. OHADA is therefore expected to provide parties with a regional legal system that allows them to form clear legal commitments with predictable consequences. A unified legal system is therefore supposed to help avoid several issues of conflicts of law and the often-difficult application of private international law and foreign substantive law. This presumably reduces legal uncertainty associated with international business and generates greater legal predictability and security.[38]

The creation of common law principles is achieved through a foundational instrument, the OHADA Treaty. Through this instrument, the Member States have agreed upon a delegation of power to regional organs and institutions in charge with the formulation and enforcement of those unified laws. The ultimate goal sought by OHADA in establishing these unified laws is to encourage trade and industry and promote economic development.[39] In conducting unification within its territory, OHADA's objective is the substitution of better rules in each Member State's legal system.[40] The adopted uniform laws provide the Member States with deficient legal regimes with ready-to-adopt instruments meant to be simple and modern compared to their own national laws.[41] More importantly, this is meant to provide the Member States with an opportunity to dispose of their colonial laws in favour of *modern* laws, which are intended to improve on the status quo with respect to various normative social goals, such as economic development. Through this process, the goals of unification blend with law reform which, in the context of West and Central Africa, may prove to be critical insofar as it can strengthen the economies of the countries in the region before they can be integrated effectively.[42]

However, unification endeavours raise several issues which might hinder economic integration efforts and sustainable economic growth rather than promoting them within the OHADA area. Although the substitution of a uniform set of rules for the variety of rules provided by different national legal systems is said to increase legal predictability and reduce transaction costs, there is little empirical evidence that the existence of different sets of domestic laws constitutes a significant impediment to cross-border business.

As discussed in the context of the European Economic Community, businesses are more concerned with the consistency of decision-making and with enforceability of the rules applicable to business. The impact of differences in dispositive rules can easily be eliminated by contractual provisions or model laws which lay down a common set of rights and duties in all relevant jurisdictions.[43] Moreover, as it was examined in the context of the EAC, the adoption of adequate policies, including regional industrial and investment legal instruments, may be more appropriate to promote economic growth in the context of African regional schemes.

To achieve its objectives and built a regional community aimed at strengthening its Member States' economies, OHADA has established an institutional framework similar to that of the European Economic Community, with regional institutions which are dedicated either to produce or to apply common rules to regulate or promote business across the OHADA area. The Treaty has therefore provided for five institutions, three of which are directly or indirectly involved in the OHADA legislative process (Conference of Heads of States, Council of Ministers and Permanent Secretariat, which is assisted by the Regional Training Centre for Legal Officers), while a Common Court is responsible for the application of common rules adopted by the Member States.

III.2.1. OHADA Uniform Acts

The OHADA Member States, bound by an international convention—the OHADA Treaty, use the Uniform Acts with the intent to provide obligatory rules of regional application and aimed at achieving uniformity within the OHADA territory.[44] The Uniform Acts, which are the main sources of OHADA law alongside the Treaty, are the primary means used by the organisation to achieve its goal of *harmonising* the business laws of its Member States. They are the core of the organisation, with every institution working either to formulate them or to implement them across the OHADA area.[45]

Uniform Acts are slightly different from other types of regional laws such as Regulations and Directives examined in the context of the European Economic Community. Although the Uniform Acts are similar to the EEC Regulations by the fact that they are both supposed to overrule and take precedence over national legislation, the Uniform Acts are distinguished by the fact that they are designed to take the form of regular national laws instead of complementing them or establishing a set of standards to be followed across the OHADA area.[46] Through its process, OHADA, therefore, produces Uniform Acts that are not particular to any of its Member States' legal systems but are nevertheless supposed to apply across their boundaries.[47]

Inspired from the modernisation theory and the functionalist approach to regionalism, this mechanism adopted by OHADA places law at the centre of the development discourse and is based on the general assumption that by adopting a set of legal rules and principles originating from *developed* societies, there is a likelihood that developing countries will be able to promote their development and catch up with more advanced countries.[48] By adopting this approach, the OHADA Member States were motivated by the desire to provide a secure and reliable legal framework in which market activities can securely take place and private actors can operate more efficiently.[49] The legislation produced by OHADA is primarily made up of rules applying directly across national borders—thereby based on a top-down approach—rather than a coordination of substantive rules that may differ among its Member States.[50] This attitude can be explained by the multiplication of regional integration projects in the second half of the twentieth century and the tendency for countries involved in these projects to delegate their law-making roles to regional organisations.[51] Nine Uniform Acts have been adopted by OHADA to date, including, inter alia, corporate governance, general commercial law, securities, accounting, enforcement measures, transportation, bankruptcy, cooperatives and arbitration.[52]

III.2.2. The Uniform Acts' Drafting Process

As provided by the Treaty, Uniform Acts are elaborated by the Permanent Secretariat, in collaboration with Member States' governments.[53] Articles 6 to 9 of the OHADA Treaty provide for a robust drafting process which is meant to ensure that Uniform Acts are both sophisticated and relevant to each Member State's situation, thereby ensuring their implementation. In practice, the Permanent Secretariat delegates the task of drafting a new Uniform Act to an institution or a group of experts/consultants specialised in a specific field of law.[54] As a result, several factors and considerations are involved in the overall process and often influence the outcome of the procedure and both the content and design of a new Uniform Act.

On the one hand, funding, which in most cases originates from external donors in the context of bilateral or international assistance to law reform in developing countries, constitutes one of the key factors that influence the drafting process. This often includes the direct involvement of donor countries in the drafting process of new Uniform Acts.[55] Consequently, there is a likelihood that the law chosen as a model and inspiration for a new Uniform Act may not be based on laws originating from the OHADA Member States but instead be largely influenced by the legal tradition of the donor country/funding institution or any other law to which legal consultants involved in the drafting process are more familiar with.[56]

This situation can be explained by the general tendency by developing countries to borrow legal norms and concepts from jurisdictions that are considered as more advanced, mainly Europe in the case of African countries.[57] In the OHADA context, borrowing legal concepts from other legal systems is considered as a method of speeding up the process of finding legal solutions to similar problems and is motivated by the desire to have laws that are deemed better, modern or superior. A prestigious model may, therefore, be preferred, as there is a general assumption that it will influence the development of the Member States legal systems by shaping legal ideas, institutions, categories, and rules.[58]

Upon reception of the preliminary draft of a new Uniform Act, the Permanent Secretariat initiates an extended revision process which involves the Member States' Governments, which are expected to make comments and propose amendments on the new law.[59] This stage of the procedure is marked by the participation of the OHADA National Commissions, which were established in each Member State especially for this purpose. The commissions, which consist of a group of national stakeholders including practising lawyers, judges and academics, work closely with the OHADA Permanent Secretariat and participate in the drafting process by providing comments and proposing modification to the OHADA laws to be adopted by the Council of Ministers.[60] The Common Court of Justice and Arbitration is involved in a later stage of the drafting process and delivers an opinion on the conformity of the new law with OHADA law in general.[61] The final draft of the Uniform Act is then presented to the Council of Ministers for adoption.

However, despite its sophistication and its apparent effectiveness, this drafting process is nevertheless affected by various limitations, including the rather strong dependence on foreign aid and, consequently, the adoption of Uniform Acts which do not always reflect the needs and views of local businesses and are instead based on legal rules whose suitability is decided by donor-countries or development agencies. Moreover, despite the establishment of the OHADA national commissions, the process nevertheless appears to lack sufficient national participation. By entrusting the direction of the entire process solely to the Permanent Secretariat (administrative body), the Council of Ministers (intergovernmental body), with minimal participation from national elites and none from representatives of the Member States' populations, one incurs the risk of producing "vaguely drafted rules for the purpose of achieving political compromise".[62]

To ensure the effective and uniform application of the Uniform Acts, the OHADA Treaty has provided for both direct effect and supremacy of OHADA law, two doctrines which have been identified as key factors which influenced the advancement of the European integration.

III.2.3. Direct Effect and Supremacy of the Uniform Acts

Article 9 of the OHADA Treaty provides that the Uniform Acts are published in the OHADA Official Journal 60 days after their adoption and come into force ninety days after their publication unless otherwise provided by the provisions of an individual Uniform Act.[63] Consequently, Uniform Acts become enforceable in each Member State and can be invoked by parties in local courts' proceedings after the 90-day period has passed. Moreover, the supremacy of OHADA law has been provided by article 10 of the OHADA Treaty, which provides that the Uniform Acts are "directly applicable and overriding in the Contracting States notwithstanding any conflict they may give rise to in respect of previous or subsequent enactment of municipal laws".

The application of the two doctrines was further reinforced by CCJA in its opinion of 30 April 2001 in which, at the request of Cote d'Ivoire, the Court provided that article 10 established the *supranationality* of Uniform Acts by making them directly applicable, i.e. applicable without the need to pass special law for their ratification, in all Member States, and giving them priority in case of conflict with any national law anterior and posterior to their adoption.[64] In addition, the majority of Uniform Acts are equipped with provisions relating to their *supranationality* and the fact that they are aimed at replacing any conflicting national legislation.[65]

The direct effect and supremacy aspects of the Uniform Acts, therefore, require that Member States' authorities and local courts ensure that both the content and the application of their national laws or any other administrative decisions are consistent with the content of the Uniform Acts. As discussed in the context of European Community law, these two doctrines were used to ensure that regional law was binding on the Member States, but could also govern relations between individuals who could thereby invoke them in case of a dispute, given the various rights and obligations conferred upon them by the said rules. However, it should be noted that, unlike the case of European Community law, in the context of OHADA these two doctrines have been provided in the OHADA Treaty and the provisions of the Uniform Acts.[66] The drafters of the OHADA Treaty have therefore established the two doctrines as fundamental Treaty principles, with a view to ensuring the effective implementation of the common rules in every Member State.

Despite the adoption of both direct effect and supremacy, the unification endeavours conducted by OHADA run the risk of being hindered by the fact that national courts and administrative authorities might interpret the Uniform Acts and subsequent OHADA law under the influence of their domestic legal culture and factors which are particular to each Member State.[67] This is likely to result in significant divergences in the interpretation of the Uniform Acts. This might, therefore, cause law in action to be very different from the law in the books, as these regional norms would be interpreted differently across the region. To address this particular issue, article 14 of the OHADA Treaty has provided for the establishment of the CCJA, which was created to ensure a uniform application of OHADA law in every Member State.

III.3. The Common Court of Justice and Arbitration

The OHADA Treaty has provided for the establishment of a CCJA, which is responsible for ensuring and monitoring the application and implementation of the Uniform Acts as well as their uniform interpretation in all the OHADA Member States.[68] The CCJA was therefore created as a supranational institution which is responsible for monitoring the Member States' national courts on matters covered by the Treaty and Uniform Acts. This is supposed to ensure that national courts' decisions are reviewed by a regional authority in order to ensure their conformity with OHADA law and thereby protect local and foreign investors against any arbitrary and biased decisions made by national courts or local administrations. This procedure is expected to improve the business environment in the OHADA region by providing a reliable judicial framework likely to attract more foreign investment.[69]

In addition to being established as a judicial institution intended to monitor the implementation of OHADA law in the Member States, the CCJA is also expected to act as the region's arbitration centre. Given the rise in recent decades of international arbitration as an alternative dispute resolution mechanism deemed to be cost and time efficient, neutral and impartial, the drafters of the OHADA Treaty have placed a great emphasis on the role of arbitration in the OHADA strategy and entrusted the CCJA with monitoring the arbitration procedure provided for at title IV of the Treaty. This section, therefore, focuses on both judicial and arbitral functions of the Court.

III.3.1. CCJA as a Regional Court of Appeals

As OHADA judicial institution, the CCJA is the highest court of the organisation, established to ensure a common and harmonised application and interpretation of the Treaty, Uniform Acts and subsequent Regulation in all the Member States.[70] The Court assumes these duties through two separate procedures: consultation and dispute settlement.

III.3.1.1. CONSULTATION

This procedure is aimed at ensuring the uniform interpretation of the Uniform Acts throughout the OHADA region. For this purpose, the Court may be requested to give its opinion on the Uniform Acts by several institutions, including the Member States, the Council of Ministers or national courts. As mentioned above, the Court's opinion is requested by the Permanent Secretariat regarding the draft of a new Uniform Act, before its adoption by the Council of Ministers.[71] This consultation is made to ensure the conformity of the new law with OHADA legislation as a whole.

The Court may also be consulted by the Council of Ministers or any Member States with regard to the exact meaning or the application of a Uniform Act.[72] The opportunity for the Court to give its opinion has arisen several times, including through Opinion No 002/99/E of 13 October 1999 at the request of the President of Mali regarding the conformity of specific provision of a national law with the provisions of the Uniform Act on Bankruptcy; or Opinion No 02/2000/EP of 26 April 2000 given at the request of Senegal regarding the scope of application of the Uniform Act on Corporate Governance.

The Court may also be consulted by Member States' courts dealing with dispute settlement concerning the application of OHADA law.[73] This procedure may be used by national courts obtain clarification from the CCJA regarding a specific provision of a particular Uniform Act. Even though it is not binding in nature, the Court's opinion may be relied upon by national courts when they decide the case. Despite the major role that it could play in the process carried out by OHADA, national courts make seldom use of this procedure when applying OHADA law in dispute settlement cases.[74] This consultation procedure under OHADA law is similar to the preliminary reference procedure under EU law to the extent that it allows the Court to ensure that the provisions of the Uniform Acts receive a uniform interpretation throughout all the Member States.[75] However, despite the various questions that OHADA law may potentially raise, this procedure has not been used as much as the preliminary reference in the EU. This situation might be due to a lack of information on this function of the CCJA, as a greater emphasis is placed on the Court's involvement in the dispute settlement procedure; budgetary and logistics problems might also prevent national courts from using this procedure, given the location of the CCJA in Cote d'Ivoire and the amount of time that it would therefore take for a national court to receive an opinion from the CCJA.

III.3.1.2. DISPUTE SETTLEMENT

Concerning dispute settlement, the Court's jurisdiction is limited to cases involving OHADA law[76] and every part of business law which falls within the scope of the organisation.[77] The OHADA Treaty has provided for a two-tier procedure which involves national jurisdictions in the first stage and the CCJA in the last stage.

One the one hand, article 13 of the OHADA Treaty provides that "litigation regarding the implementation of Uniform Acts is settled in the first instance and on appeal within the courts and tribunals of the Contracting States". National courts, therefore, play a critical role in this procedure, to the extent that disputes involving OHADA law are brought to them in the first and second instances. In case the dispute is still not settled after the appeal level, the jurisdiction to decide the case is conferred to the CCJA instead of national supreme courts.[78] This procedure may have been established in order to give to the CCJA direct access into the Member States' judiciary, therefore an opportunity to correct eventual errors and abuses which may have characterised the procedure at the national level. This procedure seems to have the merit of making national judicial systems more reliable, as national courts' decisions are supposed to be under the scrutiny of the CCJA. The CCJA's role as a jurisdiction of last resort was therefore established to provide the organisation with a secure and reliable judicial system, which would be more attractive to foreign investment.

However, these functions of the CCJA, which are sometimes considered as exorbitant and beyond the normal duties of a regional court, raise several issues relating to national sovereignty. In some cases, national courts are reluctant to refer cases covered by the Uniform Acts to the CCJA or to accept OHADA's supranational decisions. In addition, because of financial constraints and logistical limitations, parties not based in Abidjan, Cote d'Ivoire, where the CCJA is located, are not particularly encouraged to appeal to the CCJA.[79] This attitude is, to some extent, due to the national courts' attachment to their sovereignty, a situation which has the potential of inhibiting the powers of the CCJA and thereby impeding the effective and uniform application of OHADA law. This situation could, over time, significantly hinder the achievement of OHADA's objectives.[80]

A different mechanism has been provided for in the European Economic Community, which has managed to avoid this issue. Unlike the CCJA, the ECJ was not supposed to be directly involved in the dispute settlement procedure within the EEC, its role being limited to monitoring the European integration process. For this purpose, the ECJ was used only to ensure a uniform application of EU law through the preliminary reference procedure or to compel the EEC countries and institutions to fulfil their obligations under the EEC Treaty.[81] Although this role played by the CCJA may be explained by the fact that, beyond legal integration OHADA, is aimed at providing the Member States with a secure and reliable legal system, it would be preferable to limit the CCJA's duties to monitoring the regional integration process by using a procedure which does not trample unnecessarily on the Member States' sovereignty.

III.3.2. CCJA as a Regional Arbitration Centre

In addition to its role as a regional judicial institution, Article 21 of the OHADA Treaty has established the CCJA as a regional arbitration centre which is responsible for any disputes concerning business activities taking place within the OHADA region, or when one of the parties involved is domiciled in an OHADA Member State. This reflects the importance attached to arbitration in the context of OHADA, given that it is considered as a neutral mechanism which is meant to be cost-efficient, free of unnecessary publicity and providing the parties with the expertise of arbitrators who are experts in a specific economic area.[82] In addition, arbitration also has the merit of providing the parties with some degree of control over the procedure, through the appointment of arbitrators and their agreement over the arbitral award.

As an arbitration centre, the CCJA does not handle the cases itself but rather administers the arbitration proceedings through the appointment or the confirmation of arbitrators for a specific case.[83] In addition to the administration of arbitral proceedings, and similar to the Permanent Review Tribunal in the context of MERCOSUR, the Court also reviews draft arbitral awards before they are adopted by arbitral tribunals and is responsible for the recognition and the enforcement of the same awards.[84] This specific task performed by the CCJA proves particularly important in the context of the regional processes conducted under the AEC, as it provides for a dispute settlement mechanism designed to accommodate the sovereignty concerns of its Member States, while also ensuring that the Court can monitor the application of regional rules through its appeal procedure. Moreover, the issue of the effective implementation of regional law has been addressed through the provision of a regional application of arbitral awards once they have been recognised and confirmed by the CCJA.[85]

IV. Conclusion

As mentioned above, the extended study of the harmonisation process carried by OHADA proved to be important to the extent that, with its seventeen Member States, OHADA is the largest harmonisation project in Africa and allows us to summarise the analysis of the different aspects of the issue of harmonisation within the AEC conducted in this chapter. Article 53 of the OHADA Treaty provides that the organisation was established with a view to expanding to other states in Africa and therefore opens the way for the consideration of the expansion of the OHADA experience to other regional schemes in the context of the AEC and the use of legal integration to foster a deeper and more effective economic integration on the continent.

However, as noted above, the harmonisation process conducted by OHADA has had a relative success to date given that it involves countries which share the same legal tradition.[86] As the majority of OHADA Member States are former French colonies, one would assume that the OHADA system is mostly influenced by French law and can, therefore, be considered as being part of the Civil Law tradition.[87] In Civil Law countries, legislation is seen as one coherent national confined system that is essentially statutory, as such complete, and explainable from within. In this view, legislation is seen as capable to cover all eventualities and capable of resolving all issues arising.[88] This might explain the choice of unification as the main means for OHADA to achieve its goals, and the general tendency of the drafters of OHADA law to produce laws which are very detailed and all-encompassing.

However, as discussed in the context of NAFTA, producing rules which are very detailed does not leave enough room for the courts in charge of their application to manoeuvre and thereby advance regional integration projects or promote regional development.[89] As discussed in the context of the EEC, the ECJ's involvement in European integration through legal purposive interpretation of the general provided in the EEC Treaty ensured the development of the European Community. This could be explained by the fact that EEC law was never meant to replace national laws, but rather to complement them and promote increased convergence between the Member States' legal systems.[90] As argued in the first section of this chapter, this approach is more appropriate for the RECs that make up the AEC, as it allows them to use harmonisation as an instrument to advance economic integration in key sectors, rather than an objective to achieve at all cost.

The situation is completely different in the context of OHADA Uniform Acts, which are aimed at replacing the Member States' national laws and are very detailed (maximal harmonisation), therefore leaving insufficient room for the CCJA to interpret OHADA laws in favour of a deeper and more effective regional integration. Furthermore, by entrusting the CCJA with the task of a regional supreme court instead of a regional guardian and monitor of regional integration efforts, the OHADA Treaty has both hampered the Court of the power to foster a deeper integration and unnecessarily impinged on Member States' sovereignty.

Furthermore, in the context of OHADA, there is also an overemphasis on the need to attract foreign investment, which is believed to promote economic development given that it is supposed to provide the Member States with capital, resources and new technologies which are necessary to promote economic growth and industrialisation. However, in a majority of countries, foreign investment has tended to focus predominantly on the extraction of minerals and production of a few primary commodities, thereby hindering the African states' goal of diversifying their production and exports.[91]

Despite the fact that it constitutes a remarkable example of harmonisation—with well-functioning institutions which are somehow involved in the production and application regional rules—the OHADA legal framework presents a model of regionalism which is not likely to adequately support the establishment of an AEC and thereby promote regional development in Africa. The harmonisation model adopted by the EAC, which targets specific sectors and is aimed at accommodating various legal systems rather than replacing them, is more adapted to the needs and circumstances of the AEC Member States, as it allows them to take targeted measures to promote cross-border business transactions and projects more likely to promote regional integration and development, while also focusing on their own national economic priorities and particularities.

Nevertheless, the arbitration process provided under the CCJA jurisdiction offers an interesting regional dispute settlement mechanism which, similar to the Permanent Review Tribunal provided in the context of MERCOSUR, could prove adequate in the context of African regional schemes with concerns over autonomy and sovereignty are shared by a majority of participating countries.

Notes

1. The coordination and harmonisation of policies between existing and future RECs are provided in article 3(l) of the AU Constitutive Act and in article 4(1)(d) of the Treaty of Abuja as one of the objectives of the continent's efforts towards regional integration.
2. This constitutes one of the key aspects of the concept of integration through law developed in Augenstein, D. (2013), *Integration Through Law Revisited: The Making of The European Polity*, Farnham, Surrey, England; Burlington, VT: Ashgate, p. 75.

3. See, generally, Tharani, A. (2017) 'Harmonisation in the EAC' in Ugirashebuja, E., Ruhangisa, J.E., Ottervanger, T. and Cuyvers, A. (eds) *East African Community Law: Institutional, Substantive and Comparative EU Aspects*, Brill, p. 486.
4. Ibid, p. 487.
5. See Foster, N.G. (2006), *Foster on EU Law*, Oxford, OUP, pp. 263–264.
6. Ferreira-Snyman, MP., Ferreira, GM. (2010) 'The Harmonisation of Laws within the African Union and the Viability of Legal Pluralism as an Alternative' 73 *Journal of Contemporary Dutch-Dutch Law* 608, p. 614. See also Kähler, L., (2007) 'Conflict and Compromise in the Harmonization of European Law' in Wilhelmsson et al. (eds) *Private Law and the Many Cultures of Europe*, Kluwer Law International, p. 126.
7. See Berman, PS. (2007) 'Global Legal Pluralism' 80 *Southern California Law Review* 1155, pp. 1162–1163. See also Burke-White, W. (2005) 'International Legal Pluralism' 25 *Michigan Journal of International Law* 977.
8. See Thomas, PJ. (2008) 'Harmonizing the Law in a Multilingual Environment with Different Legal Systems: Lessons to Be Drawn from the Legal History of South Africa' 14 *Fundamina* 133.
9. See Article 71 (1) (e) of the EAC Treaty.
10. This approach is different from the one adopted by SADC, for example, which has opted for harmonisation through the adoption of special Protocols by its Member States.
11. The "commitment in favour of the establishment of an African Economic Community" is highlighted in the preamble of the OHADA Treaty.
12. See Mancuso, S. (2007) 'Trends on the Harmonization of Contract Law in Africa' 13(1) *Annual Survey of International and Comparative Law*, p. 157. See also Fagbayibo, B. (2009) 'Towards the Harmonisation of Laws in Africa: is OHADA the Way to Go?' 42(3) *Comparative and International Law Journal of Southern Africa* 309, p. 310.
13. The signatories of the OHADA Treaty have particularly expressed, in the preamble, their particular concern to support the establishment of an African Economic Community through the process carried out by OHADA.
14. See preamble of the OHADA Treaty. Emphasis added.
15. This assumption (the relevance of OHADA rules to each Member State's particular circumstances) is provided in article 1 of the OHADA Treaty.
16. See, for example, Fagbayibo (2009) and Frilet, M. (2012) 'Legal Innovation for Development: The OHADA Experience' in Cisse, H., Muller, S., Thomas, C. and Wang, C. (eds) *World Bank Legal Review Volume 4: Legal Innovation and Empowerment for Development*, which note the significant progress achieved by OHADA and even label it as "one of the more successful legal harmonisation experiments in Africa" (Fagbayibo in particular); and Shumba, T. (2015) *Harmonising Regional Trade Law in the Southern African Development Community (SADC): A Critical Analysis of the CISG, OHADA and CESL*, Baden-Baden, Germany: Nomos/Hart Publishing, where the author considers the expansion of the OHADA model and experience to other African regional schemes.
17. See Martor, B., Pilkington, N., Sellers, D. et al. (2004) *Le Droit Uniforme Africain des Affaires Issu de l'OHADA*, Paris: Lexis Nexis, p. ix. This is reflected in the emphasis on economic development as one of the objectives in most of the treaties establishing Regional Economic Communities in Africa, which provide for either the promotion, the acceleration or the fostering of sustainable growth and economic and social development in these RECs. See, for example, article 3(a) of the EAC Treaty; preamble and article 3(1) of the ECOWAS Treaty; article 5, 1(a) of the SADC Treaty; etc.

18. Mbaye, K. (2004) 'L'Histoire et Les Objectifs de l'OHADA' *Petites Affiches* n°205, p. 4.
19. See Martor et al. (2004), p. ix.
20. Current Member States include Benin, Burkina Faso, Cameroon, Central African Republic, Chad, Comoros, Congo, D.R. Congo, Cote d'Ivoire, Equatorial Guinea, Gabon, Guinea, Guinea-Bissau, Mali, Niger, Senegal and Togo.
21. Mbaye (2004), p. 4.
22. Simo Thumde, M. (2009) 'OHADA as Experienced in Cameroon: Addressing Areas of Particular Concern to Common Law Jurists' in Dickerson, C.M. (ed.) *Unified Business Laws for Africa: Common Law Perspectives on OHADA*, p. 70.
23. Martor, B., Pilkington, N., Sellers, D. et al. (2007) *Business Law in Africa: OHADA and the Harmonization Process*, 2nd edition, p. 59.
24. See Mbaye, K. (2004). See also Carbonara, E. and Parisi, F. (2007) 'The Paradox of Legal Harmonization' 132 (3–4) *Public Choice* 367, p. 369. For further thoughts on this aspect of legal harmonisation in developing countries, see also Estrella Faria, J.A. (2009), Future Directions of Legal Harmonisation and Law Reform: Stormy Seas or Prosperous Voyage?, *Uniform Law Review*, p. 17.
25. See Issa-Sayegh, J. (1999) 'Quelques aspects techniques de l'intégration juridique: Exemple des Actes Uniformes de l'OHADA' *Revue de Droit Uniforme*.
26. Ouattara, A. (2001) 'De la nature juridique des Actes Uniformes de l'OHADA' *Revue mensuelle de l'AIDD*, No.20, p. 9.
27. Issa-Sayegh, J. and Lohoues-Obles, J. (2002) *OHADA, Harmonisation du Droit des Affaires*, Brussels : Bruylant—Juriscope, p. 44.
28. Andersen, C.B. (2007) 'Defining Uniformity in Law' *Uniform Law Review* 1, p. 15.
29. Allot, A. (1965) 'Towards the Unification of Laws in Africa' 14(2) *The International and Comparative Law Quarterly*, p. 377.
30. Estrella Faria. (2009), p. 10. See also Hartkamp, A. (2003) 'Modernisation and Harmonisation of Contract Law: Objectives, Methods and Scope' *Uniform Law Review*; and Goode, R. (2005) 'Rule, Practice, and Pragmatism in Transnational Commercial Law' 54(3) *The International and Comparative Law Quarterly*, p. 555.
31. See Oppong (2011), p. 106. See also Schwenzer, I. (2011) 'Regional and Global Unification of Law' 13(3–4) *European Journal of Law Reform*, p. 17.
32. Yakubu, A. (1999), p. 35. See also Goode (2005), p. 554.
33. Ndulo, M. (1993), p. 107. See also Akinbote, A. (2010) 'The OHADA and ECOWAS Treaties as Tools for Regional Integration and Regulatory Norms' Network of Reformers' Workshop, Kampala 19–21 January 2010, p. 20.
34. See Mbaye (2004). See also Bamodu, G. (1994) 'Transnational Law, Unification and Harmonization of International Commercial Law in Africa' 38 *Journal of African Law*, pp. 125–143.
35. Carbonara and Parisi (2007), p. 368.
36. See Zweigert and Kötz (1998), *An Introduction to Comparative Law*, 3rd edition, Oxford: Clarendon Press, p. 24
37. Further discussions and details on unification processes are provided in Andersen (2007), p. 18.
38. See Carbonara and Parisi (2007), p. 369.
39. Andersen (2007), pp. 19–20.
40. This contrasts with the adoption of Community law in the context of the European Economic Community where Community law was adopted with a view to complementing the Member States' national rules rather than replacing them.

41. Gopalan, S. (2003) 'Transitional Commercial Law: The Way Forward' 18(4) *American University International Law Review* p. 805.
42. Stephan, P.B. (1999) 'The Futility of Unification and Harmonization in International Commercial Law' *University of Virginia School of Law Legal Studies Working Papers, Working Paper No. 99–10*, p. 5.
43. See Goode, R. (2005) 'Rule, Practice, and Pragmatism in Transnational Commercial Law' 5(3) *The International and Comparative Law Quarterly*, p. 555.
44. Gopalan (2003), p. 814.
45. Abarchi, D. (2000) 'La supranationalité de l'OHADA' 44 *Revue EDJA*, p. 7. See also Issa-Sayegh (2008), p. 6.
46. See article 9 of the OHADA treaty.
47. This aspect of unified laws applicable beyond boundaries and across a specific region, is discussed in Cotterrell, R. (2012) 'What is Transnational Law?' *Queen Mary University of London School of Law, Legal Studies Research Paper No.103/2012*, p. 2. On the same topic, see also Tietje, C., Brouder, A. and Nowrot, K. (eds) (2006), *Philip C. Jessup's Transnational Law Revisited—On the Occasion of the 50th Anniversary of its Publication*, Halle-Wittenberg, pp. 45–55.
48. See Parsons, T. (1966) *Societies: Evolutionary and Comparative Perspectives*, Englewood Cliffs, New Jersey: Prentice-Hall, p. 27.
49. See generally Trubek, D. (1972) 'Max Weber on Law and the Rise of Capitalism' *Wisconsin L.Rev.*, pp. 742–743. The author discusses the adoption by developing countries of common rules with a view to achieving greater efficiency.
50. Ibid.
51. See Mistelis, L. (2001) 'Is Harmonisation a Necessary Evil? The Future of Harmonisation and New Sources of International Trade Law' in Fletcher, I., Mistelis, L. And Cremona, M. (eds) *Foundations and Perspectives of International Trade Law*, London: Sweet and Maxwell, p. 4.
52. The choice of these different areas of law is based on article 2 of the OHADA Treaty, which provides for a comprehensive list of matters which fall within the scope of business law under OHADA.
53. Article 6 of the OHADA Treaty.
54. For further comments on this aspect of the OHADA drafting process, see also Sawadogo, F.M. (2001) 'Les Actes uniformes de l'OHADA: aspects techniques et généraux' 39–40 Revue Burkinabé de Droit, Numero special, p. 3.
55. See, generally, Estrella Faria, (2009), p. 28.
56. Ibid.
57. See Allott (1965), p. 386. See also Dickerson (2005) 'Harmonizing Business Law in Africa: OHADA calls the tune' 44(17) *Columbia Journal of Transnational Law*, p. 59.
58. This is evidenced, for example, in the drafting process of a new OHADA Uniform Act on Contract Law which was initiated in 2004. This process was funded by the Swiss Government and delegated by the Permanent Secretariat to the International Institute for the Unification of Private Law (UNIDROIT) Despite the fact that illiteracy and a poor level of legal culture were identified by the legal consultant responsible for drafting the new law as the main "uniquely African features" shared by countries across the OHADA region, the UNIDROIT Principles on International Commercial Contracts were chosen as model for the new Uniform Act, a decision which was in contrast with the objective of the organisation which is meant to adopt common rules supposed to be simple and therefore accessible to all types of businesses within the OHADA region. Further discussions on the various factors which

influence the transfer of various legal rules and principles from industrialised countries to developing countries, see Graziadei, M. (2008) 'Comparative law as the Study of Transplants and Receptions' in Reinmann, M. and Zimmermann, R. (eds), *The Oxford Handbook of Comparative Law*, Oxford: Oxford University Press, p. 458.

59. See article 7 of the OHADA Treaty.
60. Dickerson, C.M. (2009) 'Perspectives on the Future' in Dickerson, C.M. (ed.) *Unified Business Laws for Africa: Common Law Perspectives on OHADA*, London; Philadelphia, PA: GMB Publishing Ltd, p. 96.
61. See Article 7 of the OHADA Treaty.
62. This issue has been raised in Estrella Faria (2009), p. 10, when discussing the limitation of law reform processes in general.
63. For any country joining OHADA, both the Treaty and the Uniform Acts come into force 60 days after submission of the instruments for admission. The 90-day rule for the entry into force of the Uniform Acts have a few exceptions, including the Uniform Act on Company Law, the Uniform Act on Securities and the Uniform Act on General Commercial Law which were adopted on 17 April 1997 but came into force nine months after their adoption.
64. The Court developed a similar reasoning in its opinion No 002/99/EP of 13 October 1999 made at the request of Mali, in which it considers incompatible and contrary to OHADA law the provisions of a draft legislation prepared by the Malian Government which was in variance with article 39 of the Uniform Act on Simplified Recovery Procedures and Enforcement Measures. A similar argument is used by the same CCJA in its decision No 012/2002 of 18 April 2002, Société Elf Oil Cote d'Ivoire v Société Cotracom in which the Court reversed a decision by the President of the Court of Appeals of Abidjan regarding the determination of the jurisdiction of national judges by a national law contrary to the provisions of the Uniform Act on Simplified Recovery Procedures and Enforcement Measures.
65. This is evidenced in several provisions, including article 35 of the Uniform Act on Arbitration, article 1 of the Uniform Act on General Commercial Law and articles 916 and 917 of the Uniform Act on Company law.
66. As mentioned in chapter five, these two doctrines were developed by the CJEU through its jurisprudence in cases such as Van Gend Loos and Costa.
67. See Gopalan (2003), p. 806.
68. OHADA Treaty, article 1.
69. Fagbayibo (2009), p. 314.
70. See article 14 of the OHADA Treaty.
71. Article 7 para 2 of the OHADA Treaty.
72. Article 14 para 2 of the OHADA Treaty.
73. Ibid.
74. See Issa-Sayegh (2008), p. 38. For example, this procedure was used in 1999 when, at the request of the president of a tribunal of the first instance in Libreville, Gabon, the Court gave its Opinion No 001/99/JN providing some clarifications as to the judge who was competent to decide a procedure provided for in the Uniform Act on Enforcement Measures.
75. In the context of the EU, beyond the uniform interpretation of EU law, the preliminary reference has also been used by the CJEU to establish several principles which were critical in the development of the European Union.
76. The functions of the CCJA are provided in article 14 of the Treaty. The article gives details on the litigation role of the Court as well as on its role as an advisory body.
77. Article 2 of the Treaty lists all areas of law that fall within the scope of business law as construed by OHADA. These areas are company law, clearing of debts,

securities, enforcement measures, rules on bankruptcy, arbitration, labour law, accounting, sales, transportation and any matter that the Council of Ministers may decide to add later on. The CCJA's jurisdiction is therefore limited to matters falling within those areas of law.

78. See article 14, para 3 of the OHADA Treaty.
79. Ibid. See also Fagbayibo (2009), p. 315.
80. This concern regarding the stripping of national supreme courts of their jurisdiction over disputes at the last resort in favour of the CCJA has been expressed by the Colloquium organised by the African Association of Francophone High Courts in 2006 on the theme "Relations between national supreme courts and the OHADA Common Court of Justice and Arbitration: Assessment and Prospects". The minutes of the Colloquium contained several recommendations, including a proposed amendment of the OHADA Treaty in order to reinstate the jurisdiction of national supreme courts over matters covered by the Uniform Acts. This amendment would entrust the CCJA the sole task of promoting harmonisation within the OHADA region, more particularly by reviewing national supreme courts' decisions made in violation of a Uniform Act.
81. This role of the ECJ can be summarised in five procedures: the preliminary reference procedure to ensure a uniform interpretation of EEC law; proceedings initiated by the EEC Commission for failure to fulfil an obligation by a member state; actions for annulment of any particular EEC law that seems illegal, which is submitted by any EEC member state, the Council, the Commission or the Parliament; actions for failure to act which are lodged by member states, other Community institutions, individuals or companies against the EEC institutions if they fail to make certain decisions under certain circumstances; and direct actions lodged by individuals or companies who have been affected by the action or inaction of the Community.
82. See Bashi Rudahindwa, J. (2012) 'From Port-Louis to Panama and Washington DC: Two Regional Approaches to International Commercial Arbitration' 14(1) *European Journal of Law Reform*, p. 45. See also Teynier, E. and Yala, F. (2001) 'Un nouveau centre d'arbitrage en Afrique Sub-Saharienne' 37 *Acomex*, p. 1.
83. OHADA Treaty, article 2.
84. See article 2 of the CCJA rules on the mission of the Court. This particular provision reflects the originality of the CCJA arbitration procedure, as it confers the Court with the authority to both monitor the arbitral proceedings and to ensure the enforcement of the arbitral awards in the Member States.
85. M'Bosso, J.M. (2001) 'Le fonctionnement du Centre d'Arbitrage CCJA et le déroulement de la procédure arbitrale' *Revue Camerounaise de l'Arbitrage*, Special Issue, October 2001.
86. See Allott (1965), p. 383.
87. The majority of founding members of the organisation were former French colonies, which inherited their legal systems from France. Guinea-Bissau, Equatorial-Guinea and the Democratic Republic of Congo, the three Member States which joined OHADA later on, inherited their legal systems from Portugal Spain and Belgium, which are also considered to belong to the Civil law tradition. For further discussion on the civil law character of OHADA Member States, see Fagbayibo (2009), p. 318. See also Martor et al. (2007), p. 3 and Dickerson (2005), p. 20.
88. David, R. and Brierley, J.E.C. (eds) (1985), *Major Legal Systems in the World Today: An Introduction to the Comparative Study of the Law*, 3rd edition, London: Stevens & Sons, p. 19.

89. Krapohl, S., Fraude, B. and Dinkel, J. (2010) 'Judicial Integration in the Americas?: A Comparison of Dispute Settlement in NAFTA and MERCOSUR' in Laursen, F. (ed.) *Comparative Regional Integration*, p. 172.
90. See Allott (1965), p. 377. This process has been referred to in the literature as the Europeanisation of the legal systems across the EEC. Further details on this aspect of EEC law have been provided in Miller, L. (2011) *The Emergence of EU Contract Law: Exploring Europeanization*, Oxford; New York: Oxford University Press, p. 10.
91. See Alves, P., Draper, P. and Khumalo, N. (2009) 'Africa's Challenges in International Trade and Regional Integration: What Role for Europe?' *SAIIA Occasional Paper No 32*, p. 5. See also Vandervelde, K.J. (1998) 'The Political Economy of a Bilateral Investment Treaty' 92(4) *The American Journal of International Law* 621, p. 625.

8 Conclusion

I. Summary of the Analysis

This study was set out to explore the various ways in which law can be used to support the effective establishment of an African Economic Community (AEC). Taking into account the particular circumstances within which the majority of African regional schemes are conducted, and highlighting the various factors which influence particular models of and various approaches towards regionalism, the monograph was used to evaluate the particular mechanism adopted by the Treaty of Abuja to achieve its objective of promoting sustainable economic growth and development across the African continent. The analysis conducted throughout the monograph was built upon two key concepts—regional developmentalism and integration through law—which provided the general conceptual framework which allowed us to explore the various aspects and characteristics that law could take to support regionalism efforts as well as to address particular issues arising in the African context.

Each chapter of the analysis was therefore aimed at unpacking the various components of the monograph' main conceptual framework, with a view to considering the application of the identified legal norms, mechanisms and policies in the context of the various regional processes conducted under the banner of the AEC, whilst assessing their ability to promote economic growth and regional development in light of the particular issues and challenges faced by the majority of African economies. In particular, while Chapters 2, 4 and 5 were used to unpack the concept of integration through law by clarifying the various roles that law can play in the context of regionalism and the specific way in which those are expected to correspond to the underlying economic and political conditions of a particular region, Chapters 3, 6 and 7 provided further details on the concept of regional developmentalism and were used to adapt the various components of our hypothesis to the various processes provided in the Treaty of Abuja. These various points were used to elaborate our thesis, which can be encapsulated in the concept of *regional developmentalism through law*.

The development of the monograph was organised as follows:

Chapter 2: Regionalism, Law and Development

This chapter provided the theoretical framework upon which the analysis was developed by examining the theoretical considerations underlying the correlation between law, regionalism and development. The various aspects of this correlation were used to develop the concept of regional developmentalism through law.

The first section of the chapter provided the historical context in which regionalism efforts were initiated in Africa, placing a strong emphasis on the colonial period and the particular goal that early forms of regionalism were expected to achieve. This discussion allowed us to observe a distinctive trend across the continent, including the establishment of both national and regional central administrations especially designed for the exploitation of the African colonies' natural and human resources with a view to serving European metropoles' capitalist interests. These considerations were used to identify the distant origins of the various economic and political challenges which would shape the second wave of regional schemes which emerged upon the independence of the majority of African states.

The second section provided further insights on the link between law and regional development, here focusing initially on the old regionalism model followed by most countries upon independence and providing for state-led development and regional cooperation. This section also focused more specifically on trade theory and comparative advantage which were identified as the key theories underlying the concept of regional integration.

The third section accounted for the shift from old regionalism to new regionalism and the subsequent focus on market-led regional processes and the strong emphasis on the promotion of trade liberalisation. Here the concept of regional integration was analysed in light of both economic and political approaches to the concept, emphasising the specific role that law is expected to play under both perspectives. This section allowed us to engage with the dichotomy between supranational and intergovernmental regional governance and to evaluate the advantages and limitations of both approaches. It is against such backdrop that this section also provided an initial insight into the African Regional Economic Communities (RECs), highlighting the limited progress that they have achieved to date.

In light of these observations, the last section of the chapter was used to introduce the concept of regional developmentalism through law, which is based on the developmental state paradigm and provides for an understanding of regional processes in light of their ability to adopt legal frameworks that are adapted to the circumstances and needs of a particular region.

This particular conceptual framework was developed with a view to ensuring that the study of the concept of integration through law provided throughout the monograph was conducted in light of the particular needs and circumstances of the African economies involved in the regional schemes which form the AEC.

Chapter 3: Political Economy of Regionalism in Africa

In light of the analyses provided in the previous chapter, which emphasised the need for regional legal frameworks to be adapted to both the objectives and the actual circumstances of the countries involved in regional schemes, this chapter was particularly aimed at providing a clear insight into the specific circumstances within which the AEC is expected to be established. In particular, the chapter highlighted the various constraints and limitations experienced by the majority of countries members of the various African RECs upon which the AEC is expected to be built. The chapter focused more particularly on the various factors which have influenced the various approaches to regionalism followed by the African countries with a view to understanding the particular model of regionalism adopted by the Treaty of Abuja.

For this purpose, the chapter focused on the various waves of regionalism which have been experienced since the independence era (1950s–1960s) and highlighted the move from a focus on economic *cooperation* and regional *self-reliance* under the Organisation of African Unity to economic *integration* and *trade liberalisation* under the Treaty of Abuja. The chapter was also used to identify external factors which have influenced this particular shift in regionalism efforts in Africa, including the application across the continent of the Washington Consensus paradigm through the implementation of neoliberal policies suggested by the Bretton Woods system and the overemphasis on market-led development.

This discussion was used to understand the alteration of the meaning of development, which now includes the adoption by developing countries of particular models and mechanisms considered as *ideal* and *universal*, deemed to be particularly suitable to promote economic growth irrespectively of the particular circumstances and specific context of various regions. In this context, state intervention is expected to be limited to the establishment of an appropriate legal framework to encourage private sector activities, as well as the adoption of market-friendly norms, principles and mechanisms.

This chapter also highlighted the same focus on the promotion of trade liberalisation and freer trade under the WTO rules, which apply to a majority of African countries. The chapter focused particularly on GATT 94 article XXIV, which provides for the establishment of Free Trade Areas and Customs Unions. However, the chapter also presented various alternatives to article XXIV, including the Enabling Clause and Article XVIII, which offers safeguard measures especially adapted to the needs of regional schemes among less-developed countries.

Lastly, this analysis was used to place emphasis on the key aspects of regional developmentalism through law in the African context, including self-reliance and industrialisation under the Organisation of African Unity and the focus on regional policies particularly designed to address the major issues faced by the majority of African countries under the New Partnership for Africa's Development (NEPAD), the Action Plan for Boosting Intra-African Trade (BIAT) and the Programme for Infrastructure Development in Africa (PIDA). The issues identified include the over-dependence on the production of a few commodities, the inability to properly compete in the world economy and the consequent marginalisation of African economies created by this situation.

The considerations highlighted in this chapter provided the backdrop against which the various components of the concept of regional developmentalism through law examined in the previous chapter were applied in the remaining chapters.

Chapter 4: Contextualisation of the Concept of Integration Through Law

This chapter was aimed at providing a better insight into the concept of integration through law, focusing more particularly on the various roles that law can play in the context of regional integration and the particular way in which it is supposed both to reflect the particular circumstances of the countries involved in a regional scheme and to determine success in the achievement of their objectives.

For this purpose, the first section of the chapter focused on the various features of law in the context of regional integration, including both regulatory and institutional frameworks adopted to coordinate specific regional schemes. These various features were used to conduct an analysis of three particular regional processes, namely the North American Free Trade Agreement (NAFTA), the Common Market of the Southern Cone (MERCOSUR) and the Association of Southeast Asian Nations (ASEAN), which allowed us to identify various legal instruments adopted in order to address particular issues likely to arise at various stages of regional integration.

In particular, while the minimalist approach adopted by NAFTA—which follows a rules-based coordination mechanism and a political dispute settlement mechanism—was considered appropriate for a regional process aimed at providing market access and conducting trade liberalisation among the participating countries, a more interventionist approach was deemed more suitable for a process such as MERCOSUR, which provided for a deeper economic integration among its Member States, including through the adoption of a Common External Tariff and the coordination of the Member States' macroeconomic policies. The lack of elaboration of common legal instruments and special techniques to ensure the enforcement of regional policies was identified as the key issue which could potentially undermine a regional process such as MERCOSUR. These two cases, which represent two different approaches to the concept of economic integration analysed in chapter two, were used to highlight the fact that models that place a strong emphasis on economic integration and trade liberalisation are likely to present serious limitations in light of the particular needs of the African economies, given the detrimental effect that they could have on the African economies if they were not combined with interventionist measures aimed at promoting structural transformation.

The process conducted under ASEAN was presented as a nuanced model of regionalism in which a particular emphasis was placed on the adoption of suitable legal instruments aimed at achieving the participating countries' objectives. In this context, both economic integration and trade liberalisation were considered as means to achieve the ASEAN countries' aim of enhancing their economies' international competitiveness, as well as creating a regional production base. This approach, which was understood to be inspired from the developmental state paradigm applied in several countries in the region, used state intervention to regulate both regional investments and market activities with a view to promoting specific sectors and areas more likely to help the participating countries achieve their goal. The examination of these three approaches to regional integration were therefore used to emphasise the need for the legal frameworks adopted by regional schemes to be adapted to their objectives and particular circumstances, a consideration which was used to inform the methodology adopted in the remaining chapters of the monograph, more particularly in the investigation for an appropriate legal framework to support the establishment of an AEC that is relevant to the economies of its Member States.

Chapter 5: The Establishment of a Common Market Within the European Community

Following on from the analysis provided in the previous chapter, this chapter was used to further unpack the concept of integration through law, examining the various ways in which law was used in the context of European integration, focusing on the way in which law contributed to the gradual transformation of the European Economic Community (EEC) into a Common Market. The chapter focused more particularly on the specific techniques and methods, as well as the specific mechanisms that were used to help the Community achieve its objectives. This analysis proved especially important, given the fact that the majority of African regional schemes are designed to emulate the European model of regionalism. The various aspects of this analysis were used to underline the fact that the Vinerian model of regionalism followed by the European process, which places a particular emphasis on gradual economic integration through the removal of tariff and non-tariff barriers to the free movement of goods, services and factors of production, was particularly suitable for countries which had already achieved a certain level of economic growth, a situation which is different in the context of the African countries for which economic transformation and industrialisation constitute a higher priority.

A particular emphasis was placed on legal integration—consisting in legislative harmonisation, mutual recognition and judicial integration through the enforcement of Community law—which provided for specific techniques that helped advance the European integration process, especially after the stagnation observed in the early 1970s. Both the regulatory framework adopted by the Community, as well as the supranational institutions established by the EEC Treaty were considered as key factors that promoted the of achievement of the regional objectives. Given the fact that the majority of African RECs aim to emulate the process conducted by the EEC, the extended analysis conducted in this chapter was aimed at grasping the particular context that prompted the adoption of the various principles, techniques and mechanisms used by the EEC as well as the specific way in which they were supposed to be used to support the overall European project. A stronger emphasis was placed on the judicial integration conducted by the European Court of Justice which, through the adoption of the three doctrines of direct effect, supremacy and mutual recognition in the context of the preliminary reference procedure, managed to give Community law the necessary authority in order to ensure its effective and uniform application in all Member States.

The various aspects of law analysed in the two previous chapters were therefore provided with a view to informing the analysis in the remaining chapters of the monograph.

Chapter 6: Regional Developmentalism Through Law Within SADC, ECOWAS and EAC

A sixth chapter of the monograph was used to identify the particular ways in which the findings of the previous chapters can be applied in the context of the AEC. Through the examination of the processes conducted in the context of the Southern African Development Community (SADC), the Economic Community of African States (ECOWAS) and the East African Community (EAC), this chapter was used to highlight the need for the African RECs, which are part of the AEC, to follow a model of regionalism that is more adapted to their specific needs and particular circumstances.

Moreover, the analysis in this chapter placed a strong emphasis on the critical need for the adoption of an appropriate legal framework upon which regional processes can be built and which are more likely to promote sustainable economic growth in the specific context of the AEC. For this purpose, the chapter identified the adoption of appropriate regional development strategies and the effective coordination of regional processes as prerequisites for the effective establishment of an AEC which would be relevant to the African context. The chapter was also used to identify the key features of both regulatory and institutional frameworks that are necessary to achieve the objectives provided in the Treaty of Abuja. A strong emphasis was placed on two key features identified in the context of the East African Community, including the need to establish an efficient and well-organised regulatory framework to ensure the effective implementation of regional law, including Treaty provisions and secondary rules, and the importance of the binding effect of regional regulatory frameworks, likely to guarantee the implementation of AEC law.

While the case of both SADC and ECOWAS' early years was used to highlight the disadvantages and limitations that regional schemes based solely either on a state-led coordination process or a market-led economic integration, the EAC was presented as an actual example of comprehensive regionalism based on regional developmentalism through law, in which deeper economic integration is used to support the participating countries' efforts towards economic transformation, capacity-building and industrialisation. This analysis also highlighted the crucial role played by regional institutions with increased autonomy and more powers to coordinate the participating countries' collective actions as well as to ensure the effective implementation of regional policies and their uniform application across a specific region. Lastly, and more importantly, the chapter underlined the need for African RECs to adopt appropriate development strategies based on key legal instruments such as regional industrial and investment policies directed towards regional capacity-building and the enhancement of the participating countries' product diversification.

Chapter 7: The Issue of Harmonisation Within the AU/AEC

The last chapter was dedicated to the issue of harmonisation within the AEC, given the prominent role that is it expected to play to advance regional efforts across the continent. While the first section focused on the rationale of any harmonisation process, the different methods and techniques used in order to achieve this objective and the experience of the EAC, the second section focused on the process conducted by the Organisation for Harmonisation of Business Law in Africa (OHADA), which provides for a rules-based model of regionalism intended, indirectly, to support the efforts towards the establishment of the AEC. The section was used especially to assess the suitability of a regional process based on a stand-alone process of legislative harmonisation to the specific context of the AEC.

OHADA is particularly aimed at promoting economic growth and deeper economic integration through legal integration—which involves legislative harmonisation and judicial integration. For this purpose, the OHADA Treaty has provided for the adoption of common rules, the Uniform Acts, which are expected to be simple, modern and adapted to every Member State particular circumstances. The adoption of these Uniform Acts is expected to promote increase legal certainty and predictability within the OHADA region and thereby to help the Member States attract more foreign investment deemed to be essential in order to promote their sustainable economic growth and development.

In light of the particular circumstances of the African economies which were underlined in the previous chapter, the analysis conducted in this section was used to highlight the issues likely to arise in a legal integration process which is conducted outside of a wider regional process with clear objectives. These issues include, *inter alia*, the limitation of a regional court established to ensure the uniform application of regional law by acting as a regional supreme court and the adoption of various legal norms and principles based on market-friendly economic models through a top-down approach which often do not reflect the particular circumstances of a specific region.

This section was used to argue that legal integration is more suitable when used in the context of wider regional processes, including those aimed at the establishment of Customs Unions and Common Markets.

II. Theoretical Implication

These various considerations were examined with a view to identifying the key components of the main argument developed throughout the monograph, which was encapsulated in the concept of regional developmentalism through law. The key aspects of this concept, which is believed to be suitable to address the various issues arising in the context of regionalism in Africa, can be summarised as follows:

II.1. Rules-Based and Extensive vs. Open-Ended Regulatory Frameworks

Highlighting the need for legal processes to be adapted to the particular circumstances of the countries involved in specific regional schemes, the analysis identified various strategies adopted in different regions in order to promote economic growth and sustainable development. These strategies include market access, trade liberalisation, sectoral integration, the establishment of a regional production base and trade facilitation.

The monograph was also used to identify specific legal frameworks corresponding to these strategies; while a rules-based coordination mechanism seemed suitable for processes which are limited to the promotion of market access and the establishment of a Free Trade Area (such as the Tripartite Free Trade Area and the Continental Free Trade Area), open-ended regulatory frameworks were deemed appropriate for regional processes requiring deeper economic integration and a certain degree of state intervention (such as the EAC). These open-ended regulatory frameworks are believed to be flexible and designed to be further developed through the elaboration of additional legal instruments which are expected to address new issues arising in the course of the regional process.

Open-ended regulatory frameworks or Regional Trade Agreements in the form of *incomplete contracts* were considered to be particularly suitable in the context of the AEC, where regional processes are expected to promote regional development through the structural transformation and the industrialisation of the African economies. These objectives are expected to be achieved through the adoption of particular legal instruments which are designed to regulate both regional trade and investment and to create a dynamic comparative advantage in sectors that are considered as particularly favourable to promote economic growth and sustainable regional development. These legal instruments include, inter alia, appropriate Rules of Origin, Common External Tariffs, Common Policies, Regional Industrial and Investment rules (as is the case under the EAC and ASEAN), as well as measures aimed at promoting a harmonious regional development among countries belonging to the same region such as the Regional Policy examined in the context of the EEC.

The analysis was also used to place a strong emphasis on the need to provide for specific rules regarding the application and enforcement of the regional rules, to ensure the effective unpacking of the Regional Trade Agreements. Here the focus was particularly on the doctrines of direct effect and supremacy, which can be used in the context of the AEC to ensure the effective and uniform application of the rules developed by the African RECs.

II.2. Intergovernmental vs. Supranational Institutional Framework

Given the crucial role that regional institutions can potentially play to further the participating countries' efforts toward regional integration, the monograph has also argued for the establishment in the African RECs of hybrid institutional frameworks in which intergovernmental institutions would be responsible for providing the general vision and direction of the regional schemes, while a very limited number of supranational institutions would be in charge of coordinating state interventions directed towards infrastructure and capacity-building, as well as the harmonisation of the relevant rules. As observed in the context of the EAC, such an arrangement is particularly designed to ensure the smooth progression of regional processes while also accommodating sovereignty concerns of the participating countries. While supranational institutions could be used to coordinate various programmes and projects conducted under a specific regional scheme, intergovernmental institutions often provide the general vision and main objectives to be achieved by the region.

II.3. Interstate and Quasi-Judicial vs. Judicial Dispute Settlement Mechanisms

The monograph was also used to emphasise the crucial role played by appropriate dispute settlement mechanisms (DSM) to support the successful achievement of the objectives of regional initiatives by solving any conflicts likely to arise between participating countries regarding the application or the interpretation of regional rules. Whether through interstate conciliatory mechanisms including negotiations, consultation or mediation (as is the case under ASEAN and NAFTA), quasi-judicial arrangements (OHADA, MERCOSUR) or regional adjudication processes conducted by a regional court (EAC, EEC), the adoption of an appropriate dispute settle mechanism proves important in the context of regionalism as it is used to determine the effective implementation of Regional Trade Agreements. Here a particular emphasis was placed on the need to adopt a DSM that reflects the concerns shared by the participating countries, which will determine either the supranational or the intergovernmental nature of a particular region's DSM.

These three key components constitute the key aspects of the concept of regional developmentalism through law which was used throughout the monograph, to consider the use of law to support the effective establishment of an AEC which corresponds to the particular circumstances of the African economies.

Bibliography

I. Official Documents

Africa

African Economic Community Treaty (Treaty of Abuja), 3 June 1991
African Union Constitutive Act, 11 July 2000
Charter of the Organisation of African Unity, 25 May 1963
East African Community Industrialisation Strategy 2012–2032
East African Community Model Investment Code, 2006
East African Community Treaty, 30 November 1999
Economic Community of West African States Treaty, 28 May 1975
Economic Community of West African States Revised Treaty, 24 July 1993
Economic Community of West African States Agricultural Policy (ECOWAS), 2005
Economic Community of West African States Common Industrial Policy (WACIP), 2010
Lagos Plan of Action for the Economic Development of Africa 1980–2000
New Partnership for Africa's Development (NEPAD) Framework, July 2001
Organisation for the Harmonisation of Business Law in Africa (OHADA) Treaty, 17 October 1993
Organisation for the Harmonisation of Business Law in Africa (OHADA) Revised Treaty, 17 October 2008
Southern African Development Coordination Conference Memorandum of Understanding, 01 April 1980
Southern African Development Community Regional Indicative Strategic Development Plan, August 2003
Southern African Development Community Trade Protocol, 01 August 1996
Southern African Development Community (SADC) Treaty, 17 August 1992
Southern African Development Community Tribunal Protocol, 07 August 2000
Treaty for East African Co-operation, 6 June 1967

Asia

Agreement on the Common Effective Preferential Tariff, 28 January 1992
ASEAN Charter, 20 November 2007
ASEAN Comprehensive Investment Agreement (ACIA), 26 February 2009

ASEAN Framework Agreement for the Integration of Priority Sectors (AFAIP), 29 November 2004
ASEAN Framework Agreement on Services (AFAS), 15 December 1995
ASEAN Trade in Goods Agreement (ATIGA), 26 February 2009
Bangkok Declaration establishing the Association of Southeast Asian Nations, 08 August 1967
Framework Agreement on the ASEAN Investment Area (AIA), 15 December 1995
Protocol to the ASEAN Charter on Dispute Settlement Mechanisms, 08 April 2010

North America

North American Free Trade Agreement (NAFTA), 17 December 1992
North American Agreement on Environmental Cooperation (NAAEC), September 1993
North American Agreement on Labour Cooperation (NAALC), September 1993

Latin America

Olivos Prorocol, February 2002
Protocol of Brasilia, 17 December 1991
Protocol of Ouro Preto, 17 December 1994
Treaty of Asunción, 26 March 1991

Europe

Treaty of Paris establishing the European Coal and Steel Community, 18 April 1951
Treaty of Rome establishing the European Economic Community, 25 March 1957
Single European Act revising the Treaties of Rome, 17 February 1986

II. Secondary Sources

Books

Amsden, A.H., 2001. *The Rise of "The Rest": Challenges the West From Late-Industrializing Economies* (Oxford: Oxford University Press).
Arndt, H.W., 1987. *Economic Development: The History of an Idea* (Chicago; London: University of Chicago Press).
Asante, S.K., 1986. *The Political Economy of Regionalism in Africa: A Decade of the Economic Community of West African States (ECOWAS)* (New York: Praeger).
Balassa, B., 1962. *The Theory of Economic Integration* (London: Allen and Unwin).
———., 1989. *Comparative Advantage, Trade Policy and Economic Development* (London: Harvester Wheatsheaf).
Barnard, C., 2013. *The Substantive Law of the EU: The Four Freedoms*, 4th ed. (Oxford: Oxford University Press).
Betts, R.F., 2004. *Decolonization* (London; New York: Routledge).
Bhagwati, J.N. and Krueger, A.O., 1995. *The Dangerous Drift to Preferential Trade Agreements* (Washington, DC: AEI Press).
Birkinshaw, P., 2003. *European Public Law* (London: Butterworths).

Biswaro, J.M., 2005. *Perspectives on Africa's Integration and Cooperation: From OAU to AU: Old Wine in New Bottle?* (Dar-es-Salaam: Tanzania Publishing House).

———., 2012. *The Quest for Regional Integration in the Twenty First Century: Rhetoric Versus Reality: A Comparative Study* (Dar Es Salaam: Mkuki na Nyota).

Bobo, B.H. and Sintim-Aboagye, H. (eds), 2012. *Neo-Liberalism, Interventionism and the Developmental State: Implementing the New Partnership for Africa's Development* (Trenton, NJ; London: Africa World Press).

Boone, C., 2003. *Political Topographies of the African State: Rural Authority and Institutional Choice* (Cambridge: Cambridge University Press).

Broberg, M. and Fenger, N., 2010. *Preliminary References to the European Court of Justice*, (Oxford: Oxford University Press).

Cappelletti, M., Seccombe, M. and Weiler, J., 1986. *Integration Through Law: Europe and the American Federal Experience—Vol. 1: Methods, Tools and Institutions, Bk 2: Political Organs, Integration Techniques and Judicial Process* (Berlin; New York: W. de Gruyter).

Cardoso, F.H. and Faletto, E., 1978. *Dependency and Development in Latin America* (Berkeley; London: University of California Press).

Carreau, D., Juillard, P. and Flory, T., 1980. *Droit international économique*, 2nd ed. (Paris: Librairie Generale de droit et de jurisprudence).

Chang, H-J. and Rowthorn, R. (eds), 1995. *Role of the State in Economic Change* (Oxford: Clarendon Press; New York: Oxford University Press).

Chatterjee, P., 1993. *Nationalist Thought and the Colonial World: A Derivative Discourse* (Tokyo: Zed Books for the United Nations University).

Chauffour, J-P. and Maur, J-C., 2011. 'Beyond Market Access' in J-P. Chauffour and J-C. Maur (eds) *Preferential Trade Agreement Policies for Development: A Handbook* (Washington, DC: The World Bank).

Clapham, C., 1996. *Africa and the International System: The Politics of State Survival* (Cambridge: Cambridge University Press).

Cooley, A. and Spruyt, H., 2009. *Contracting States: Sovereign Transfers in International Relations* (Princeton, NJ; Woodstock: Princeton University Press).

Craig, D. and Porter, D., 2006. *Development Beyond Neoliberalism? Governance, Poverty Reduction and Political Economy* (London; New York: Routledge).

Darby, P., 1987. *The Three Faces of Imperialism* (New Haven, CT: Yale University Press).

David, R. and Brierley, J.E.C. (eds), 1985. *Major Legal Systems in the World Today: An Introduction to the Comparative Study of the Law*, 3rd ed. (London: Stevens & Sons).

Davies, K., 2013. *Understanding European Union Law*, 5th ed. (London: Routledge).

De Waart, P., Peters, P. and Denters, E., 1988. *International Law and Development* (Dordrecht; Boston; London: Martinus Nijhoff Publishers).

Dehousse, R., 1998. *The European Court of Justice: The Politics of Judicial Integration* (Basingstoke: Palgrave Macmillan).

Dickson, J. and Eleftheriadis, P. (eds), 2012. *Philosophical Foundations of European Union Law* (Oxford: Oxford University Press).

Downs, G.W. and Rocke, D.M., 1995. *Optimal Imperfection? Domestic Uncertainty and Institutions in International Relations* (Princeton, NJ: Princeton University Press).

Duina, F., 2013. *Social Construction of Free Trade: The European Union, NAFTA and MERCOSUR* (Princeton; Oxford: Princeton University Press).

Evans, P., Rueschemeyer, D. and Skocpol, T. (eds), 1985. *Bringing the State Back In* (Cambridge: Cambridge University Press).

Ferguson, J., 2006. *Global Shadows: Africa in the Neoliberal World Order* (Durham; London: Duke University Press).

Franck, T.M., 1964. *East African Unity Through Law* (New Haven; London: Yale University Press).

Frank, A.G., 1966. *The Development of Underdevelopment* (New York: Monthly Review Press).

Freund, B., 1988. *The Making of Contemporary Africa* (Houndmills: Palgrave Macmillan).

Fujita, M., Kuroiwa, I. and Kumagai, S. (eds), 2011. *The Economics of East Asian Integration: A Comprehensive Introduction to Regional Issues* (Cheltenham; Northampton: Edwar Elgar).

Fullbrook, E., 2007. *Real World Economics: A Post-Autistic Economics Reader* (London: Athem Press).

Gambari, J.A., 1991. *Political and Comparative Dimensions of Regional Integration: The Case of ECOWAS* (Atlantic Highlands, NJ; London: Humanities Press International).

Gantz, D.A., 2009. *Regional Trade Agreements: Law, Policy and Practice* (Durham, NC: Carolina Academic Press).

Gathii, J.T., 2011. *African Regional Trade Agreements as Legal Regimes* (Cambridge: Cambridge University Press).

Giplin, R., 2000. *Global Political Economy: Understanding the International Economic Order* (Princeton, NJ: Princeton University Press).

Glick, L.A., 1994. *Understanding the North American Free Trade Agreement: Legal and Business Consequences of NAFTA*, 2nd ed. (Alphen aan den Rijn; London: Kluwer Law International).

Haas, E., 1964. *Beyond the Nation-State: Functionalism and International Organization* (Stanford, CA: Stanford University Press).

Hansen, J.D. and Nielsen, J.W., 1997. *An Economic Analysis of the European Union*, 2nd ed. (London: The McGraw-Hill Companies).

Harrison, G., 2000. *Neoliberal Africa: The Impact of Social Engineering* (London; New York: Zed Books).

Hart, M., 1990. *A North American Free Trade Agreement—the Strategic Implications for Canada* (Ottawa: Centre for Trade Policy and Law and the Institute for Research on Public Policy).

Haufbauer, G.C. and Schott, J.J., 2005. *NAFTA Revisited: Achievements and Challenges* (Washington, DC: Institute for International Economics).

Heater, D., 1992. *The Idea of European Unity* (Leicester: Leicester University Press).

Herbst, J., 1990. 'War and the State in Africa' 14 *International Security* 126.

Hermann, C. and Terhechte, J.P., 2009. *European Yearbook of International Economic Law 2010* (Dordrecht: Springer).

Hirst, M., 1992. *Avances y desafios en la formacion del Mercosur* (Buenos Aires: FLASCO).

Hoekman, B. and Kostecki, M.M., 2001. *The Political Economy of the World Trading System: The WTO and Beyond*, 2nd ed. (Oxford: Oxford University Press).

Hoekman, B., Mattoo, A. and English, P. (eds), 2002. *Development, Trade and the WTO: A Handbook* (Washington, DC: World Bank).

Hogan, M.J., 1987. *The Marshall Plan: America, Britain and the Reconstruction of Western Europe, 1947–1952 (Studies in Economic History and Policy: USA in the Twentieth Century)* (Cambridge: Cambridge University Press).

Holland, R.F., 1985. *European Decolonization 1918–1981: An Introductory Survey* (Basingstoke; London: Palgrave Macmillan).

Inama, S. and Sim, E.W., 2015. *The Foundation of the ASEAN Economic Community: An Institutional and Legal Profile* (Cambridge: Cambridge University Press).

Issa-Sayegh, J. and Lohoues-Obles, J., 2002. *OHADA, Harmonisation du Droit des Affaires* (Brussels: Bruylant—Juriscope).

Jackson, J.H., 1997. *The World Trading System: Law and Policy of International Economic Relations*, 2nd ed. (Cambridge, MA: MIT Press).

Jomo, K.S., Chung, C.Y., Folk, B.C., Ul-Haque, I., Phongpaichit, P., Simatupang, B. and Tateishi, M., 1997. *Southeast Asia's Misunderstood Miracle: Industrial Policy and Economic Development in Thailand, Malaysia and Indonesia* (Boulder, CO and Oxford: Westview Press).

Jones, C.A., 1983. *The North-South Dialogue: A Brief History* (London: Frances Pinter).

Kaahwa, A., 2008. *Reforming Justice in East Africa: A Comparative Review of Legal Sector Processes* (Kampala: Fountain Publishers).

Kalaba, M., Willcox, O., Fundira, T., Williams, B. and Alves, P., 2006. *Deepening Integration in SADC: South Africa—SADC's Economic Engine* (Gaborone: Friedrich Ebert Foundation).

Kaplinsky, R., 2005. *Globalisation, Poverty and Inequality: Between a Rock and a Hard Place* (Cambridge: Polity).

Kapur, D. et al., 1997. *The World Bank: Its First Half Century* (Washington, DC: Brookings Institution).

Kararach, G., 2014. *Development Policy in Africa, Mastering the Future?* (Basingstoke: Palgrave Macmillan).

Kothari, U. and Minogue, M. (eds), 2002. *Development Theory and Practice: Critical Perspectives* (Basingstoke: Palgrave Macmillan).

Krueger, A., 1995. *Trade Policies and Developing Nations* (Washington, DC: Brookings Institution).

Kufuor, K.O., 2006. *The Institutional Transformation of the Economic Community of West African States* (Aldershot: Ashgate).

Kyambalesa, H. and Houngnikpo, M., 2006. *Economic Integration and Development in Africa* (Aldershot: Ashgate).

Ladan, M.T., 2009. *Introduction to ECOWAS Community Law and Practice: Integration, Migration, Human Rights, Access to Justice, Peace and Security* (Zaria, Kaduna, Nigeria: Ahmadu Bello University Press).

Langhammer, R. and Hiemenz, U., 1990. *Regional Integration Among Developing Countries: Opportunities, Obstacles, and Options* (Tübingen: JCB Mohr).

Laski, H.J., 1930. *Liberty in the Modern State* (Harmondsworth, Middlesex: Penguin Books).

Leifer, M., 1989. *ASEAN and the Security of South-East Asia* (London; New York: Routledge).

Lipsey, R.G. and Smith, M.G., 1987. *Global Imbalances and US Policy Responses* (Toronto: C.D. Howe Institute).

Lowenfeld, A.F., 2008. *International Economic Law*, 2nd ed. (Oxford; New York: Oxford University Press).

Maduro, M.P., 1998. *We the Court: The European Court of Justice and the European Economic Constitution. A Critical Reading of Article 30 of the EC Treaty* (Oxford: Hart Publishing).

Malanczuk, P., 1997. *Akehurst's Modern Introduction to International Law*, 7th ed. (New York: Routledge).

Martor, B., et al., 2004. *Le Droit Uniforme Africain des Affaires Issu de l'OHADA* (Paris: Lexis Nexis).

———., 2007. *Business Law in Africa: OHADA and the Harmonization Process*, 2nd ed. (Paris: Lexis Nexis).

Matambalya, F.A.S.T., 1995. *The Impact of Regionalisation Schemes on the Export and Economic Performance of Developing Countries: A Case Study of the Southern African Development Community (SADC)* (Frankfurt: Brandes & Apsel).

Mattli, W., 1999. *The Logic of Regional Integration: Europe and Beyond* (Cambridge: Cambridge University Press).

Mensah, J. (ed.), 2008. *Neoliberalism and Globalization in Africa: Contestations From the Embattled Continent* (New York: Palgrave Macmillan).

Miller, L., 2011. *The Emergence of EU Contract Law, Exploring Europeanization* (Oxford; New York: Oxford University Press).

Mitrany, D., 1944. *A Working Peace System* (version published in 1966) Chicago: Quadrangle Books.

Mutharika, B., 1972. *Toward Multinational Economic Cooperation in Africa* (New York; London: Praeger).

Nnoli, O. (ed.), 1981. *Path to Nigeria Development* (Dakar: CODESRIA).

Noman, A., Botchwey, K., Stein, H. and Stiglitz, J.E., 2012. *Good Growth and Governance in Africa: Rethinking Development Strategies* (Oxford: Oxford University Press).

Novakovic, M., 2013. *Basic Concepts of Public International Law: Monism and Dualism* (Belgrade: Faculty of Law, University of Belgrade).

Nyang'oro, J.E. and Shaw, T.M., 1992. *Beyond Structural Adjustment in Africa: The Political Economy of Sustainable and Democratic Development* (New York; London: Praeger).

Ofstad, A. et al., 1986. *SADCC Intra-Regional Trade Study* (Gaborone: SADCC).

O'Keefe, T.A., 2007. *Latin American Trade Agreements* (Boston: Brill/Martinius Nijhoff).

Onwuka, R. and Sesay, A., 1985. *The Future of Regionalism in Africa* (London: Palgrave Macmillan).

Oppong, R.F., 2011. *Legal Aspects of Economic Integration in Africa* (Cambridge: Cambridge University Press).

Ortergaard, T., 1989. *SADCC, Beyond Transportation: The Challenge of Industrial Co-Operation* (Uppsala: CDR Publications No.8).

Pahuja, S., 2011. *Decolonising International Law: Development, Economic Growth and the Politics of Universality* (Cambridge: Cambridge University Press).

Parsons, T., 1966. *Societies: Evolutionary and Comparative Perspectives* (Englewood Cliffs, NJ: Prentice-Hall).

Peet, R. (ed.), 2003. *Unholy Trinity: The IMF, World Bank and WTO* (London; New York: Zed Books).

Pelkmans, J., 1986. *Completing the Internal Market for Industrial Products* (Luxembourg: Office for Official Publications of the European Communities).

———., 1997. *European Integration, Methods and Economic Analysis* (London: Longman).

Peters, W.C., 2010. *The Quest for an African Economic Community: Regional Integration and its Role in Achieving African Unity: The Case of SADC* (Frankfurt am Main: Peter Lang).

Pollack, M.A., 2002. *The Engines of European Integration: Delegation, Agency and Agenda Setting in the EU* (Oxford: Oxford University Press).

Przeworski, A., 1991. *Democracy and the Market: Political and Economic Reforms in Eastern Europe and Latin America* (Cambridge: Cambridge University Press).

Rapley, J., 1996. *Understanding Development: Theory and Practice in the Third World* (Boulder, CO; London: Lynne Rienner).

Ricardo, D., 1817. *On the Principles of Political Economy* (London: John Murray).

Rist, G., 1997. *The History of Development: From Western Origin to Global Faith* (London: Zed Books).

Robson, P., 1968. *Economic Integration in Africa* (London: Allen and Unwin).

Rodney, W., 1974. *How Europe Underdeveloped Africa* (Cape Town; Dakar; Nairobi; Oxford: Pambazuka Press; originally published in 1972 by Bogle-L'Ouverture Publications).

Rostow, W.W., 1960. *Stages of Economic Growth: A Non-Communist Manifesto* (Cambridge: Cambridge University Press).

Saitoti, G., 2002. *The Challenges of Economic and Institutional Reforms in Africa* (Aldershot: Ashgate).

Schmidt, S. and Kelemen, R.D. (eds), 2013. *The Power of the European Court of Justice* (London: Routledge).

Schultz, T.W., 1964. *Transforming Traditional Agriculture* (New Haven: Yale University Press).

Schwarzenberger, G., 1970. *Economic World Order? A Basic Problem of International Economic Law* (Manchester: Manchester University Press).

Shapiro, M.M., 1981. *Courts: A Comparative and Political Analysis* (Chicago: University of Chicago Press).

Shumba, T., 2015. *Harmonising Regional Trade Law in the Southern African Development Community (SADC): A Critical Analysis of the CISG, OHADA and CESL* (Baden-Baden, Germany: Nomos/Hart Publishing).

Smith, A., 1904. *The Wealth of Nations*, 5th ed. (London: Methuen & Co Ltd, first published in 1776).

Stiglitz, J.E., 2002. *Globalisation and Its Discontents* (New York: W.W. Norton & Co).

Swann, D., 1996. *European Economic Integration: The Common Market, European Union and Beyond* (Cheltenham; Brookfield: Edward Elgar).

Tietje, C., Brouder, A. and Nowrot, K. (eds), 2006. *Philip C. Jessup's Transnational Law Revisited—On the Occasion of the 50th Anniversary of its Publication* (Halle-Wittenberg: Faculty of Law, Martin-Luther-University Halle-Wittenberg).

Tinbergen, J., 1954. *International Economic Integration* (Amsterdam: Elsevier).

Trebilcock, M.J. and Prado, M.M., 2014. *Advanced Introduction to Law and Development* (Cheltenham: Edward Elgar).

van de Walle, N., 2001. *African Economies and the Politics of Permanent Crisis, 1979–1999* (Cambridge: Cambridge University Press).

Ver Loren van Themaat, P., 1981. *The Changing Structure of International Economic Law: A Contribution of Legal History, of Comparative Law and of General Legal Theory to the Debate on a New International Economic Order* (The Hague; Boston; London: Martinus Nijhoff Publishers).

Viner, J., 1950. *The Customs Union Issue* (London; Lancaster, PA: Stevens and Sons).

Wade, R., 1990. *Governing the Market: Economic Theory and the Role of Government in East Asian Industrialisation* (Princeton: Princeton University Press).

Ward, I., 2009. *A Critical Introduction to European Law*, 3rd ed. (Cambridge: Cambridge University Press).

Weggoro, N.C., 1995. *Effects of Regional Economic Integration in Southern Africa and the Role of the Republic of South Africa: A Study of Project Coordination Approach in Industry and Trade in SADCC/SADC* (Berlin: Köster).

Witulski, U., 1990. *Macroeconomic Linkages Among Southern African Countries* (Munich; London: Weltforum-Verl.).

Yahuda, M., 2004. *The International Politics of the Asia Pacific since 1945* (London: Routledge).

Zweigert, K. and Kötz, H., 1998. *An Introduction to Comparative Law*, 3rd ed. (Oxford: Clarendon Press).

Book Chapters

Aka, P.C., 2012. 'Political Analysis of the Genesis of NEPAD' in B.H. Bobo and H. Sintim-Aboagye (eds), *Neo-Liberalism, Interventionism and the Developmental State: Implementing the New Partnership for Africa's Development* (Trenton, NJ; London: Africa World Press).

Alter, K.J., 2012. 'Understanding the European Court's Political Power' in H. Zimmerman and A. Dur (eds), *Key Controversies in European Integration* (Basingstoke: Palgrave Macmillan).

Andriamananjara, S., 2011. 'Customs Unions' in J-P. Chauffour and J-C. Mau (eds), *Preferential Trade Agreement Policies for Development: A Handbook* (Washington, DC: The World Bank).

Armstrong, K., 2002. 'Mutual Recognition' in C. Barnard and J. Scott (eds), *The Law of the Single European Market* (Oxford: Hart).

Arnull, A., 2009. 'European Community Legal Instruments' in P. Cane and J. Conaghan (eds), *The New Oxford Companion to Law* (Oxford: Oxford University Press).

Asante, S.K.B., 1984. 'ECOWAS, the EEC and the Lome Convention' in D. Mazzeo (ed.), *African Regional Organizations* (Cambridge: Cambridge University Press).

Bach, D., 1998. 'Régionalisme et mondialisation en Afrique subsaharienne: le retournement d'un paradigme' in D. Bach (ed.), *Régionalisation, mondialisation et fragmentation en Afrique subsaharienne* (Paris: Karthala).

Birkinshaw, P., 2012. 'National Courts and European Union Courts' in J. Hayward and R. Wurzel (eds), *European Disunion: Between Sovereignty and Solidarity* (Basingstoke: Palgrave Macmillan).

Boughton, J.M., 2006. 'Who's in Charge? Ownership and Conditionality in IMF-Supported Programs' in G. Ranis, J.R. Vreeland and S. Kosack (eds), *Globalisation of the Nation State: The Impact of the IMF and the World Bank* (London: Routledge).

Bouzas, R. and Soltz, H., 2001. 'Institutions and Regional Integration: The Case of MERCOSUR' in V. Bulmer-Thomas (ed.), *Regional Integration in Latin America and the Caribbean: The Political Economy of Open Regionalism* (London: University of London, Institute of Latin American Studies).

Browne, R.S., 1996. 'How Africa Can Prosper' in D.N. Balaam and M. Veseth (eds), *Readings in International Political Economy* (Upper Saddle River, NJ: Prentice Hall; London: Prentice-Hall International).

Burfisher, M.E. and Missiaen, M.B., 1990. 'Intraregional Trade in West Africa' in J.E. Okolo and S. Wright (eds), *West African Regional Cooperation and Development* (Boulder; Oxford: Westview Press).

Cahill, M., 2012. 'European Integration and European Constitutionalism: Consonances and Dissonances' in D. Augenstein (ed.), *'Integration Through Law' Revisited: The Making of the European Polity* (Farnham, Surrey, UK: Burlington, VT: Ashgate).

Cammack, P., 2002. 'Neoliberalism, the World Bank and the New Politics of Development' in U. Khotari and M. Minogue (eds), *Development Theory and Practice: Critical Perspectives* (Basingstoke: Palgrave Macmillan).

Castells, M., 1992. 'Four Asian Tigers With a Dragon Head: A Comparative Analysis of the State, Economy and Society in the Asian Pacific Rim' in R. Henderson and J. Applebaum (eds), *State and Development in the Asian Pacific Rim* (London: Sage Publications).

Chang, H-J., 2004. 'Institutional Foundations for Effective Design and Implementation of Trade and Industrial Policies in Least Developed Economies' in C. Soludo, O. Ogbu and H-J. Chang (eds), *The Politics of Trade and Industrial Policy in Africa: Forced Consensus?* (Trenton, NJ: Africa World Press).

———., 2015. 'Is Industrial Policy Necessary and Feasible in Africa? Theoretical Considerations and Historical Lessons' in A. Noman and J.E. Stiglitz (eds), *Industrial Policy and Economic Transformation in Africa* (New York: Columbia University Press).

Clark, J.M. Jr., 1992. 'The Sovereign Debt Crisis: A Lawyer's Perspective' in H. Fox (ed.), *International Economic Law and Developing States: An Introduction* (London: British Institute of International and Comparative Law).

Craig, P., 2002. 'The Evolution of the Single Market' in C. Barnard and J. Scott (eds), *The Law of the Single European Market: Unpacking the Premises* (Oxford: Hart Publishing).

Cummings, R.J., 1992. 'A Historical Perspective on the Lagos Plan of Action' in J.E. Nyang'oro and T.M. Shaw (eds), *Beyond Structural Adjustment in Africa: The Political Economy of Sustainable and Democratic Development* (New York; London: Praeger).

De la Mare, T. and Donnelly, C., 1999. 'Preliminary Rulings and EU Legal Integration: Evolution and Stasis' in P. Craig and G. Búrca (eds), *The Evolution of EU Law* (Oxford: Oxford University Press).

De Witte, B., 1999. 'Direct Effect, Primacy, and the Nature of the Legal Order' in P. Craig and G. Búrca (eds), *The Evolution of EU Law* (Oxford: Oxford University Press).

Dehousse, R. and Weiler, J.H.H., 1990. 'The Legal Dimension' in W. Wallace (ed.), *The Dynamics of European Integration* (London: Pinter for the Royal Institute of International Affairs).

Dickerson, C.M., 2009. 'Perspectives on the Future' in C.M. Dickerson (ed.), *Unified Business Laws for Africa: Common Law Perspectives on OHADA* (London; Philadelphia, PA: GMB Publishing).

Djuidje Kouam, R., 2008. 'APRM and the Challenges of the Implementation of Economic Governance Standards in Africa: A Critical Assessment' in S.H. Boko and D. Seck (eds), *NEPAD and the Future of Economic Policy in Africa* (Trenton, NJ; London: Africa World Press).

Edge, W.A., 1998. 'Botswana, a Developmental State' in W.A. Edge and M.H. Lekorwe (eds), *Botswana: Politics and Society* (Pretoria: J.L. van Schaik).

Fine, B., 2013. 'Beyond the Developmental State: An Introduction' in B. Fine, J. Saraswati and D. Tavasci (eds), *Beyond the Developmental State: Industrial Policy Into the Twenty-First Century* (London: Pluto Press).

Finger, J.M and Schuler, P., 2002. 'Implementation of WTO Commitments: The Development Challenge' in B. Hoekman, A. Mattoo and P. English (eds), *Development, Trade and the WTO: A Handbook* (Washington, DC: World Bank).

Fox, H., 1992. 'The Definition and Sources of International Economic Law' in H. Fox (ed.), *International Economic Law and Developing States: An Introduction* (London: British Institute of International and Comparative Law).

Frilet, M., 2012. 'Legal Innovation for Development: The OHADA Experience' in H. Cisse, S. Muller, C. Thomas and C. Wang (eds), *World Bank Legal Review Volume 4: Legal Innovation and Empowerment for Development* (Washington, DC: World Bank).

Fujita, M. and Hamagushi, N., 2011. 'Regional Integration of Production Systems and Spatial Income Disparities in East Asia' in M.N. Jovanovic (ed.), *International Handbook on the Economics of Integration, Volume II: Competition, Spatial Location of Economic Activity and Financial Issues* (Cheltenham; Northampton: Edward Elgar).

Gormley, L., 1985. *Prohibiting Restrictions on Trade Within the EEC* (Amsterdam; New York: North-Holland; New York, NY: Elsevier Science).

Graziadei, M., 2008. 'Comparative Law as the Study of Transplants and Receptions' in M. Reinmann and R. Zimmermann (eds), *The Oxford Handbook of Comparative Law* (Oxford: Oxford University Press).

Gunder Frank, A., 1970. 'The Development of Underdevelopment' in R. Rhodes (ed.), *Imperialism and Underdevelopment* (New York; London: Monthly Review Press).

Hansen, J.D. and Schroder, P.J.H., 2001. 'Economic Integration in Europe: Setting the Stage' in J.D. Hansen (ed.), *European Integration: An Economic Perspective* (Oxford: Oxford University Press).

Helpman, E., 2010. 'Labor Market Frictions as a Source of Comparative Advantage, With Implications for Unemployment and Inequality' in R.M. Solow and J-P. Touffut (eds.), *The Shape of The Division of Labour: Nations, Industries and Households* (Cheltenham: Edward Elgar Publishing).

Hervey, T., 2009. 'European Treaties' in P. Cane and J. Conaghan (eds), *The New Oxford Companion to Law* (Oxford: Oxford University Press).

Hu, R.W., 2011. 'China, the US and Regional Institution Building in East Asia' in R.P. Buckley, R.W. Hu and D.W. Arner (eds), *East Asian Economic Integration: Law, Trade and Finance* (Cheltenham; Northampton: Edward Elgar).

Hurrell, A., 2001. 'The Politics of Regional Integration in MERCOSUR' in V. Bulmer-Thomas (ed.), *Regional Integration in Latin America and the Caribbean: The Political Economy of Open Regionalism* (London: University of London, Institute of Latin American Studies).

Ilorah, R., 2012. 'The Realities of Regional Integration: The NEPAD Perspective' in B.H. Bobo and H. Sintim-Aboagye (eds), *Neo-Liberalism, Interventionism and the Developmental State: Implementing the New Partnership for Africa's Development* (Trenton, NJ; London: Africa World Press).

Jebuni, C.D., Ogunkola, E.O. and Soludo, C.C., 1999. 'A Case-Study of the Economic Community of West African States (ECOWAS)' in A. Oyejide, I. Elbadawi and S. Yeo (eds), *Regional Integration and Trade Liberalization in SubSaharan Africa, Vol. 3: Regional Case-Studies* (Basingstoke: Palgrave Macmillan).

Kasekende, L.A., Ng'eno, N. and Lipumba, N., 1999. 'Regional Integration and Economic Liberalization in Eastern and Southern Africa' in A. Oyejide, I. Elbadawi and S. Yeo (eds), *Regional Integration and Trade Liberalization in Sub-Saharan Africa, Vol. 3: Regional Case-Studies* (Basingstoke: Palgrave Macmillan).

Kelly, D., 2005. 'Trade, Security and Globalisation' in D. Kelly and D. Grant (eds), *The Politics of International Trade in the Twenty-First Century: Actors, Issues and Regional Dynamics* (Houndmills; Basingstoke; Hampshire; New York: Palgrave Macmillan).

Kennes, W., 1999. 'Africa Regional Economic Integration and the European Union' in D. Bach (ed.), *Regionalisation in Africa: Integration and Disintegration* (Oxford: James Curry).

Keohane, R.O., 2003. 'Political Authority After Intervention—Gradation in Sovereignty' in J.K. Holzrefe and R.O. Keohane (eds), *Humanitarian Intervention: Ethical, Legal and Political Dilemmas* (Cambridge: Cambridge University Press).

Khan, M., 2012. 'Beyong Good Governance: An Agenda for Developmental Governance' in J.K. Sundaram and A. Chowdhury (eds), *Is Good Governance Good for Development* (London: Bloomsbury Academic).

Khor, M., 2008. 'The World Trading System and Development Concerns' in N. Serra and J. Stiglitz (eds), *The Washington Consensus Reconsidered: Towards A New Global Governance* (Oxford: Oxford University Press).

Killick, T. and Hewitt, A., 1996. 'Bilateral Aid Conditionality and Policy Leverage' in O. Stokke (ed.), *Foreign Aid Towards the Year 2000: Experiences and Challenges* (London: Frank Cass).

Krapohl, S., Fraude, B. and Dinkel, J., 2010. 'Judicial Integration in the Americas? A Comparison of Dispute Settlement in NAFTA and MERCOSUR' in F. Laursen (ed.), *Comparative Regional Integration* (Surrey: Ashgate).

Lall, S., 2004. 'Selective Industrial and Trade Policies in Developing Countries: Theoretical and Empirical Issues' in C. Soludo, O. Ogbu and H-J. Chan (eds), *The Politics of Trade and Industrial Policy in Africa: Forced Consensus?* (Trenton, NJ: Africa World Press).

Laursen, F., 2010. 'Regional Integration: Some Introductory Reflections' in F. Laursen (ed.), *Comparative Regional Integration: Europe and Beyond* (Surrey: Ashgate).

Mac Amhlaigh, C.S., 2011. 'Concepts of Integration Through Law (and the Price of Constitutional Pluralism)' in D. Augenstein (ed.), *Integration Through Law Revisited: The Making of European Polity* (Farnham, Surrey, UK; Burlington, VT: Ashgate).

Malewezi, J., 2001. 'Regional Integration: The Path to Prosperity?' in C. Clapham, G. Mills, A. Morner and E. Sidiropoulos (eds), *Regional Integration in Southern Africa: Comparative International Perspectives* (Johannesburg: SAIIA).

Matsuyama, K., 1998. 'Economic Development as Coordination Problems' in M. Aoki, H-K. Kim and M. Okuno-Fujiwara (eds), *The Role of Government in East Asian Economic Development: Comparative Institutional Analysis* (Oxford: Clarendon Press).

Mazzeo, D., 1984. 'The Experience of the East African Community: Implications for the Theory and Practice of Regional Cooperation in Africa' in D. Mazzeo (ed.), *African Regional Organizations* (Cambridge: Cambridge University Press).

Mercurio, B., 2011. 'Bilateral and Regional Trade Agreements in Asia: A Sceptic's View' in R.P. Buckley, R.W. Hu and D.W. Arner (eds), *East Asian Economic Integration: Law, Trade and Finance* (Cheltenham; Northampton: Edward Elgar).

Mistelis, L., 2001. 'Is Harmonisation a Necessary Evil? The Future of Harmonisation and New Sources of International Trade Law' in I. Fletcher, L. Mistelis and M. Cremona (eds), *Foundations and Perspectives of International Trade Law* (London: Sweet and Maxwell).

Moravcisk, A. and Schimmerlfenning, F., 2009. 'Liberal Intergovernmentalism' in A. Wiener and T. Diez (eds), *European Integration* (Oxford: Oxford University Press).

Mtengeti-Migiro, R., 1992. *Institutional Arrangements for Economic Integration in Eastern and Southern Africa: A Study of SADCC and the PTA With Experiences From the EEC* (Konstanz: Hartung-Gore).

Mvungi, S.E.A., 1994. *Constitutional Questions in the Regional Integration Process: The Case of the Southern African Development Community With References to the European Community* (Hamburg: Freidrich Naumann Foundation Southern Africa Regional Office).

Newton, S., 2006. 'The Dialectics of Law and Development' in D.M. Trubek and A. Santos (eds), *The New Law and Economic Development: A Critical Appraisal* (Cambridge: Cambridge University Press).

Nicolaides, P., 2011. 'EU Policies and Policy-Making' in M.N. Jovanovic (ed.), *International Handbook on the Economics of Integration, Volume I: General Issues and Regional Groups* (Cheltenham; Northampton: Edward Elgar).

Ninsin, K.A., 2008. 'West Africa's Integration: The Logic of History and Culture' in S. Adejumobi and A. Olukoshi (eds), *The African Union and New Strategies for Development in Africa* (Amherst, NY: Cambria Press).

Nishikimi, K. and Kuroiwa, I., 2011. 'Analytical Framework for East Asian Integration (1): Industrial Agglomeration and Concentrated Dispersion' in M. Fujita., I. Kuroiwa and S. Kumagai (eds), *The Economics of East Asian Integration: A Comprehensive Introduction to Regional Issues* (Cheltenham; Northampton: Edward Elgar).

Nnadozie, E., 2008. 'NEPAD, APRM, and Institutional Change in Africa' in S. Adejumobi and A. Olukoshi (eds), *The African Union and New Strategies for Development in Africa* (Amherst; New York: Cambria Press).

Odhiambo, W., 2005. 'The East African Customs Union and Its Implications' in R. Ajulu (ed.), *The Making of a Region—the Revival of the East African Community* (Midrand, South Africa: Institute for Global Dialogue).

Odularu, G.O., 2008. 'The Challenges of Globalisation and Regional Integration: Lessons From Africa' in S.H. Boko and D. Seck (eds), *NEPAD and the Future of Economic Policy in Africa* (Trenton, NJ; London: Africa World Press).

Okamoto, J., 2011. 'Institution Building For Economic Integration in East Asia: A Brief History' in M. Fujita, I. Kuroiwa and S. Kumagai (eds), *The Economics of East Asian Integration: A Comprehensive Introduction to Regional Issues* (Cheltenham; Northampton: Edward Elgar).

Oloo, A.G.R., 2005. 'The EALA and the National Assemblies of Partner States: Conflict or Harmony? in R. Ajulu (ed.), *The Making of a Region—The Revival of the East African Community* (Midrand, South Africa: Institute for Global Dialogue).

Olukoshi, A.O., 2004. 'Democratisation, Globalisation an Effective Policy Making in Africa' in C. Soludo, O. Ogbu and H-J. Chan (eds), *The Politics of Trade and Industrial Policy in Africa: Forced Consensus?* (Trenton, NJ: Africa World Press).

Pitelis, C.N., 2011. 'Foreign Direct Investment and Economic Integration' in M.N. Jovanovic (ed.), *International Handbook on the Economics of Integration*, Vol. III: Factor Mobility, Agriculture, Environment and Quantitative Studies (Cheltenham and Northampton: Edward Eldgar).

Pomfret, R., 2011. 'Regional Integration in Asia' in M.N. Jovanovic (ed.), *International Handbook on the Economics of Integration, Volume I: General Issues and Regional Groups* (Cheltenham; Northampton: Edward Elgar).

Porges, A., 2011. 'Dispute Settlement' in J-P. Chauffour and J-C. Mau (eds), *Preferential Trade Agreement Policies for Development: A Handbook* (Washington, DC: The World Bank).

Pririe, I., 2013. 'Globalisation and the Decline of the Developmental State' in B. Fine, J. Saraswati and D. Tavasci (eds), *Beyond the Developmental State: Industrial Policy Into the Twenty-First Century* (London: Pluto Press).

Radkin, J., 2012. 'The European Court of Justice: A Strange Institution' in H. Zimmerman and A. Dur (eds), *Key Controversies in European Integration* (Basingstoke: Palgrave Macmillan).

Robson, P., 1997. 'Integration in Sub-Saharan Africa' in A.M. El-Agraa (ed.), *Economic Integration Worldwide* (Basingstoke: Palgrave Macmillan).

Shapiro, M., 1999. 'The European Court of Justice' in P. Craig and G. Búrca (eds), *The Evolution of EU Law* (Oxford: Oxford University Press).

Sidaway, J. and Gibb, R., 1998. 'SADC, COMESA, SACU: Contradictory Formats for Regional Integration in Southern Africa' in D. Simon (ed.), *Reconfiguring the Region: South Africa in Southern Africa* (London: James Currey).

Simon, D., 2003. 'Regional Development-Environment Discourses, Policies and Practices in Post-Apartheid Southern Africa' in A. Grant and F. Soderbaum (eds), *The New Regionalism in Africa* (Aldershot: Ashgate).

Simo Thumde, M., 2009. 'OHADA as Experienced in Cameroon: Addressing Areas of Particular Concern to Common Law Jurists' in C.M. Dickerson (ed.),

Unified Business Laws for Africa: Common Law Perspectives on OHADA (London; Philadelphia, PA: GMB Publishing).

Smith, M.G., 2011. 'The North American Free Trade Agreement: *fait accompli?*' in M.N. Jovanovic (ed.), *International Handbook on the Economics of Integration, Volume I: General Issues and Regional Groups* (Cheltenham; Northampton: Edward Elgar).

Tamm, D., 2012. 'The History of the Court of Justice of the European Union Since Its Origin' in A. Rosas, E. Levits and Y. Bot (eds), *The Court of Justice and the Construction of Europe: Analyses and Perspectives on Sixty Years of Case-law—La Cour de Justice et la Construction de l'Europe: Analyses et Perspectives de Soixante Ans de Jurisprudence* (Dordrecht: Springer).

Toohey, L., 2011. 'When "failure" Indicates Success: Understanding Trade Disputes Between ASEAN Members' in R.P. Buckley, R.W. Hu and D.W. Arner (eds), *East Asian Economic Integration: Law, Trade and Finance* (Cheltenham; Northampton: Edward Elgar).

Trubek, D.M. and Santos, A., 2006. 'Introduction: The Third Moment in Law and Development Theory and the Emergence of a New Critical Practice' in D.M. Trubek and A. Santos (eds), *The New Law and Economic Development: A Critical Appraisal* (Cambridge: Cambridge University Press).

Usman, M.T., 2008. 'NEPAD and the Economic Integration Agenda in Africa—Reflection on the Prospect and Constraints' in S.H. Boko and D. Seck (eds), *NEPAD and the Future of Economic Policy in Africa* (Trenton, NJ; London: Africa World Press).

Van Langhenhove, L., 2013. 'Why We Need to "Unpack" Regions to Compare Them More Effectively' in L. Fioramonti (ed.), *Regionalism in a Changing World* (London: Routledge).

Van Waeyenberge, E., 2006. 'From Washington to Post-Washington Consensus: Illusions of Development' in B. Fine and K.S. Jomo (eds), *The New Development Economics: After the Washington Consensus* (New Delhi: Tulika Books; London: Zed Books).

Wanyande, P., 2005. 'The Role of the East African Assembly' in R. Ajulu (ed.), *The Making of a Region—the Revival of the East African Community* (Midrand, South Africa: Institute for Global Dialogue).

Weatherill, S., 2004. 'Why Harmonise?' in T. Tridimas and P. Nebbia (eds), *European Union Law for the Twenty-First Century* (Oxford: Hart Publishing).

Williamson, J., 1990. 'What Washington Means by Policy Reform' in J. Williamson (ed.), *Latin American Adjustment: How Much Has Happened?* (Washington, DC: Institute for International Economics).

Journal Articles

Abarchi, D., 2000. 'La supranationalité de l'OHADA' 44 *Revue EDJA*.

Abbott, F.M., 2000. 'NAFTA and the Legalisation of World Politics: A Case Study' 54(3) *International Organization* 519.

Abbott, K.W. and Snidal, D., 2000. 'Hard and Soft Law in International Governance' 54(3) *International Organization* 421.

Abott, K.W. et al., 2000. 'The Concept of Legalisation' 54(3) *International Organization* 401.

Afadameh-Adeyemi, A. and Kalula, E., 2010. 'SADC at 30: Re-Examining the Legal and Institutional Anatomy of the Southern African Development Community' in *Monitoring Regional Integration in Southern Africa Yearbook 2010*, pp. 5–22 (Stellenbosch: Trade Law Centre for Southern Africa, the Konrad-Adenauer-Stiftung).

Ajulo, S.B., 2001. 'Sources of Law of the Economic Community of West African States (ECOWAS)' 45(1) *Journal of African Law* 73.

Akinrinsola, I., 2004. 'Legal and Institutional Requirements for West African Economic Integration' 10 *Law and Business Review of the Americas* 493.

Alavi, J.S., 2011. 'Regional Trade Agreements Among Developing Countries: Enabling Clause Re-visited', *SSRN Electronic Journal*.

Allot, A., 1965. 'Towards the Unification of Laws in Africa' 14(2) *The International and Comparative Law Quarterly*.

Alter, K.J., Helfer, L.R. and McAllister, J.R., 2013. 'A New International Human Rights Court for West Africa: The ECOWAS Community Court of Justice' 107 *American Journal of International Law* 737.

Andersen, C.B., 2007. 'Defining Uniformity in Law' 12(1) *Uniform Law Review* 1.

Arieti, A., 2006. 'The Role of MERCOSUR as a Vehicle for Latin American Integration' 6 *Chicago Journal of International Law* 761.

Baldwin, R.E., 2005. 'Sequencing and Depth of Regional Economic Integration: Lessons for the Americas From Europe' 31(1) *World Economy* 5.

Bamodu, G., 1994. 'Transnational Law, Unification and Harmonization of International Commercial Law in Africa' 38 *Journal of African Law* 125.

Barkan, J.D., 1994. 'Resurrecting Modernisation Theory and the Emergence of Civil Society in Kenya and Nigeria' in D.E. Apter and C.G. Rosberg (eds) *Political Development and the New Realism in Sub-Saharan Africa* (Charlottesville; London: University Press of Virginia).

Bashi Rudahindwa, J., 2012. 'From Port-Louis to Panama and Washington DC: Two Regional Approaches to International Commercial Arbitration' 14(1) *European Journal of Law Reform* 44.

Berman, P.S., 2007. 'Global Legal Pluralism' 80 *Southern California Law Review* 1155.

Blecker, R.A., 2005. 'The North American Economies After NAFTA: A Critical Appraisal' 33(3) *International of Political Economy* 5.

———, 2009. 'External Shocks, Structural Change, and Economic Growth in Mexico, 1979–2007' 37(7) *World Development* 1274.

Boldorini, M.C. and Zalduendo, S., 1995. 'La estructura juridico-institutional del MERCOSUR despues del Protocolo de Ouro Preto' 283 *Boletin Informativo Techint*.

Bowles, P. and MacLean, B., 1996. 'Understanding Trade Bloc Formation: The Case of the ASEAN Free Trade Area' 3(2) *Review of International Political Economy* 319.

Burke-White, W., 2005. 'International Legal Pluralism' 25 *Michigan Journal of International Law* 977.

Carbonara, E. and Parisi, F., 2007. 'The Paradox of Legal Harmonization' 132(3/4) *Public Choice* 367.

Carubba, C.J. and Murrah, L., 2005. 'Legal Integration and Use of the Preliminary Ruling Process in the European Union' 59(2) *International Organization* 399.

Chingono, M. and Nakana, S., 2009. 'The Challenge of Regional Integration in Southern Africa' 3 *African Journal of Political Science and International Relations* 396.

Coastworth, J., 2005. 'Structures, Endowments and Institutions in the Economic History of Latin America' 40(3) *Latin America Research Review* 126.

Collier, P. and Gunning, J.W., 1999. 'Why Has Africa Grown Slowly?' 13(3) *The Journal of Economic Perspectives* 3.

Comaroff, J. and Comaroff, J.L., 2000. 'Millennial Capitalism: First Thoughts on a Second Coming' 12(2) *Public Culture* 291.

Cooke, B., 2003. 'A New Continuity With Colonial Administration: Participation in Development Management' 24(1) *Third World Quarterly*.

Coutts, S.D., 2011. 'The Lisbon Treaty and the Area of Freedom, Security and Justice as an Area of Legal Integration' 7 *Croatian Yearbook of European Law and Policy* 87.

Davidson, P., 2004. 'The ASEAN Way and the Role of Law in ASEAN Economic Cooperation' 8 *Singapore Year Book of International Law*.

DeGhetto, K., Gray, J.R. and Kiggundu, M.N., 2016. 'The African Union's Agenda 2063: Aspirations, Challenges, and Opportunities for Management Research' 2 *African Journal of Management* 1.

De Waele, H., 2010. 'The Role of the European Court of Justice in the Integration Process: A Contemporary and Normative Assessment' 6(1) *Hanse Law Review* 3.

Dickerson, C.M., 2005. 'Harmonizing Business Law in Africa: OHADA Calls the Tune' 44 *Columbia Journal of Transnational Law* 17.

Du Plessis, M. and Malebakeng, F., 2010. 'Enforcing the SADC Tribunal's Decisions in South Africa: Immunity: South African Judicial Decisions' 35 *South African Yearbook of International Law* 265.

Eleftheriadis, P., 1998. 'Begging the Constitutional Question' 36 *Journal of Common Market Studies* 255.

Estrella Faria, J.A., 2009. 'Future Directions of Legal Harmonisation and Law Reform: Stormy Seas or Prosperous Voyage?' *Uniform Law Review* 5.

Fagbayibo, B., 2009. 'Towards the Harmonisation of Laws in Africa: Is OHADA the Way to Go?' 42(3) *Comparative and International Law Journal of Southern Africa* 309.

Ferreira-Snyman, M.P. and Ferreira, G.M., 2010, 'The Harmonisation of Laws Within the African Union and the Viability of Legal Pluralism as an Alternative' 73 *Journal of Contemporary Dutch-Dutch Law* 608.

Garret, G., Kelemen, D.R. and Schulz, H., 1998. 'The European Court of Justice, National Governments, and Legal Integration in the European Union' 52(1) *International Organization* 149.

Gathii, J.T., 2000. 'Retelling Good Governance Narratives on Africa's Economic and Political Predicaments: Continuities and Discontinuities in Legal Outcomes Between Markets and States' 45 *Villanova Law Review* 971.

Gattamorta, M.E., 2005. 'The Evolution of Development Strategies for Africa: From the Lagos Plan of Action to the Report of the Commission for Africa' 1 *CeMiSS Quarterly* 94.

Gibbon, P., 1993. 'The World Bank and the New Politics of Aid' 5(1) *European Journal of Development Research* 35.

Goh, G., 2000. 'The ASEAN Way: Non-Intervention and ASEAN Role in Conflict Management' *Stanford Journal of East Asian Affairs* 113.

Goode, R., 2005. 'Rule, Practice, and Pragmatism in Transnational Commercial Law' 54(3) *The International and Comparative Law Quarterly* 539.

Gopalan, S., 2003. 'Transitional Commercial Law: The Way Forward' 18(4) *American University International Law Review* 803.

Gupta, K.R., 2007. 'Objectives of GATT and Developing Countries' 35(2) *South African Journal of Economics* 126.

Hartkamp, A., 2003. 'Modernisation and Harmonisation of Contract Law: Objectives, Methods and Scope' 8(1–2) *Uniform Law Review* 81.

Hayashi, S., 2010. 'The Developmental State in the Era of Globalisation: Beyond the Northeast Asian Model of Political Economy' 23(1) *The Pacific Review* 45.

Hazlewood, A., 1979. 'The End of the East African Community: What Are the Lessons for Regional Integration Schemes?' 18(1) *Journal of Common Market Studies* 40.

Hemel, D. and Schalkwyk, A., 2010. 'Tyranny on Trial: Regional Courts Crack Down on Mugabe's Land "Reform"' *The Yale Journal of International Law* 517.

Hope, R.K., 2002. 'From Crisis to Renewal: Towards a Successful Implementation of the New Partnership for Africa's Development' 101 *African Affairs* 387.

Ikejiaku, B-V., 2009. 'The Concept of "Development" Revisited Towards Understanding: In the Context of Sub-Saharan Africa' 2(1) *Journal of Politics and Law* 31.

Issa-Sayegh, J., 1999. 'Quelques aspects techniques de l'intégration juridique: Exemple des Actes Uniformes de l'OHADA' *Revue de droit uniforme.*

Joerges, C., 1996. 'Taking the Law Seriously: On Political Science and the Role of Law in the Process of European Integration' 2(2) *European Law Journal* 105.

Jourdan, P., 1998. 'Spatial Development Initiatives (SDIs)—the Official View' 15(5) *Development Southern Africa.*

Kaltenthaler, K. and Mora, F.O., 2002. 'Explaining Latin American Economic Integration: The Case of MERCOSUR' 9(1) *Review of International Political Economy* 72.

Kelemen, R.D., 2012. 'The Political Foundations of Judicial Independence in the European Union' 19(1) *Journal of European Policy* 43.

Keohane, R.O., Moravcsik, A. and Slaughter, A.M., 2000. 'Legalized Dispute Resolution: Interstate and Transnational'54(3) *International Organization* 457.

Khondker, H., 2008. 'Globalisation and State Autonomy in Singapore' 36(1) *Asian Journal of Social Science* 35.

Kouassi, R.N., 2007. 'The Itinerary of the African Integration Process: An Overview of Historical Landmarks' 1 *African Integration Review* 1.

Leipziger, D.M., Frischtak, C., Kharas, H.M. and Normand, J.F., 1997. 'MERCOSUR: Integration and Industrial Policy' 20(5) *The World Economy* 585.

Lenz, C.O., 1994. 'The Role and Mechanism of the Preliminary Ruling Procedure' 18(2) *Fordham International Law Journal* 389.

Lodge, J. and Herman, V., 1980. 'The Economic and Social Committee in EEC Decision-Making' 34(2) *International Organization* 265.

Mahiou, A., 1993. 'La Communauté Economique Africaine' 39(1) *Annuaire français de droit international.*

Mancuso, S., 2007. 'Trends on the Harmonization of Contract Law in Africa' 13(1) *Annual Survey of International and Comparative Law*.

Mansfield, E.D. and Milner, H.V., 1999. 'The New Wave of Regionalism' 53 *International Organization* 589.

Manzetti, L., 1992. 'Economic Integration in the Southern Cone' *North South Focus* 1.

Marangos, J., 2009. 'What Happened to the Washington Consensus? The Evolution of International Development Policy' 38 *The Journal of Socio-Economics* 197.

Mbaku, J.M., 2004. 'NEPAD and Prospects for Development in Africa' 41(4) *International Studies* 387.

Mbaye, K., 2004. 'L'Histoire et les objectifs de l'OHADA' *Petites Affiches* n°205.

Meisenhelder, T., 1997. 'The Developmental State in Mauritius' 35(2) *Journal of Modern African Studies* 279.

Merry, S.E., 1991. 'Law and Colonialism' 25(4) *Law and Society Review* 890.

Mkandawire, T., 2001. 'Thinking About Developmental States in Africa' 25 *Cambridge Journal of Economics* 289.

Mytelka, L., 1977. 'The Lome Convention and a New International Division of Labour' 1(1) *Journal of European Integration* 63.

Nesadurai, H.E.S., 2003. 'Attempting Developmental Regionalism Through AFTA: The Domestic Sources of Regional Governance' 24(2) *Third World Quarterly* 235.

Ngugi, J.M., 2005. 'Policing Neo-Liberal Reforms: The Rule of Law as an Enabling and Restrictive Discourse' 26 *University of Pennsylvania Journal of International Law*513.

Nicholaidis, K., 2007. 'Mutual Recognition "on trial" the Long Road to Services Liberalisation' 14(5) *Journal of European Public Policy* 717.

Omilola, B., 2011. 'To What Extent Are Regional Trade Agreements in Africa Fulfilling the Conditions for Successful RTAs?' 3(6) *Journal of African Studies and Development* 105.

Omogorobe, Y., 1992. 'The Legal Framework for Economic Integration in the ECOWAS Region: An Analysis of the Trade Liberalisation Scheme' 5 *African Journal of International and Comparative Law* 355.

Osiemo, O., 2014. 'Lost in Translation: The Role of African Regional Courts in Regional Integration in Africa' 1 *Legal Issues of Economic Integration* 87.

Ouattara, A., 2001. 'De la nature juridique des Actes Uniformes de l'OHADA' 20 *Revue mensuelle de l'AIDD*.

Ovrawah, O.A., 1994. 'Harmonisation of Laws Within the Economic Community of West African States (ECOWAS)' 6 *African Journal of International & Comparative Law* 76.

Parrenas, J.C., 1998. 'ASEAN and Asia-Pacific Economic Cooperation' 11(2) *Pacific Review* 233.

Paul, J.R., 2003. 'Do International Trade Institutions Contribute to Economic Growth and Development?' 44(1) *Virginia Journal of International Law*.

Pierson, C., 1992. 'Democracy, Market and Capital: Are There Necessary Economic Limits to Democracy?' *40 Political Studies*, Special Issue.

Prempeh, H.K., 2006. 'Marbury in Africa: Judicial Review and the Challenge of Constitutionalism in Contemporary Africa' 80(4) *Tulane Law Review*.

Radice, H., 2008. 'The Developmental State Under Global Neoliberalism' 29(6) *Third World Quarterly* 1153.

Ruggie, J., 1982. 'International Regimes, Transactions, and Change: Embedded Liberalism in the Postwar Economic Order' 36(2) *International Organization*.

Salacuse, J.W., 1999. 'From Developing Countries to Emerging Markets: A Changing Role for Law in the Third World' 33 *International Lawyer* 875.

Sawadogo, F.M., 2001. 'Les Actes uniformes de l'OHADA: aspects techniques et généraux' 39–40 *Revue Burkinabé de droit*, Numéro spécial.

Schmitt, S.K., 2007. 'Mutual Recognition as a New Mode of Governance' 14(5) *Journal of European Public Policy*.

Sherman, F.C., 2009. 'Law and Development Today: The New Developmentalism' 10(09) *German Law Journal* 1257.

Smith, J.M., 2000. 'The Politics of Dispute Settlement Design: Explaining Legalism in Regional Trade Pacts' 54(1) *International Organization* 137.

Snidal, D., 1985. 'Coordination Versus Prisoners' Dilemma: Implications for International Cooperation and Regimes' 79 *American Political Science Review* 923.

Soderbaum, F., 2004. 'Modes of Regional Governance in Africa: Neoliberalism, Sovereignty Boosting, and Shadow Networks' 10(4) *Global Governance* 419.

Starr-Deelen, D. and Deelen, B., 1996. 'The European Court of Justice as a Federator' 26(4) *Publius*.

Stein, E., 1981. 'Lawyers, Judges, and the Making of a Transnational Constitution' 75(1) *The American Journal of International Law* 1.

Stone Sweet, A., 2010. 'The European Court of Justice and the Judicialization of EU Governance' 5(2) *Living Reviews in EU Governance* 5.

Stubbs, R., 2009. 'Whatever Happened to the East Asian Developmental State? The Unfolding Debate' 22(1) *Pacific Review* 1.

Sweet, A.S. and Brunell, T.L., 1998. 'Constructing a Supranational Constitution: Dispute Resolution and Governance in the European Community' 92(1) *The American Political Science Review* 63.

Tamanaha, B., 1995. 'Lessons of Law-and-Development Studies' 89(2) *American Journal of International Law* 470.

Tan, L.H., 2002. 'Law and Policy in ASEAN Economic Integration', 38 *Asia Business Law Review*.

Ten Kate, A., 1992. 'Trade Liberalisation and Economic Stablilisation in Mexico: Lessons of Experience' 20(5) *World Development* 659.

Teynier, E. and Yala, F., 2001. 'Un nouveau centre d'arbitrage en Afrique Sub-Saharienne' 37 *Acomex* 1.

Tickell, A., 2002. 'Neoliberalizing Space' 34(3) *Antipode* 380.

Trubek, D., 1972. 'Max Weber on Law and the Rise of Capitalism' *Wisconsin Law Review* 742.

Tsie, B., 1996. 'States and Markets in the Southern African Development Community (SADC): Beyond the Neo-Liberal Paradigm' 22 *Journal of Southern African Studies*.

Vaillant, M., 2005. 'MERCOSUR: Southern Integration Under Construction' *Internationale Politik und Gesellschaft* 2.

van der Mei, A.P., 2009. 'Regional Integration: The Contribution of the Court of Justice of the East African Community' *ZaöRV* 69.

Vandervelde, K.J., 1998. 'The Political Economy of a Bilateral Investment Treaty' 92(4) *The American Journal of International Law* 621.

Vervaele, J.A.E., 2005. 'MERCOSUR and Regional Integration in South America' 54(2) *The International and Comparative Law Quarterly* 387.

Vinuesa, R.E., 2005. 'Enforcement of MERCOSUR Arbitration Awards Within the Domestic Legal Orders of Member States' 40 *Texas International Law Journal* 425.

Williamson, J., 1993. 'Democracy and the "Washington Consensus"' 21(8) *World Development* 1334.

Research and Policy Papers

Adepoju, A., Boulton, A. and Levin, M., 2007. 'Promoting Integration Through Mobility: Free Movement and the ECOWAS Protocol' *UNHCR Paper No. 150*, Geneva: Policy Development and Evaluation Service, United Nations High Commissioner for Refugees.

Akinbote, A., 2010. 'The OHADA and ECOWAS Treaties as Tools for Regional Integration and Regulatory Norms' *Paper presented at the Network of Reformers' Workshop*, Kampala 19–21 January.

Alter, K., 2009. 'The European Court's Political Power Across Time and Space' *Northwestern Law & Econ Research Paper No. 09-03*, Northwestern University – Department of Political Science; University of Copenhagen, Faculty of Law.

Alves, P., Draper, P. and Khumalo, N., 2009. 'Africa's Challenges in International Trade and Regional Integration: What Role for Europe?' *SAIIA Occasional Paper No. 32*, South African Institute of International Affairs, Johannesburg, South Africa.

Balassa, B., 1984. 'Trade Between Developed and Developing Countries: The Decade Ahead' (3) *OECD Economic Studies.*

Belanger, L., 2009. 'Incompleteness and Maintenance of International Cooperation: The Ex-Post Politics of MERCOSUR and NAFTA' *Paper Presented at the 2009 ABRI-ISA Meeting*, Rio de Janeiro, 21–24 July.

Bond, P. and Dor, G., 2003. 'Neoliberalism and Poverty Reduction Strategies in Africa' *Discussion Paper for the Regional Network for Equity in Health in Southern Africa (EQUINET)*, Harare, Zimbabwe, March 2003.

Cotterrell, R., 2012. 'What Is Transnational Law?' 37(2) *Law and Social Inquiry* 500.

Davis, K. and Trebilcock, M.J., 1999. 'What Role Do Legal Institutions Play in Development?' *Draft prepared for the International Monetary Fund's Conference on Second Generation Reforms*, 8–9 November.

Draper, P., 2010. 'Rethinking The (European) Foundations of Sub-Saharan African Regional Economic Integration: A Political Economy Essay' *OECD Development Centre Working Papers*, No. 293, OECD Publishing, Paris.

Estevadeordal, A., 1999. 'Negotiating Preferential Market Access: The Case of NAFTA' *Working Paper 3, Institute for the Integration of Latin America and the Caribbean*, Buenos Aires.

Harvey, D., 2007. 'Neoliberlism as Creative Destruction' 610 *The Annals of the American Academy of Political and Social Science, NAFTA and Beyond: Alternative Perspectives in the Study of Global Trade and Development.*

Hoeller, P., Girouard, N. and Colecchia, A., 1998. 'The European Trade Policies and Their Economic Effects' *OECD Economic Department Working Paper No. 194*, OECD Publishing, Paris.

Kent, J.L., 1991. 'Effectiveness of the European Court of Justice and Its Role in the Process of Integration' *Paper presented at the Second International Conference on 'The Challenges of a New European Architecture: Implications for the European Community's Internal and External Agendas'*, 22–24 May 1991, George Mason University, Fairfax, VA.

Kitonsa, E., 2012. 'The Status of the EAC Legal Harmonisation Process in Uganda' *Paper presented at the Conference on Creating a Predictable and Facilitative Legal Environment For Business in The East African Community*, Arusha, Tanzania, 6–7 August.

Kowalski, P., 2011. 'Comparative Advantage and Trade Performance: Policy Implications' *OECD Trade Policy Paper No. 121*, OECD Publishing, Paris.

Law Krumm, K.L., 1985. 'The External Debt of Sub-Saharan Africa: Origins, Magnitude and Implications for Action' *Staff Working Paper No. SWP 741*, Washington, DC: The World Bank.

Moreno-Brid, J.C., 2007. 'Economic Development and Industrial Performance in Mexico Post-NAFTA' *Paper presented at the Taller Nacional sobre 'Migracion interna y destrallos en Mexico: diagnostico, perspectivas y politicas'*, Mexico City, 16 April.

Mugyenyi, O. and Zeija, F., 2006. 'The East African Customs Union Protocol: An Audit of the Stakeholders' Participation in the Negotiation Process' *ACODE Policy Research Series No. 14*, http://www.acode-u.org/Files/Publications/PRS_14.pdf (accessed on 13 March 2018).

Ndulo, M., 1992. 'The Promotion of Intra-African Trade and The Harmonisation of Laws in the African Economic Community: Prospects and Problems' *Paper presented at the conference of the African Economic Community Treaty*, Abuja, Nigeria, 27–30 January.

Nsekela, J.H.R., 2009 'The Role of the East African Court of Justice in the Integration Process' *Paper Presented During the 3rd East African Community Media Summit*, Imperial Royale Hotel, Kampala, Uganda, 21–22 August.

Olarreaga, M., Soloaga, I. and Winters, A., 1999. 'What's Behind MERCOSUR's Common External Tariff?' *World Bank Policy Research Paper No. WPS 2231*, Washington, DC: World Bank.

Oloka-Onyango, J., 2005. 'Who Owns the East African Community?' *Human Rights and Peace Centre Occasional Paper Series No. 1*, Makerere University, Kampala, Uganda.

Pacheco-Lopez, P. and Thirlwall, A.P., 2004. 'Trade Liberalisation in Mexico: Rhetoric and Reality' 57 (229) *PSL Quarterly Review* 141.

Riedel, J., 1986. 'Myths and Reality of External Constraints on Development' *Thames Essays No. 47*, London: Trade Policy Research Centre.

Shapiro, H., 2007. 'Industrial Policy and Growth' *DESA Working Paper No. 53*, New York: United Nations.

Shefaeddin, S.M., 2005. 'Trade Liberalisation and Economic Reform in Developing Countries: Structural Change of De-Industrialisation?' *UNCTAD Discussion Paper No. 179*, Geneva: United Nations.

Smith, M.P., 2003. 'From Competition to Competitiveness: A New EU Industrial Policy?' *Paper presented at the Eighth Biennal International Conference of the European Studies Association*, Nashville, TN, 27–29 March.

Stephan, P.B., 1999. 'The Futility of Unification and Harmonization in International Commercial Law' *Legal Studies Working Papers, Working Paper No. 99–10,* University of Virginia School of Law, Charlottesville, Virginia, United States.

Stiglitz, J., 1998. 'Towards a New Paradigm for Development: Strategies, Policies and Processes' *Paper presented at the Prebisch Lecture at UNCTAD*, October.

Thomas, C., 2008. 'Re-Reading Weber in Law and Development: A Critical Intellectual History of "Good Governance" Reform' *Cornell Law Faculty Publications, Paper 118.*

Trubek, D.M., 2009. 'Developmental States and the Legal Order: Towards a New Political Economy of Development and Law' *Legal Studies Research Paper Series Paper No. 1075*, University of Wisconsin Law School, Madison, Wisconsin, United States.

UNECA, Friedrich-Elbert-Stiftung, 2017. *The Continental Free Trade Area (CFTA) in Africa—a Human Rights Perspective.* Addis Ababa: United Nations Economic Commission for Africa.

van Der Mei, A.P., 2009. 'The East African Community: The Bumpy Road to Supranationalism: Some Reflections on the Judgments of the Court of Justice of the East African Community' *Anyang' Nyong'o and Others and East African Law Society and Others' Maastricht Faculty of Law Working Paper 2009–2007*, Maastricht University, Maastricht, Netherlands.

Zepeda, E., Wise, T.A. and Gallagher, K.P., 2009. *Rethinking Trade Policy for Development: Lessons From Mexico Under NAFTA* (Washington, DC: Carnergie Endowment for International Peace Policy Outlook).

Official Reports

Berman, M. and Rikap, C., 2010. 'Regional Integration and Export Diversification in MERCOSUR: The Case of Argentina and Brazil' *CEPAL Review* 100.

Hanlon, J., 1984. *SADCC: Progress, Projects and Prospects. The Trade and Investment Future of the Southern African Development Co-Ordination Conference*, Special Report No. 182, Intelligence Unit, The Economist.

Leiva, E.G. and Diaz, C.R., 2009. 'The Common External Tariff of MERCOSUR. Is It a Tool for Stimulate the Competitiveness of Its Members?' *Working Paper*, Washington, DC: Inter-American Development Bank.

Meyns, P. and Musamba, C., 2010. 'Introduction: Recent Debates on the Developmental State in Africa' in Meyns, P. and Musamba, C. (eds) *The Developmental State in Africa: Problems and Prospects, INEF-Report, 101/2010* (Institute for Development and Peace, University of Duisburg-Essen, Duisburg, Germany).

UNECA, 2008. *Assessing Economic Integration in Africa III: Towards Financial and Monetary Integration in Africa* (Addis Ababa: UNECA).

———, 2010. *Assessing Regional Integration in Africa IV: Enhancing Intra-African Trade* (Addis Ababa: UNECA).

———, 2012 *Assessing Regional Integration in Africa V: Towards an African Continental Free Trade Area* (Addis Ababa: UNECA).

———, 2013. *Assessing Regional Integration in Africa VI: Harmonising Policies to Transform the Trading Environment* (Addis Ababa: UNECA).

United Nations Development Programme, 2014. *Human Development Report*, http://hdr.undp.org/sites/default/files/hdr14-report-en-1.pdf (accessed on 18/03/2018).

Villarreal, M.A. and Fergusson, I.F., 2015. 'The North American Trade Agreement' *United State Congressional Research Service Report*, Washington, DC: Congressional Research Service.

Word Bank, 1981. *Accelerated Development in Sub-Saharan Africa: An Agenda for Action* (Washington, DC: World Bank (Berg Report)).

———, 1991. *World Development Report 1991: The Challenge of Development* (Washington, DC: World Bank).

———, 1997. *World Development Report 1997: The State in a Changing World* (Washington, DC: World Bank).

PhD Thesis

Svensson, S., 2008. 'The Role of the European Court of Justice in the Integration of the European Community' Thesis, Lund University Department of Political Science, Lund, Sweden.

Index

For Product Safety Concerns and Information please contact our EU representative GPSR@taylorandfrancis.com
Taylor & Francis Verlag GmbH, Kaufingerstraße 24, 80331 München, Germany

www.ingramcontent.com/pod-product-compliance
Ingram Content Group UK Ltd.
Pitfield, Milton Keynes, MK11 3LW, UK
UKHW022000180926
475701UK00003B/127
9780367590420